We the Students

WE THE

SUPREME COURT DECISIONS FOR

AND ABOUT STUDENTS

STUDENTS

JAMIN B. RASKIN

American University
Washington College of Law

COSPONSORED BY THE SUPREME COURT HISTORICAL SOCIETY

CQ PRESS

A DIVISION OF CONGRESSIONAL QUARTERLY INC.
WASHINGTON, D.C.

CQ Press

A Division of Congressional Quarterly Inc.

1414 22nd Street, N.W.

Washington, D.C. 20037

(202) 822-1475 ; (800) 638-1710

www.cqpress.com

Book design and cover: Jill Shimabukuro

Printed and bound in the United States of America

04 03 02 01 00   5 4 3 2 1

Photo credits: 2, 29, 31, 40 (middle, bottom), 43, 170, 172, 173, 177, 198, 227, Library of Congress; 5, National Archives; 7, 9, Ken Heinen; 13, 19, 47, 66, 80, 83, 230, Collection of the Supreme Court of the United States; 15, 50, 201, file photos; 18, Bentley Historical Library, University of Michigan; 24, 45, 81, 111, 176, 180, Corbis/Bettmann-UPI; 40, 146, *Time*; 60, 134, 236, AP/Wide World Photos; 86, 89, *Providence Journal-Bulletin*; 99, 146, Andre Lambertson/SABA; 105, *Louisville Courier-Journal*; 118, Ankers Photographers, Inc.; 129, Reuters; 151, *Columbus Evening Dispatch*; 158 (top, bottom), *Miami Herald*; 162, W & L Archive; 194, Institute of Texan Cultures; 213, Alan Weiner/NYT Pictures.

LIBRARY OF CONGRESS CATALOGING-IN-PUBLICATION DATA

Raskin, Jamin B.
    We the students : Supreme Court cases for and about students / by Jamin B. Raskin.
        p. cm.
    Includes index.
    ISBN 1-56802-570-X (h) — ISBN 1-56802-571-8 (p)
    1. Students—Legal status, laws, etc.—United States—Cases. 2. Students—United States—Civil rights—Cases. 3. Educational law and legislation—United States—Cases. I. Title.

KF4150.A7 R37 2000
344.73'079—dc21   00-029759

Contents

Preface

"One is continually aware of the importance of the public school as an arena of legal controversy."
JUSTICE WILLIAM J. BRENNAN, JR. (SEPTEMBER 29, 1964)

"In our system, state operated schools may not be enclaves of totalitarianism. School officials do not possess absolute authority over their students. Students in school as well as out of school are 'persons' under our Constitution. They are possessed of fundamental rights which the State must respect, just as they themselves must respect their obligations to the State." JUSTICE ABE FORTAS, *TINKER V. DES MOINES INDEPENDENT COMMUNITY SCHOOL DISTRICT* (1969)

This casebook is about the Constitution of the United States and how the Supreme Court and lower courts have interpreted it to govern the lives of American public school students. The cases presented here, some famous and some obscure, form a platform from which to launch young minds on a voyage of constitutional discovery. I invite America's students to learn to read and speak the language of constitutional law by studying cases that have affected them—and will continue to affect them—directly.

I know that America's young people can excel in constitutional law. In the fall of 1999, twenty-five law students at American University's Washington College of Law were named Marshall-Brennan Fellows and, with the support of the Arca Foundation and Mrs. Thurgood Marshall and Mrs. William J. Brennan, Jr., went out to teach the Constitution in the public high schools of the District of Columbia. The results were astonishing as high school students rose to the occasion and developed their constitutional vision and voices.

I first decided to write this book on a dare from high school teachers who complained that there was no collection of cases to grab the attention of their students. Every summer I address a group of thirty high school teachers from all over America who are brought to Washington, D.C., by the Street Law program to study the Supreme Court. I was amazed to learn that the teachers have no easy access to major Supreme Court decisions, much less a set of carefully edited case materials to share with their own students. One teacher challenged me to write a casebook that would be "neither too complicated nor too boring."

The 1999–2000 Marshall-Brennan Fellows at American University, with Mrs. Thurgood Marshall, Mrs. William J. Brennan, Jr., and Professor Jamin B. Raskin, in front on the right.

I believe that this book is not too complicated. I have edited away as much of the underbrush as possible while I hope not sacrificing the critical points of legal substance. And I am quite certain that readers will not find it boring. The cases presented here explore the most interesting problems facing young Americans today: censorship of high school newspapers, drug use and drug testing, racial desegregation, hate speech and the Confederate flag, religious prayer at graduation ceremonies and in other school contexts, inequality in school financing and poverty, sex education and condom distribution, privacy and responsibility, and freedom of thought and freedom of speech. In fact, a great many of our most important Supreme Court cases concern public schools; if you study them, you will know more about constitutional rights than the vast majority of adult Americans.

This casebook is designed specifically for use by high school and college instructors in social studies, history, civics, and government classes. The explanatory historical material, glossary definitions, biographical sketches, moot court exercises, and discussion questions provide classroom teachers with all the necessary material to guide their students toward constitutional literacy. As Justice William J. Brennan, Jr., noted in a remarkable address given at the University of Pennsylvania thirty-five years ago calling for constitutional education in our high schools, "a teacher need not be a lawyer to teach effectively in this area.

Stanford Law School's class of 1952. Future Supreme Court justice Sandra Day O'Connor is in the first row, second from left; future chief justice William Rehnquist is at far left in the back row.

The teacher's job is not so much to supply the kind of answer a lawyer would give, but rather to raise the difficult questions to get his students worrying and thinking about the values and interests at stake."

Constitutional Knowledge, Critical Thinking, Persuasive Argument, and Values Clarification

You must first learn the basics of what the Constitution is and how the legal system works. You can then approach these cases with an inquiring and logical mind, the kind of mindset that you would bring to algebra or geometry. Why does the Court decide a case one way rather than the other? Who has the better side of the argument in a Supreme Court decision, the majority or the dissenters, and why? What makes an argument relevant or irrelevant? How does the Supreme Court go about the business of interpreting words? Is it always consistent? Should it be? Is constitutional law about facts, rules, values, or some complex interaction of all three? Why does law change over time and what makes it change?

Future Supreme Court justice Ruth Bader Ginsburg's entry in her high school year book in 1950.

Future Supreme Court justice Clarence Thomas compares notes with a fellow high school student at St. John's.

Pretty soon you will discover that, when it comes to interpreting difficult constitutional issues, there are few "right" answers. Rather, there are different available arguments that are more or less convincing. This ambiguity requires us to make persuasive arguments about the meaning of the Constitution based on the different methods of interpretation. As you practice writing and arguing about the Constitution, you will improve your oral communication skills and persuasiveness and your written communication skills, including clarity, cogency, and subtlety.

In the final analysis, I hope that you will see that every great legal conflict has at its heart a clash over values and principles. Learning the Constitution in this way enables you to clarify what your values are and to engage in real dialogue with other people about the rules of our common life. No one knows what leads to disasters like the Columbine

Civic-minded students pick up trash outside a St. Louis homeless shelter. Like volunteer service, learning your constitutional rights and responsibilities is an important part of becoming a citizen.

High School massacre, which shook many Americans to the core, but it is hard to believe that the students responsible were taught to think for themselves as citizens and to appreciate the values and equal dignity of other people in the community.

I hope that you will gain from this text a love and appreciation for a document that has bound us together for more than two centuries. As Chief Justice John Marshall wrote in *McCulloch v. Maryland* in 1819, "we must never forget, that it is a constitution we are expounding." It belongs to all of us.

Becoming a Democratic Citizen: Rights and Responsibilities

I have written this casebook with one driving conviction: that, while you can be many things without knowing your own Constitution, you cannot be an effective citizen. Knowing your Constitution is not only a birthright; it is a rite of passage that allows you to become a responsible citizen in a modern representative democracy.

It is a splendid and wonderful thing to learn of your rights as a citizen, but rights exist only in the context of a working democratic community where we all assume corresponding responsibilities. Just as each of us has a legal right to speak and to be heard, we have a complementary moral obligation to listen to one another in a respectful way. Just as we have a right to insist that government not violate our rights and securities as individuals, government has the right to insist that each of us respect the rights and securities of our fellow citizens (or students). It is this tension between rights and responsibilities that creates much of the excitement of this text.

From my interactions with high school students, I have assumed that my young readers are mature and wise. I know that you will find nothing in this casebook as a license for irresponsibility; rather, you will view the material presented here as a complex challenge to fulfill the highest calling of democracy: to be an active, engaged, educated, and responsible citizen. When you think and talk seriously about the problems and cases raised in this book, you will finetune your moral and political sensibilities as a citizen of the nation and your community. And who knows? Perhaps, even now, this book is in the hands of a future U.S. president or Supreme Court justice.

Acknowledgments

I wish to thank the 1999–2000 Marshall-Brennan Fellows, upper-level students at the Washington College of Law, who road-tested these materials in the Washington, D.C., public schools; Mrs. William J. Brennan, Jr., and Mrs. Thurgood Marshall for their generous support of this program; the D.C. public school system and its devoted teachers and creative students; Roceal Duke for her creative support; the Supreme Court Historical Society and its sensational editor, Clare Cushman, who gave invaluable editorial suggestions; Savina Lambert, who located the wonderful photographs in this book; Smith Bagley, Janet Shenk, Michele Nelson, Steve Cobble, Donna Edwards, and the visionary people at the Arca Foundation in Washington; the ceaselessly creative Lee Arbetman and Ed O'Brien of the National Institute for Citizen Education in the Law, whose invitation to address high school teachers every summer prompted me to write this casebook; Dean Claudio Grossman and my colleagues Angela Davis, Elliott Milstein, Ann Shalleck, Leti Volpp, Peter Cicchino, and Mark Niles; John Deist of the California Attorney General's Office; Steve Wermiel, who has been instrumental at every turn of this project; Terry Hickey at the Community Law in Action program at the University of Maryland School of Law, Dar Williams, for musical inspiration; the good people at the National Youth Leadership Forum, the National Institute for Legal Education in Florida, and the Oak Hill Juvenile Detention Center in Laurel, Maryland, for giving me opportunities to interact with high school students; my mother, Barbara Raskin (1935–1999), who showed me how words could become windows to ideas and feelings, and my father, Marcus Raskin, who showed me how ideas can change things; my brother, Noah Raskin, brothers-in-law, Keith Littlewood and Kenneth Bloom, sisters, Eden Raskin and Erika Raskin Littlewood, and sisters-in-law, Mina Raskin and Abby Bloom; my three naughty and wonderful children, Hannah Grace, Thomas Bloom, and Tabitha Claire; my nieces and nephews, Emily Blair, Zachary Gaylin, Maggie Ryan, Mariah Sophia, Phoebe Rose, and Boman Grant; and my mother-in-law and father-in-law, Arlene and Herbert Bloom. I would also like to thank my able research assistants Michelle Priestly, Danielle Fagre, Justin Antonipillai, Kelly Skoloda, Fei Khajawi, Wilder Leavitt, Kara Mather, Ben Jackson, Eva Lopez-Paredes, Danielle Kono, Adam Hill, and Jennifer McKeever; and, finally, my editor at CQ Press, Patricia Gallagher, copy editor, Tracy Villano, and production editor, Talia Greenberg.

This book is dedicated to my wife, Sarah Bloom Raskin, the beautiful and mysterious woman who sat across from me in Professor Laurence Tribe's Constitutional Law class at Harvard in Langdell North in the fall of 1986.

For Further Information

If you have a question that you cannot answer, consult your school librarian or a law librarian at a nearby law school or university. There are also extensive bibliographies and suggestions for other contacts at the end of each chapter. You may also call the Student Press Law Center at (703) 807-1904 if your question relates to the free speech or free press rights of students. Or, you may e-mail me at *Raskin@wcl.american.edu* and I will get back to you with an answer as soon as I can.

Remember: It's your Constitution, and it's up to you to make it work.

Jamin B. Raskin
Professor of Law
Washington College of Law
American University
Washington, D.C.

THE CONSTITUTION AND THE COURTS OF THE UNITED STATES

1

The Constitution: What Is It?

The American Constitution sets forth our nation's governing structure, establishing both the powers of government and the basic rights of the people. The modern world's first written constitution, it is the glue that has held the nation together through civil war; recession; depression; world war; and profound social, economic, political, racial, sectional, and cultural conflict.

When the delegates to the Constitutional Convention in Philadelphia approved the document on September 17, 1787, its provisions principally concerned structural issues—namely, the *separation of powers,* which refers to the distribution of powers among the legislative, executive, and judicial branches of the national government, and *federalism,* or the allocation of powers between the national government and the states.

Three years later, in 1791, the Constitution expanded to address individual liberty. In that year, the states ratified the first ten amendments, called the *Bill of Rights,* laying down the constitutional rights of the people. The Bill of Rights had been championed by Anti-Federalists, who feared a tyrannical central government. Under these amendments, Congress could not establish a church or deny free exercise of religion, deny the right to assemble and petition for a redress of grievances, violate free speech or free press, conduct unreasonable or warrantless searches and seizures, or punish people twice for the same offense (*double jeopardy*).

Read through the Constitution and Bill of Rights in the Appendix and ask yourself: what values were important to our Founders?

The Constitution: Whose Is It?

The Constitution begins "We the People," and these may be the three most important words in the whole document. For our Constitution incorporated the ideas of John Locke and Thomas Paine by assuming that *all people* begin with inalienable rights and that people only create governments to secure those rights and promote the common good. Thus, as Thomas Jefferson put it earlier in the Declaration of Independence, governments derive "their just Powers from the Consent of the Governed." The Constitution belongs to all of us because all of us are, through a process of moral and political imagination, consenting parties to it.

President Abraham Lincoln returned to this democratic principle in the Gettysburg Address, perhaps the greatest speech in our history, when he poetically proclaimed dedication to the idea that "government of the people, by the people, for the people, shall not perish from the earth." It was indeed the Civil War and the resulting Thirteenth, Fourteenth, and Fifteenth Amendments that ended the horrors of slavery and launched the nation on a path that ultimately saw all Americans become consenting members of its social contract.

Our government belongs to all of us, but it is the Supreme Court that is generally the final interpreter of the meaning of the Constitution. The Court must be the constant guardian of our civil rights against government abuse. Congress and the people of the states have the power to amend the Constitution on "great and extraordinary occasions," as urged by James Madison in *Federalist* No. 49.

The Constitution defined the structure and powers of the national government and, in short order, set forth a Bill of Rights for the people. Here the founders take turns signing their names.

THE FOUNDATION OF AMERICAN GOVERNMENT

And in fact, the people have exercised this power seventeen times since the Bill of Rights was ratified. But it is the Court that is charged with interpreting the meaning of the written document along the way. This is the power of *judicial review,* by which the courts may declare *unconstitutional* any federal or state laws and policies that violate rights, rules, or principles set forth in the Constitution.

The principle and practice of judicial review were first established in the great case of *Marbury v. Madison* (1803), where the chief justice of the United States, John Marshall, declared: "[i]t is emphatically the province and duty of the judicial department to say what the law is."

The Constitution: What Does It Mean?

In some places, the Constitution is very clear and specific, such as where it says that citizens must be thirty-five years old in order to become president. In other places, the Constitution speaks in broad, majestic generalities, such as where it says that states may not deprive persons of "equal protection of the laws" or abridge the "freedom of speech."

How exactly the Court should interpret broad constitutional terms is an issue of enduring and fascinating controversy, but the major sources of interpretation that we all must use are

- the text of the Constitution itself;
- *precedent,* or rulings from factually similar cases that illuminate the Constitution's meaning;
- the intentions of the Framers;
- the history of the nation and its institutions;
- the general structure of the constitutional design based on the division of national, state, and local powers through federalism and the separation of powers among the legislative, executive, and judicial branches at the national level;
- the spirit and values of the Constitution embodied in the Bill of Rights; and
- practical concerns and requirements.

The Constitution does not enforce itself, nor do judges go out searching for constitutional violations. If people think that their constitutional rights are being violated, they must summon up the courage to go to court and bring a case. Under the Constitution's case-or-controversy requirement, which is set out in Article III's description of the judicial branch, the Court may only take cases brought by people who have an active controversy involving an actual *injury,* that is, a violation of their legally protected rights. Our Court is not permitted to issue an *advisory opinion,* which is an opinion that states how the Court would rule on a legal matter that is not actually ripe. *Ripeness* is a doctrine requiring that a case or controversy be present—as opposed to hypothetical or potential—in order for it to be heard. One of the "passive virtues" of the Supreme Court is that it deals with specific public conflicts and controversies only when they are ripe. At the same time, a case cannot be *moot,* or no longer fit for judicial resolution because no actual controversy exists anymore. If there is no real injury alleged in a plaintiff's complaint, or the government is not responsible for it, or there is nothing the Court can do about it anyway, the Court will say that the plaintiff lacks *standing.* If the Court believes that it does not have proper jurisdiction over an issue because the Constitution leaves the resolution of that issue entirely up to the executive or legislative branches, the Court may decline to decide the case on the merits because the case presents a *political question.*

The Incorporation of the Bill of Rights

Although the provisions of the Bill of Rights originally applied only against Congress ("*Congress* shall make no law . . ."), the Supreme Court has decided that the Bill of Rights binds all of the states and localities as well. The reason for this is that, in 1868, the Fourteenth Amendment was added to the Constitution. The Fourteenth Amendment's *Due Process Clause* provides that "No state shall . . . deprive any person of life, liberty, or property, without due process of law; nor deny to any person within its jurisdiction the equal protection of the laws." The Court has found that the "liberty" guaranteed by "due process of law" includes almost all of the specific rights granted to the people against Congress by the Bill of Rights. Thus, state governments cannot abridge the rights recognized in the Bill of Rights—such as the right to speak, or publish a newspaper, or practice religion, or be free from unreasonable searches and seizures—any more than Congress can. This assimilation of Bill of Rights protections to citizens facing state power is called "incorporation" through the Due Process Clause.

The State Action Requirement

It is important to remember that, while the Constitution does apply against both Congress and the states (and localities), it applies only to actions of *government.* Specifically, it applies to what we call a *state action*—an action undertaken by a government agency or actor, whether federal, state, or local. This is known as the state action requirement. A private entity is not ordinarily subject to constitutional restraints. (One exception is the Thirteenth Amendment's ban on slavery and involuntary servitude even where the offending actor is a private person or entity acting outside of law.)

Thus, unlike public schools, which are an arm of government, private schools are not bound directly by the Constitution. Private schools may be found to be in violation of a *statute,* or law passed by a federal or state legislature, such as

The Constitution's opening words "We the People" may be not only the largest but the most important in the whole document, infusing the meaning of the entire text.

those forbidding discrimination on the basis of race, gender, ethnicity, and disability, but private schools may not themselves be found to be in direct violation of the U.S. Constitution.

Judicial Architecture: How Our Court System Works

To understand the cases that appear in the chapters that follow, some background information will be useful, beginning with an overview of the judicial process.

There are two major branches of the judicial system in the United States: the federal courts and the state courts in each of the fifty states (as well as the equivalent in the District of Columbia and the Territories). Depicted graphically, our judiciary looks something like this:

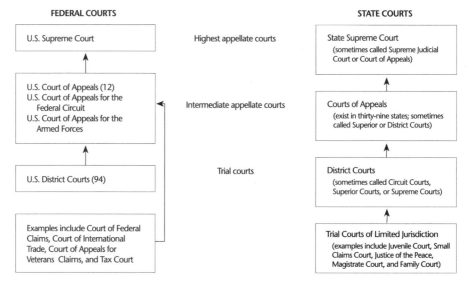

Source: Adapted from Lee Epstein and Thomas G. Walker, *Constitutional Law for a Changing America: Rights, Liberties, and Justice,* 2d ed. (Washington, D.C.: CQ Press, 1995), 865.

Federal courts decide issues of federal law, which means controversies relating to the United States Constitution, federal laws (or statutes) passed by Congress, and regulations issued by federal agencies. The federal system has three levels of courts. The *United States District Courts* are trial courts that make findings of fact and law in civil cases and render verdicts in federal criminal cases. The *United States Circuit Courts of Appeal* are those courts where people appeal decisions and verdicts reached in district courts. In the courts of appeals, there are no juries; judges decide all of the issues.

The U.S. Supreme Court is housed in a beautiful building across the street from the Capitol. When the Court is in session the plaza in front is filled, both before and after oral arguments, with interested parties, journalists, spectators, lawyers, and, sometimes, protesters.

The *United States Supreme Court* is the highest court of appeals. The Supreme Court is the final step in the appeals process; its decisions become the supreme law of the land on constitutional issues.

The state system also usually has three levels of courts, comprised of trial, appellate, and supreme courts. The decisions of the state supreme courts may be appealed to the United States Supreme Court if there is a federal question involved. State courts may decide issues relating to both state law and federal law. In most cases, however, the issues in question concern the former. Most crimes, such as assault, murder, rape, and burglary, are prosecuted in state court. Each state also has its own constitution that provides its citizens with additional protections beyond those afforded by the United States Constitution.

Courts hear two types of cases: criminal and civil. In a *criminal prosecution* charges are brought by a government prosecutor against a person who has allegedly violated a state or federal criminal statute. For example, if you attack your neighbor, the county or district attorney will prosecute you for violating the state's criminal code; if you are convicted, you might go to jail. *Civil suits*, in contrast, are brought by one person, company, or government entity against another for a civil wrong, property invasion, or breach of contract. For example, if you don't take care of your tree, and it falls on your neighbor's house, he can bring a negligence action against you for damages. This is called a *tort.*

Courts will hear the facts and legal claims presented by two parties. The *petitioner,* or *plaintiff,* is the party that initiates the lawsuit; the *respondent,* or *defendant,* is the party that responds to the lawsuit. (In a case that has been appealed, the appealing party is known as the *appellant* and the responding party as the *appellee.*) The courts will then either dismiss the case or grant *relief*—that is, some monetary benefit or other restitution—based on the evidence and the arguments presented. Depending on the kind of case, courts utilize different resources to reach their verdicts and make decisions. Courts analyze the Constitution and other relevant rules of law, such as a *statutory* law, which is passed by the state legislatures or Congress; an *ordinance,* which is enacted by a city, suburb, town, municipality or other local entity; or the *common law,* which is developed over time from the judgment of courts, as well as prior case precedent.

Majority and Dissenting Opinions

You will notice that most of the case excerpts in this book present both majority and dissenting opinions. A *majority opinion* will typically first summarize the *procedure* of the case, which is the path the case took to get to the Supreme Court, and then the *facts* of the case—that is, what happened that led the parties to a court battle. The procedure and facts are normally followed by the justice's analysis of the issues posed in the case. The majority opinion represents the views of a majority of justices on the nine-member Court. It is sometimes joined by a *concurring opinion,* in which one or more justices express agreement with the majority's result but demonstrate a different analysis or give the law or facts a different emphasis. A *dissenting opinion* expresses a different point of view on major or minor issues in the case and rejects the result reached by the majority of the Court.

It is important to read dissenting opinions along with majority opinions. Many decisions are decided on the slender margin of 5–4, and the simple change of one justice's mind—or the replacement of an outgoing or deceased justice with a newly appointed one—can create a new 5–4 majority in the opposite direction. Well-argued dissenting opinions are often the seeds of a later reversal. An example of a realignment of views took place between 1940 and 1943. In *Minersville School Dist. v. Gobitis* (1940) the Supreme Court upheld compulsory flag salute rituals. But a strong dissenting opinion laid the groundwork for a reversal that followed three years later in *West Virginia v. Barnette* (1943) (see Chapter 2). In the latter case, the Court overruled *Gobitis,* finding that the First Amendment does not allow public schools to force students to pledge allegiance to the flag.

Dissenting opinions register the diversity of legal and political thought in our society and remind us that the law is not a "hard science." A court is not a computer that prints out right answers once you enter all of the facts. The law

The justices of the Supreme Court. From left, Clarence Thomas, Antonin Scalia, Sandra Day O'Connor, Anthony M. Kennedy, David H. Souter, and Stephen G. Breyer; Chief Justice William H. Rehnquist; and Ruth Bader Ginsburg.

is a field of contests among competing theories, ideas, analogies, values, interpretations, and beliefs. As Justice Robert H. Jackson once famously put it, "We are not final because we are infallible, but we are infallible only because we are final."

How to Brief a Case

When law students read cases, they often take notes on them and outline them in a way that has come to be known as "briefing a case." You might find it useful to brief cases as you start your own habits of case-reading and analysis. To effectively brief a case, you must

State the procedure—Where did this case come from? A state supreme court after a state appeals court after a state district court? A federal appeals court after a federal district court? What happened in those lower courts? Who won? Who lost? The procedural history of the case is a very quick statement about the path the case has followed in the courts.

Name the parties—Who is the plaintiff? Who is the defendant?

State the facts—Write down the facts of what happened to the parties. What is the story between them? Who did what to whom? What happened that is of legal significance, that is, what happened that is relevant to deciding the legal issues?

State the issue (or issues)—What are the legal issues that the court must decide in order to arrive at a decision?

State the holding—What does the court hold or decide? What is the "rule" that it comes up with in answer to the legal issues posed?

State the court's reasoning or rationale—Why does the court decide the way it does? What is the logic or rationale of its holding? What is its analysis?

There is no single right way to brief a case, but these basic features might be useful to you as you dip your toes in the water. If you become really interested in the process of case-briefing and outlining—and do it as part of a study group—consider renting the classic movie about students at Harvard Law School called *The Paper Chase*. It might make you determined to go to law school—or to avoid the experience at all costs!

Read On

Cushman, Clare. *The Supreme Court Justices*. Washington, D.C.: Congressional Quarterly, 1995.

Hall, Kermit. *The Oxford Companion to the Supreme Court of the United States*. New York: Oxford University Press, 1992.

THE HEART AND SOUL OF THE CONSTITUTION: THE FIRST AMENDMENT AND FREEDOM OF EXPRESSION

2

"Congress shall make no law . . . abridging the freedom of speech. . . ." THE FIRST AMENDMENT

"If there is any principle of the Constitution that more imperatively calls for attachment than any other it is the principle of free thought—not free thought for those who agree with us but freedom for the thought that we hate." JUSTICE HOLMES, DISSENTING IN *UNITED STATES V. SCHWIMMER*

"In our system, students may not be regarded as closed-circuit recipients of only that which the State chooses to communicate. They may not be confined to the expression of those sentiments that are officially approved. In the absence of a specific showing of constitutionally valid reasons to regulate their speech, students are entitled to freedom of expression of their views. . . ."
JUSTICE FORTAS, *TINKER V. DES MOINES INDEPENDENT COMMUNITY SCHOOL DISTRICT*

Many people today believe that the First Amendment captures what it means to be an American. This deep identification with the First Amendment is ironic because free speech received almost no protection from the Supreme Court until the middle of the twentieth century. Originally, the First Amendment applied only to congressional actions, and even then it was restricted to cases involving *prior restraints* by government against political speech. Prior restraint refers to the restriction of speech or press before it is actually published.

Nonetheless, today the First Amendment both represents and guarantees the thoroughgoing American commitment to freedom of speech, thought, and conscience. Since the 1940s, the Supreme Court has upheld the right of citizens to engage in speech that is sexual, offensive, indecent, hostile, radical, reactionary, anti-war, and even aggressively anti-government in content. But the Court has also permitted government to censor and punish obscenity, fighting words, and incitement of imminent lawless activity. Speaking generally, the United States of America tolerates more freedom of expression than almost any other nation on Earth.

The text of the First Amendment reads:

> Congress shall make no law respecting an establishment of religion, or prohibiting the free exercise thereof; or abridging the freedom of speech, or of the press, or of the right of the people peaceably to assemble, and to petition the Government for a redress of grievances.

Although the First Amendment refers to Congress, the rights contained in the text apply also against states and localities. This is the effect of the "incorporation" doctrine discussed in Chapter 1.

There are six major rights protected by the First Amendment. These can be readily recalled by thinking of the word "GRAPES."

*G*rievances, Right to petition for a redress of
*R*eligion, Right to no Establishment of
*A*ssembly, Right to peaceful
*P*ress, Freedom of the
*E*xercise, Freedom of Religious
*S*peech, Freedom of

What images does the First Amendment evoke in your mind?

POINTS TO PONDER

How does the basic First Amendment liberty of free expression apply to students in public schools?

- Should students be required to salute and pledge allegiance to the American flag?
- Should students be prevented from wearing clothing with political messages?
- Should students be allowed to wear their hair however they please?
- Should students be able to make speeches and presentations with vulgar or profane language?

Expressive Conduct and the Right Not to Speak

The right to "speak" actually implies a broader right of free expression. The First Amendment protects not only written or spoken words, but what the Court calls *expressive conduct,* that is, actions that do not literally involve speaking or writing but that nonetheless send a message. Picketing a store, wearing a political button, or painting a picture are all examples of expressive conduct.

The following Supreme Court case, *West Virginia v. Barnette* (1943), one of many dealing with flags in our communities, articulated the idea that the First Amendment protects not just speech and written words, but actions that communicate meaning. The case also established that free speech includes a right *not* to speak when a citizen so chooses.

In *Barnette,* the Court found that public school students who choose not to join in the Pledge of Allegiance flag salute ritual for reasons of conscience cannot be forced to participate. The case reversed the Supreme Court's earlier decision in *Minersville School Dist. v. Gobitis* (1940), which upheld the expulsion of the child of a Jehovah's Witness who refused to join in the pledge ritual.

In the three years between Gobitis and the Court's change of heart in *Barnette,* the children of Jehovah's Witnesses in public schools across the country faced widespread persecution and harassment for their continuing refusal to salute the flag during a time of national mobilization against Adolph Hitler. The Jehovah's Witnesses saw flag salutes as violating the prohibitions in the Ten Commandments against idol worship and graven images. They also wanted to show solidarity with Jehovah's Witnesses in Germany who had refused to participate in the "Heil Hitler" salute.

The Court's turnaround on the flag salute issue illustrates that, when it comes to critical public questions, the Court has often changed its mind about what the Constitution provides. While we might be tempted to think of the Court as operating like a computer—plug in the facts and the legal answer

The author of this landmark opinion, **JUSTICE ROBERT H. JACKSON** (1892–1954), was born and raised in the farm country outside Jamestown, New York. He actually graduated from two high schools, Frewsburg High and Jamestown High, where he spent an extra year. He never went to college, and finished a two-year course at Albany Law School in only one year. He learned the practice of law through apprenticeship, and always considered himself a country lawyer. After a distinguished career during Franklin Delano Roosevelt's New Deal administration that included stints as *General Counsel* of the Internal Revenue Bureau, *Solicitor General of the United States,* and *Attorney General,* Jackson was appointed to the Supreme Court by FDR in 1941. He served until 1954.

HIGHLIGHTS

➤   President Roosevelt tried to entice Jackson into electoral politics, encouraging him to run for governor of New York in 1938. His name was even floated as a potential vice-presidential running mate for FDR, but Jackson's true passion was for law, not politics.

➤   Speaking of his high school English teacher Mary Willard, who inspired in him a love of language and oratory, Justice Jackson would later say: "her influence would be hard to overestimate."

prints out—the concepts of the Constitution, in truth, develop over time in reaction to events and in response to new legal arguments about how to define democracy and make the Constitution serve justice.

WEST VIRGINIA STATE BOARD OF EDUCATION
v.
BARNETTE

Supreme Court of the United States
Argued March 11, 1943.
Decided June 14, 1943.

Justice JACKSON delivered the opinion of the Court.

. . . The Board of Education on January 9, 1942, . . . order[ed] that the salute to the flag become "a regular part of the program of activities in the public schools," that all teachers and pupils "shall be required to participate in the salute honoring the Nation represented by the Flag; provided, however, that refusal to salute the Flag be regarded as an Act of insubordination, and shall be dealt with accordingly."[1]

The resolution originally required the "commonly accepted salute to the Flag" which it defined. Objections to the salute as "being too much like Hitler's" were raised by the Parent and Teachers Association, the Boy and Girl Scouts, the Red Cross, and the Federation of Women's Clubs. Some modification appears to have been made in deference to these objections, but no concession was made to Jehovah's Witnesses. What is now required is the "stiff-arm" salute, the saluter to keep the right hand raised with palm turned up while the following is repeated: "I pledge allegiance to the Flag of the United States of America and to the Republic for which it stands; one Nation, indivisible, with liberty and justice for all."

Failure to conform is "insubordination" dealt with by expulsion. Readmission is denied by statute until compliance. Meanwhile the expelled child is "unlawfully absent" and may be proceeded against as a delinquent. His parents or guardians are liable to prosecution, and if convicted are subject to fine not exceeding $50 and jail term not exceeding thirty days.

. . . [C]itizens of the United States and of West Virginia, brought suit in the United States District Court for themselves and others similarly situated asking its *injunction* to restrain enforcement of these laws and regulations against Jehovah's Witnesses. The Witnesses are an unincorporated body teaching that the obligation imposed by law of God is superior to that of laws enacted by temporal government. Their religious beliefs include a literal version of Exodus, Chapter 20, verses 4 and 5, which says: "Thou shalt not make unto thee any graven image, or any likeness of anything that is in heaven above, or that is in the earth beneath, or that is in the water under the earth; thou shalt not bow down

In *Barnette* the Court found that, under the First Amendment, public school students who choose not to join in the Pledge of Allegiance for reasons of conscience cannot be forced to participate. Still, the flag salute continues to be a daily ritual practiced in many states and school districts.

thyself to them nor serve them." They consider that the flag is an "image" within this command. For this reason they refuse to salute it.

Children of this faith have been expelled from school and are threatened with exclusion for no other cause. Officials threaten to send them to reformatories maintained for criminally inclined juveniles. Parents of such children have been prosecuted and are threatened with prosecutions for causing delinquency.

. . .

. . . [T]he compulsory flag salute and pledge requires affirmation of a belief and an attitude of mind. It is not clear whether the regulation contemplates that pupils forego any contrary convictions of their own and become unwilling converts to the prescribed ceremony or whether it will be acceptable if they simulate assent by words without belief and by a gesture barren of meaning. It is now a commonplace that censorship or suppression of expression of opinion is tolerated by our Constitution only when the expression presents a clear and present danger of action of a kind the State is empowered to prevent and punish. It would seem that involuntary affirmation could be commanded only on even more immediate and urgent grounds than silence. But here the power of compulsion is invoked without any allegation that remaining passive during a flag salute ritual creates a clear and present danger that would justify an effort even to muffle expression. To sustain the compulsory flag salute we are required to say that a Bill of Rights which guards the individual's right to speak his own mind, left it open to public authorities to compel him to utter what is not in his mind.

. . .

Nor does the issue as we see it turn on one's possession of particular religious views or the sincerity with which they are held. While religion supplies appellees' motive for enduring the discomforts of making the issue in this case, many citizens who do not share these religious views hold such a compulsory rite to infringe constitutional liberty of the individual. It is not necessary to inquire whether non-conformist beliefs will exempt from the duty to salute unless we first find power to make the salute a legal duty.

. . . The question which underlies the flag salute controversy is whether such a ceremony so touching matters of opinion and political attitude may be imposed upon the individual by official authority under powers committed to any political organization under our Constitution.

. . .

The very purpose of a Bill of Rights was to withdraw certain subjects from the vicissitudes of political controversy, to place them beyond the reach of majorities and officials and to establish them as legal principles to be applied by the courts. One's right to life, liberty, and property, to free speech, a free press, freedom of worship and assembly, and other fundamental rights may not be submitted to vote; they depend on the outcome of no elections.

. . .

National unity as an end which officials may foster by persuasion and example is not in question. The problem is whether under our Constitution compulsion as here employed is a permissible means for its achievement.

Struggles to coerce uniformity of sentiment in support of some end thought essential to their time and country have been waged by many good as well as by evil men. Nationalism is a relatively recent phenomenon but at other times and places the ends have been racial or territorial security, support of a dynasty or regime, and particular plans for saving souls. As first and moderate methods to attain unity have failed, those bent on its accomplishment must resort to an ever-increasing severity. As governmental pressure toward unity becomes greater, so strife becomes more bitter as to whose unity it shall be. Probably no deeper division of our people could proceed from any provocation than from finding it necessary to choose what doctrine and whose program public educational officials shall compel youth to unite in embracing. Ultimate futility of such attempts to compel coherence is the lesson of every such effort from the Roman drive to stamp out Christianity as a disturber of its pagan unity, the Inquisition, as a means to religious and dynastic unity, the Siberian exiles as a means to Russian unity, down to the fast failing efforts of our present totalitarian enemies. Those who begin coercive elimination of dissent soon find themselves exterminating dissenters. Compulsory unification of opinion achieves only the unanimity of the graveyard.

It seems trite but necessary to say that the First Amendment to our Constitution was designed to avoid these ends by avoiding these beginnings. There is no mysticism in the American concept of the State or of the nature or origin of its authority. We set up government by consent of the governed, and the Bill of Rights denies those in power any legal opportunity to coerce that consent. Authority here is to be controlled by public opinion, not public opinion by authority.

The case is made difficult not because the principles of its decision are obscure but because the flag involved is our own. Nevertheless, we apply the limitations of the Constitution with no fear that freedom to be intellectually and spiritually diverse or even contrary will disintegrate the social organization. To believe that patriotism will not flourish if patriotic ceremonies are voluntary and spontaneous instead of a compulsory routine is to make an unflattering estimate of the appeal of our institutions to free minds. We can have intellectual individualism and the rich cultural diversities that we owe to exceptional minds only at the price of occasional eccentricity and abnormal attitudes. When they are so harmless to others or to the State as those we deal with here, the price is not too great. But freedom to differ is not limited to things that do not matter much. That would be a mere shadow of freedom. The test of its substance is the right to differ as to things that touch the heart of the existing order.

If there is any fixed star in our constitutional constellation, it is that no official, high or petty, can prescribe what shall be orthodox in politics, nationalism, religion, or other matters of opinion or force citizens to confess by word or act their faith therein. If there are any circumstances which permit an exception, they do not now occur to us.[2]

We think the action of the local authorities in compelling the flag salute and pledge transcends constitutional limitations on their power and invades the sphere of intellect and spirit which it is the purpose of the First Amendment to our Constitution to reserve from all official control.

. . .

Affirmed.

Justice MURPHY, concurring.

I agree with the opinion of the Court and join in it.

The complaint challenges an order of the State Board of Education which requires teachers and pupils to participate in the prescribed salute to the flag. . . . In effect compliance is compulsory and not optional. It is the claim of appellees that the regulation is invalid as a restriction on religious freedom and freedom of speech, secured to them against State infringement by the First and Fourteenth Amendments to the Constitution of the United States.

A reluctance to interfere with considered state action, the fact that the end sought is a desirable one, the emotion aroused by the flag as a symbol for which we have fought and are now fighting again,-all of these are understandable. But there is before us the right of freedom to believe, freedom to worship one's Maker according to the dictates of one's conscience, a right which the Constitution specifically shelters. Reflection has convinced me that as a judge I have no loftier duty or responsibility than to uphold that spiritual freedom to its farthest reaches.

The right of freedom of thought and of religion as guaranteed by the Constitution against State action includes both the right to speak freely and the right to refrain from

JUSTICE FRANK MURPHY (1890–1949) wrote a concurring opinion in *Barnette*. He was born and raised in Harbor Beach, Michigan, and graduated from the University of Michigan law school. He was mayor of Detroit and was elected governor of Michigan in 1936 at a time of tremendous labor unrest, which occupied much of his attention. President Franklin Delano Roosevelt appointed Murphy to the Supreme Court in 1940. He served until 1949.

HIGHLIGHTS

➤   As Governor, Murphy was credited with the peaceful resolution of the nation's first sit-down strike at General Motors in 1937. "Nothing in the world is going to get the governor of Michigan off the position of working it out peacefully," he said.

➤   On the Court, Justice Murphy was known as a perfect gentleman, full of humanity, kindness, and humility. Clarence Darrow, who appeared before him when he was a trial court judge in Michigan, said Murphy was "the kindliest and most understanding man I have ever happened to meet on the Bench."

speaking at all, except insofar as essential operations of government may require it for the preservation of an orderly society, as in the case of compulsion to give evidence in court. Without wishing to disparage the purposes and intentions of those who hope to inculcate sentiments of loyalty and patriotism by requiring a declaration of allegiance as a feature of public education, or unduly belittle the benefits that may accrue therefrom, I am impelled to conclude that such a requirement is not essential to the maintenance of effective government and orderly society. . . . Official compulsion to affirm what is contrary to one's religious beliefs is the antithesis of freedom of worship which, it is well to recall, was achieved in this country only after what Jefferson characterized as the "severest contests in which I have ever been engaged."

Justice FRANKFURTER, dissenting.

One who belongs to the most vilified and persecuted minority in history is not likely to be insensible to the freedoms guaranteed by our Constitution. Were my purely personal attitude relevant I should whole-heartedly associate myself with the general libertarian views in the Court's opinion, representing as they do the thought and action of a lifetime. But as judges we are neither Jew nor Gentile, neither Catholic nor agnostic. We owe equal attachment to the Constitution and are equally bound by our judicial obligations whether we derive our citizenship from the earliest or the latest immigrants to these shores. As a member of this Court I am not justified in writing my private notions of policy into the Constitution, no matter how deeply I may cherish them or how mischievous I may deem their disregard. The duty of a judge who must decide which of two claims before the Court shall prevail, that of a State to enact and enforce laws within its general competence or that of an individual to refuse obedience because of the demands of his conscience, is not that of the ordinary person. It can never be emphasized too much that one's own opinion about the wisdom or evil of a law should be excluded altogether when one is doing one's duty on the bench. The only opinion of our own even looking in that direction that is material is our opinion whether legislators could in reason have enacted such a law. In the light of all the cir-

The dissenter in this case, **JUSTICE FELIX FRANKFURTER** (1882–1965), was born in Vienna, Austria. With his family, he left Vienna at age twelve for the United States. He attended the City College of New York and Harvard Law School, an institution where he taught for more than two decades and which he loved with the same passion he held for the Supreme Court. After Frankfruter's numerous jobs in Washington and his many years of teaching at Harvard, President Franklin Delano Roosevelt appointed him to the Court in 1939, where he served until 1962.

HIGHLIGHTS

➤   As a professor at Harvard Law School, Frankfurter was deeply involved in the celebrated Sacco-Vanzetti case, in which two Italian-American anarchists, Nicola Sacco and Bartolomeo Vanzetti, were prosecuted on murder charges. Though they proclaimed their innocence, Sacco and Vanzetti were convicted in a politically charged trial and executed by the state of Massachusetts. Frankfurter helped fight, unsuccessfully, to have their convictions overturned and wrote a book critical of the unfairness of their criminal trial. The experience of the Sacco-Vanzetti case, in part, led Frankfurter to join others in establishing the American Civil Liberties Union (ACLU), now America's leading civil liberties organization.

➤   During the post–World War I Paris Peace Conference, Frankfurter represented Dr. Chaim Weizmann and the Zionist leaders in negotiations with the Arab states. Frankfurter was himself Jewish, which he alludes to in the *Barnette* case, and a lifelong Zionist supporter of Israel.

➤   Although he was seen as a liberal when he was a law professor, Justice Frankfurter's career on the Court actually pleased conservatives because of his interest in federalism and judicial restraint, wherein judges defer to the political branches and decline to invalidate democratically chosen public policies and laws.

cumstances, including the history of this question in this Court, it would require more daring than I possess to deny that reasonable legislators could have taken the action which is before us for review. Most unwillingly, therefore, I must differ from my brethren with regard to legislation like this. I cannot bring my mind to believe that the "liberty" secured by the Due Process Clause gives this Court authority to deny to the State of West Virginia the attainment of that which we all recognize as a legitimate legislative end, namely, the promotion of good citizenship, by employment of the means here chosen.

EXERCISE 2.1. In *Barnette*, the Court held that the First Amendment prevents school officials from compelling a student to stand and salute the flag during the Pledge of Allegiance. Although public schools may continue to have a Pledge of Allegiance ceremony every morning, students may not be forced to participate or be punished for not participating. Do you think this decision was right? Write a one-page statement on your assessment of the majority's opinion in *West Virginia v. Barnette*. Was it right or wrong? Why? Read your reactions aloud and talk about them.

EXERCISE 2.2. What does the American flag represent to you? Does the flag have a single meaning or multiple meanings? If someone decides to sit out a flag salute, does it diminish the meaning of the flag in your eyes? Does it diminish the person in your eyes? What reasons might a student have for not joining in a flag salute? Do you think that businesses like Ralph Lauren, Speedo, and Tommy Hilfiger should be able to use the American flag as part of their clothing and advertising and to put it on products like underarm deodorant? Explore the use of the flag in advertising and popular culture.

EXERCISE 2.3. In *Texas v. Johnson* (1989), the Supreme Court upheld the right of the people under the First Amendment to use the American flag for expressive purposes, including even the burning of a flag at a demonstration in order to protest government policy. Since that time, there have been several attempts to add to the Constitution language that would give Congress power to enact a law making it a crime to burn or desecrate the flag. Congress has voted several times on versions of the following proposed amendment:

"Congress shall have power to prohibit physical desecration of the flag of the United States."

Although the proposed "Flag Amendment" has repeatedly won two-thirds majorities in the House of Representatives, it has consistently fallen just short of the two-thirds mark in the Senate. (Article V of the Constitution provides that new amendments must be passed by a two-thirds vote in both the House of Representatives and the Senate and then ratified by three-fourths of the states.)

The issue of flag desecration is not going away. But what does "desecration" mean? Look it up. Is it clear that flag burning is a form of desecration? Federal law today actually recommends burning flags as the proper form of disposal. Indeed, any boy scout or girl scout knows that this is proper flag protocol!

Pretend that you and your classmates are members of the Senate Judiciary Committee once again considering the proposed Flag Desecration Amendment.

Research *Texas v. Johnson* and the pros and cons of the proposed constitutional amendment to ban flag desecration. (Check magazine and newspaper articles, as well as Internet commentary.) Prepare a speech on how you plan to vote and why.

FOR THE CLASS

THE ALL-AMERICAN HIGH SCHOOL FIGHT SONG. All-American High School has a school anthem "fight song" that is played and sung at athletic events. The school requires all students to stand and sing the words. Adam and Betty are high school juniors who wear tye-died shirts and are avid vegetarians. They love to watch the All-American High football team games, but they refuse to stand and sing the fight song because they think that sports should be played for fun, non-competitively, without winners and losers. They think that the fight song is too aggressive and has excessively macho lyrics. (They particularly object to a line that says, "All-American, let's all hail/ Let's go kick some Eastern High tail/ When we fight, fight, fight/ They'll all start to bail/ All-American, hail, hail, hail!")

The school principal asserts that "Adam and Betty are causing a disturbance by setting a bad example for younger students and undermining school spirit." He suspends them for one day for failing to stand and sing. The school also bars them from going to football games until they agree to participate in the song with the rest of the school. Adam and Betty go to federal court to get an *injunction*—that is, an order from a court commanding or preventing an action—overturning their one-day suspension and the principal's order banning them from games. The district court judge strikes down the discipline but the appeals court reinstates it. Now the case is in the Supreme Court.

Select two teams of two students each to argue the case. One team should represent Adam and Betty and the other team should represent the school system. Then select nine students to serve as Supreme Court justices. The student-attorneys should compose ten-minute oral arguments to present before the Court to explain why the *Barnette* decision supports their position. (Try not to read your arguments, but speak from the heart based on an outline.)

During oral argument, the justices may jump in and interrupt at any time to ask questions about the attorneys' positions and their implications. Attorneys should answer the questions to the best of their abilities and try to keep the Court focused on their main arguments. (This process of active questioning teaches you to think on your feet and is good practice for future lawyers because this is what actually happens in oral argument in the Supreme Court and lower courts.) The chief justice should keep time and call the attorneys to argue before the bench.

At the end of the oral argument, the nine justices should meet secretly and return to deliver their opinion. Recall that it is perfectly acceptable to have a majority opinion with separate concurring opinions and a dissenting opinion (or several). Each student-justice should carefully explain his or her reasoning.

[*Hints for your first oral arguments:* Be creative and have fun! Attorneys arguing for the right not to stand and sing along might consider arguing on the basis of the *Barnette* holding that citizens are free not to be forced to speak against conscience even in the face of majority insistence. Voltaire is quoted as saying, "I disapprove of what you say, but I will defend to the death your right to say it." What values are served by a community's toleration of dissenting opinions? Is there a danger to coercing individual conformity in this way? What passages from *Barnette* can you quote on your side?

Attorneys for the school system arguing that Adam and Betty have no right to refuse to participate can distinguish this case from *Barnette* by explaining how it does not involve rights of religion or conscience. They might point out that students are asked to do things all of the time that they may disagree with (like homework) and that finding a right to refuse to participate in this case would lead down a "slippery slope" that would end with students getting out of doing anything they disliked, like writing essays on books that they disapprove of or taking tests on human evolution when they believe in creation. Moreover, *Barnette* focused on freedom of thought in politics and nationalism, but nothing so exalted is at stake here. Brainstorm what could happen if the precedent were set that students could get out of required exercises whenever they disagreed with them.]

SOFT DRINKS, HARD CHOICES. Hypothetical High School enters a national competition sponsored by Coca-Cola in which it tries to show its "Coca Cola pride" in order to receive various educational tools, such as computers and printers. On the appointed day, all Hypothetical High students wear a Coca-Cola T-shirt (donated by the company) to school—that is, all students except senior cut-up Randy Rabblerouser, who wears a Pepsi T-shirt. When told by the principal to take it off and put on a Coca-Cola T-shirt, he says, "I'm no robot, man." Randy is suspended for two days for refusing to follow the rules and policies of the school. He goes to federal court to ask for an injunction against his suspension.

Divide the classroom into two teams of students and argue before a panel of three (student) federal district judges whether the suspension is constitutional or not. How do you rule and why?

[This exercise is based on actual events that took place in Georgia. In fact, an increasing number of public high schools are signing big-dollar contracts with large corporations, selling them exclusive rights to sell and market their products on campus and at athletic events. For example, the Martin County, Florida, school district a few years ago okayed a $155,000–contract between South Fork High School and Pepsi-Cola in which South Fork contracted to "make its best effort to maximize all sales opportunities for Pepsi-Cola products."]

CHANNEL FUN. The Medium County Public School System has installed a television in every one of its schools' classrooms. The televisions were donated by the for-profit corporation Channel Fun in return for Medium County Schools' promise to broadcast daily in each homeroom at least seven minutes' worth of Channel Fun programming, which includes news and sports reports, commercials for fast food and candy, and a segment entitled "Tips for Teens." Saying that they "refuse to be part of this commercial sell-out of our education," ninth-graders Sarah Sassy and Robert Rad walk out of the classroom whenever the television is turned on. They are suspended from school after they are told to stop their protest, but they continue walking out. Sarah and Robert appeal their suspensions to federal district court.

Form two teams of students and argue whether the suspensions of Sarah and Robert should be struck down on First Amendment grounds or whether the school acted reasonably within its powers. What language in *Barnette* do you cite for your position? Select a panel of three federal appeals court judges to determine whether *Barnette* protects the students' right to walk out.

The Right to Speak Freely and Protest (But Not to Disrupt)

Just as students have a First Amendment right *not* to be forced to profess their belief in officially approved ideas, they also have a First Amendment right *to* express their own ideas, at least if they do so in a way that does not fundamentally interfere with their school's functions. This was the holding of the Court in *Tinker v. Des Moines School District* (1969), the high point of the Supreme Court commitment to free speech in the schools.

The *Tinker* case arose in the heat of national controversy over the Vietnam War, the United States' military action in Indochina in the 1960s and 1970s that caused great political division across the country. Many people supported the war as a necessary intervention on behalf of a besieged ally, South Vietnam, that was resisting Communist aggression. Others considered the long war *illegal*—that is, a violation of the Constitution. They maintained that such an undeclared intervention in the affairs of another country took place at huge human and moral cost. Historians and politicians continue to debate the Vietnam War, perhaps our most divisive military experience outside of the Civil War.

Many young Americans joined the public debate over the morality and justice of the Vietnam War. This case had its origins in November 1965 when a group of people from Iowa traveled to Washington, D.C., to join a peace march that was organized by the National Committee for a Sane Nuclear Policy (Sane) and that featured speeches by Coretta Scott King and Dr. Benjamin Spock. The Iowa marchers included teenagers Christopher Eckhardt and John Tinker, both fifteen years old and tenth-graders in Des Moines public high schools. The boys' families were steeped in progressive causes such as civil rights and the peace movement.

Upon their return to Iowa, Christopher and John decided with John's sister Mary Beth, a thirteen-year-old in eighth grade, to express their opposition to the war. Specifically, they wore black armbands to school as a way to mourn the loss of life in Vietnam and to support Sen. Robert F. Kennedy's proposal for an extended truce in the war. When dozens of other students joined in this silent

Mary Beth and John Tinker, here with their mother, Lorena, protested the Vietnam War in 1965 by wearing black armbands to school. After they were suspended by school authorities, the Supreme Court held that public school students have First Amendment rights of political expression that were violated in their case.

protest, school authorities moved to stop the protests and isolate and punish the students who wore the armbands. Even in the face of this official hostility (and taunting by other students), the Tinkers and Christopher Eckhardt stood their ground and became the plaintiffs in this famous case.

—·—

TINKER
v.
DES MOINES INDEPENDENT COMMUNITY
SCHOOL DISTRICT

Supreme Court of the United States
Argued Nov. 12, 1968.
Decided Feb. 24, 1969.

Justice FORTAS delivered the opinion of the Court.

Petitioner John F. Tinker, 15 years old, and Christopher Eckhardt, 16 years old, attended high schools in Des Moines, Iowa. Petitioner Mary Beth Tinker, John's sister, was a 13-year-old student in junior high school.

In December 1965, a group of adults and students in Des Moines held a meeting at the Eckhardt home. The group determined to publicize their objections to the hostilities in Vietnam and their support for a truce by wearing black armbands during the holiday season and by fasting on December 16 and New Year's Eve. Petitioners and their parents had previously engaged in similar activities, and they decided to participate in the program.

The principals of the Des Moines schools became aware of the plan to wear armbands. On December 14, 1965, they met and adopted a policy that any student wearing an armband to school would be asked to remove it, and if he refused he would be suspended until he returned without the armband. Petitioners were aware of the regulation that the school authorities adopted.

On December 16, Mary Beth and Christopher wore black armbands to their schools. John Tinker wore his armband the next day. They were all sent home and suspended from school until they would come back without their armbands. They did not return to school until after the planned period for wearing armbands had expired—that is, until after New Year's Day.

. . .

I

The District Court recognized that the wearing of an armband for the purpose of expressing certain views is the type of symbolic act that is within the Free Speech Clause of the First Amendment. As we shall discuss, the wearing of armbands in the circumstances of this case was entirely divorced from actually or potentially disruptive conduct by those participating in it. It was closely akin to "pure speech" which, we have repeatedly held, is entitled to comprehensive protection under the First Amendment.

First Amendment rights, applied in light of the special characteristics of the school environment, are available to teachers and students. It can hardly be argued that either students or teachers shed their constitutional rights to freedom of speech or expression at the schoolhouse gate. This has been the unmistakable holding of this Court for almost 50 years. . . .

. . .

. . . Our problem lies in the area where students in the exercise of First Amendment rights collide with the rules of the school authorities.

II

The problem posed by the present case does not relate to regulation of the length of skirts or the type of clothing, to hair style, or deportment. It does not concern aggressive, disruptive action or even group demonstrations. Our problem involves direct, primary First Amendment rights akin to "pure speech."

The school officials banned and sought to punish petitioners for a silent, passive expression of opinion, unaccompanied by any disorder or disturbance on the part of petitioners. There is here no evidence whatever of petitioners' interference, actual or nascent, with the schools' work or of collision with the rights of other students to be secure and to be let alone. Accordingly, this case does not concern speech or action that intrudes upon the work of the schools or the rights of other students.

Only a few of the 18,000 students in the school system wore the black armbands. Only five students were suspended for wearing them. There is no indication that the work of the schools or any class was disrupted. Outside the classrooms, a few students made hostile remarks to the children wearing armbands, but there were no threats or acts of violence on school premises.

The District Court concluded that the action of the school authorities was reasonable because it was based upon their fear of a disturbance from the wearing of the armbands. But, in our system, undifferentiated fear or apprehension of disturbance is not enough to overcome the right to freedom of expression. Any departure from absolute regimentation may cause trouble. Any variation from the majority's opinion may inspire fear. Any word spoken, in class, in the lunchroom, or on the campus, that deviates from the views of another person may start an argument or cause a disturbance. But our Constitution says we must take this risk[,] and our history says it is this sort of hazardous freedom—this kind of openness—that is the basis of our national strength and of the independence and vigor of Americans who grow up and live in this relatively permissive . . . society.

In order for the State in the person of school officials to justify prohibition of a particular expression of opinion, it must be able to show that its action was caused by something more than a mere desire to avoid the discomfort and unpleasantness that always accompany an unpopular viewpoint. Certainly where there is no finding and no showing that engaging in the forbidden conduct would "materially and substantially interfere with the requirements of appropriate discipline in the operation of the school," the prohibition cannot be sustained.

In the present case, the District Court made no such finding, and our independent examination of the record fails to yield evidence that the school authorities had reason to anticipate that the wearing of the armbands would substantially interfere with the work of the school or impinge upon the rights of other students. Even an official memorandum prepared after the suspension that listed the reasons for the ban on wearing the armbands made no reference to the anticipation of such disruption.[3]

On the contrary, the action of the school authorities appears to have been based upon an urgent wish to avoid the controversy which might result from the expression, even by the silent symbol of armbands, of opposition to this Nation's part in the conflagration in Vietnam. . . .

It is also relevant that the school authorities did not purport to prohibit the wearing of all symbols of political or controversial significance. The record shows that students in some of the schools wore buttons relating to national political campaigns, and some even wore the Iron Cross, traditionally a symbol of Nazism. The order prohibiting the wearing of armbands did not extend to these. Instead, a particular symbol—black armbands worn to exhibit opposition to this Nation's involvement in Vietnam—was singled out for prohibition. Clearly, the prohibition of expression of one particular opinion, at least without evidence that it is necessary to avoid material and substantial interference with schoolwork or discipline, is not constitutionally permissible.

In our system, state-operated schools may not be enclaves of totalitarianism. School officials do not possess absolute authority over their students. Students in school as well as out of school are "persons" under our Constitution. They are possessed of fundamental rights which the State must respect, just as they themselves must respect their obligations to the State. In our system, students may not be regarded as closed-circuit recipients of only that which the State chooses to communicate. They may not be confined to the expression of those sentiments that are officially approved. In the absence of a specific showing of constitutionally valid reasons to regulate their speech, students are entitled to freedom of expression of their views. . . .

. . .

The principle of these cases is not confined to the supervised and ordained discussion which takes place in the classroom. The principal use to which the schools are dedicated is to accommodate students during prescribed hours for the purpose of certain types of activities. Among those activities is personal intercommunication among the students. This is not only an inevitable part of the process of attending school; it is also an important part of the educational process. A student's rights, therefore, do not embrace merely the classroom hours. When he is in the cafeteria, or on the playing field, or on the campus during the authorized hours, he may express his opinions, even on controversial subjects like the conflict in Vietnam, if he does so without "materially and substantially interfer(ing) with the requirements of appropriate discipline in the operation of the school" and without colliding with the rights of others. But conduct by the student, in class or out of it, which for any reason—whether it stems from time, place, or type of behavior—materially disrupts classwork or involves substantial disorder or invasion of the rights of others is, of course, not immunized by the constitutional guarantee of freedom of speech.

. . .

As we have discussed, the record does not demonstrate any facts which might reasonably have led school authorities to forecast substantial disruption of or material interference with school activities, and no disturbances or disorders on the school premises in fact occurred. These petitioners merely went about their ordained rounds in school. Their deviation consisted only in wearing on their sleeve a band of black cloth, not more than two inches wide. They wore it to exhibit their disapproval of the Vietnam hostilities and their advocacy of a truce, to make their views known, and, by their example, to influence others to adopt them. They neither interrupted school activities nor sought to intrude in the school affairs or the lives of others. They caused discussion outside of the classrooms, but no interference with work and no disorder. In the circumstances, our Constitution does not permit officials of the State to deny their form of expression.

. . .

Reversed and remanded.

Justice BLACK, dissenting.

. . .

. . . While the absence of obscene remarks or boisterous and loud disorder perhaps justifies the Court's statement that the few armband students did not actually "disrupt" the classwork, I think the record overwhelmingly shows that the armbands did exactly what the elected school officials and principals foresaw they would, that is, took the students' minds off their classwork and diverted them to thoughts about the highly emotional subject of the Vietnam war. And I repeat that if the time has come when pupils of state-supported schools, kindergartens, grammar schools, or high schools, can defy and flout orders of school officials to keep their minds on their own schoolwork, it is the beginning of a new revolutionary era of permissiveness in this country fostered by the judiciary. The next logical step, it appears to me, would be to hold unconstitutional laws that bar pupils under 21 or 18 from voting, or from being elected members of the boards of education.

. . .

Change has been said to be truly the law of life but sometimes the old and the tried and true are worth holding. The schools of this Nation have undoubtedly contributed to giving us tranquility and to making us a more law-abiding people. Uncontrolled and uncontrollable liberty is an enemy to domestic peace. We cannot close our eyes to the fact that some of the country's greatest problems are crimes committed by the youth, too many of school age. School discipline, like parental discipline, is an integral and important part of training our children to be good citizens—to be better citizens. Here a very small number of students have crisply and summarily refused to obey a school order designed to give pupils who want to learn the opportunity to do so. One does not need to be a prophet or the son of a prophet to know that after the Court's holding today some students in Iowa schools and indeed in all schools will be ready, able, and willing to defy their teachers on practically all orders. This is the more unfortunate for the schools since groups of students all over the land are already running loose, conducting break-ins, sit-ins, lie-ins, and smash-ins. Many of these student groups, as is all too familiar to all who read the newspapers and watch the television news programs, have already engaged in rioting, property seizures, and destruction. They have picketed schools to force students not to cross their picket lines and have too often violently attacked earnest but frightened students who wanted an education that the pickets did not want them to get. Students engaged in such activities are apparently confident that they know far more about how to operate public school systems than do their parents, teachers, and elected school officials. . . . I dissent.

Building on *Barnette*, the Court in *Tinker* established several principles. First, it established that students do not surrender their constitutional rights simply by entering a public school; second, that symbolic dress worn for political reasons is expression protected by the First Amendment; and, third, that student expression can only be curtailed or censored where the school can show it threatens a "material and substantial interference" with the school's effective operation.

These principles were sharply limited in *Hazelwood School District v. Kuhlmeier* (1988), where the Court held that all student expression associated with official academic activities, such as the school newspaper, the school yearbook, assemblies, the student council, and athletic teams, may be regulated or censored in the interests of serving the school's reasonable academic missions and objectives. (We will explore this major caveat to the *Tinker* principle in Chapter 3.)

EXERCISE 2.4. Do you think that "political" discussion and nonviolent protests have a proper place in public schools? Should high school students be shielded from the discomforting turbulence of political controversy or should they be educated for active participation as democratic citizens in the rough-and-tumble of American society? What about junior high school students? Elementary school students? Is there any way to avoid political controversy in school? Write a one-page essay answering these questions.

EXERCISE 2.5. A student, disgruntled by a city school policy forbidding "gang colors" on campus, wears around his neck an orange-and-green bandana, colors widely associated with the Bad Boys, a local gang whose members are frequently getting into trouble with the law. The student, who is not a member of the gang himself, garners attention in the halls; several social studies classes put aside their regular work for 10-15 minutes and discuss the problems with youth gangs and the constitutionality of the citywide ban on "gang colors." There is no violence as a result of the student's bandana, but the principal learns of the student's apparel and orders him to take the bandana off. Is this student's choice of apparel protected by the First Amendment? Is the policy constitutional? Is it too vague to be enforced? What would you do if you were the principal in this situation?

JUSTICE ABE FORTAS (1910–1982) wrote the opinion for the majority in this case. Born in Memphis, Tennessee, Justice Fortas was the youngest of five children. He went to Southwestern College in Memphis and Yale Law School, where he studied under another future justice, William O. Douglas. His good friend, President Lyndon Johnson, appointed Fortas to the Court in 1965. Fortas, an accomplished violinist, remained on the Court for only four years.

HIGHLIGHTS

➤ Before going on the Court, when he was a partner at the prestigious Washington firm of Arnold and Porter, Fortas became the court-appointed advocate for Clarence Earl Gideon, the appellant in *Gideon v. Wainwright* (1963). This case established that the government must appoint lawyers for indigent criminal defendants who cannot otherwise afford one.

➤ Justice Fortas wrote the Court's opinion in *In re Gault* (1967), holding that young people in juvenile proceedings enjoy many of the same constitutional protections as adults, including the right to counsel and the right against self-incrimination.

The Confederate Flag and Other Racially Provocative Symbols

As we saw in *Barnette*, people can get very touchy about flags. As we saw in *Tinker*, people become concerned about what students wear to school. Put flags and clothes together, and you get a combustible mixture, as we see in the next case, *Melton v. Young* (1972), in which the Sixth Circuit Court of Appeals upheld the suspension of a Brainerd High School student in Chattanooga, Tennessee, for wearing to school a jacket with the Confederate flag sewn on his sleeve. Prior to the incident, there had been racial antagonism and repeated fights and disturbances over the school's use of the Confederate flag as an official school symbol. In response, the school had decided to drop the Confederate flag and the song "Dixie" from its school functions. Rod Melton protested by wearing his Confederate flag symbol to school. Watch how both the majority and the dissenting opinions invoke *Tinker* to support their decisions. Which side is more convincing?

———

MELTON

v.

YOUNG

United States Court of Appeals
Sixth Circuit
Aug. 30, 1972.

DAMON J. KEITH, District Judge.

. . .

Brainerd is a public high school in the city of Chattanooga, Tennessee. Until 1966 Brainerd was operated as an all white school which had adopted as its nickname the word "Rebel" and used the Confederate flag as the school flag along with the song Dixie as its pep song. The school has been attended by both white and black students since 1966; by 1969 the student body consisted of 170 black and 1224 white students.

. . . [W]ith the advent of the 1969 school year the student body became racially polarized as a result of continuing controversy over the use of the Confederate flag and the song Dixie at various school functions. It also appears that on October 8, 1969 demonstrations took place at the school which disrupted classes and that on the evening of the same day a motorcade drove through various parts of the city waving Confederate flags. Thereafter various disturbances took place in the city finally culminating in the imposition of a city-wide curfew for four nights from October 13 through October 17, 1969. The District Court also found that throughout the remainder of the fall semester considerable racial tension existed within the student body which continued on into the following spring. During this period it was necessary to call for police assistance amid several confrontations and also to close the school for the purpose of restoring order and calming tensions.

In May, 1970, the Brainerd school administration and P.T.A. appointed a committee of citizens to study the difficulties of the past year and recommend remedial action for the ensuing year. Among the conclusions of the committee were the nickname "Rebel," the song Dixie, and the Confederate flag were precipitating causes of tension and disorder within the school. As a corrective measure the committee recommended that the use of the Confederate flag as a school symbol and the use of the song Dixie as the school pep song be discontinued but that the nickname "Rebel" be retained. These recommendations were adopted as official policy by the School Board at its meeting on July 8, 1970 along with the directive to school administrators that each principal develop and disseminate within the student body a "code of conduct"[4] consistent with the recommendations by the opening of the school in September, 1970. It is this code and the consequences of its enforcement that gave rise to this lawsuit.

Appellant, after both he and his parents were informed of the new rules, wore a jacket to school with an emblem depicting a Confederate flag on one sleeve. He was asked to remove the emblem or cease wearing the jacket while in school by the principal but declined to do so. After he was allowed to return to class several complaints from both faculty and students caused the principal to call appellant to his office and request him to remove the jacket, which request was again refused. The principal then indicated that it was his judgment that the emblem was "provocative" and in violation of the school code and thereupon he directed that appellant either remove the jacket or leave the school. Appellant chose to absent himself from the campus.

Mississippi governor Ross Barnett smiles while Confederate flags wave in the background at a University of Mississippi football game. The Confederate battle flag made a strong reappearance in the South after the Supreme Court's desegregation holding in *Brown v. Board of Education* in 1954.

The following day appellant presented himself at the school with the same jacket and emblem and upon being sent to the principal's office and being requested to remove the jacket stated that he was merely demonstrating pride in his Confederate heritage by the wearing of the flag and that he had no other motive. Appellant was then told to leave school and not return until he was willing to stop displaying the Confederate emblem while in school. The above two suspensions occurred on September 8 and September 9, 1970 respectively and letters were sent to appellant's parents on both occasions stating the reasons for the suspension.

. . .

. . . In our view the only question for determination is whether a public high school student's suspension for his unwillingness to stop wearing a Confederate flag patch was violative of the First and Fourteenth Amendments under the circumstances in existence at the time of the suspension?

This is a troubling case; on the one hand we are faced with the exercise of the fundamental constitutional right to freedom of speech, and on the other with the oft conflicting, but equally important, need to maintain decorum in our public schools so that the learning process may be carried out in an orderly manner. It is abundantly clear that this Court will not uphold arbitrary or capricious restrictions on the exercise of such jealously guarded and vitally important constitutional tenets. However, it is contended here that the circumstances at the time of appellant's suspension were such that the District Court could properly find that

> "[t]he Principal had every right to anticipate that a tense, racial situation continued to exist at Brainerd High School as of the school [sic] in September of 1970 and that repetition of the previous year's disorders might reoccur if student use of the Confederate symbol was permitted to resume."

It is our view after an independent examination of the record that the conclusions of the District Court are fully supported by the evidence.

In the leading case of *Tinker v. Des Moines Independent Community School District,* the Supreme Court stated . . . that student conduct which "materially disrupts class work or involves substantial disorder or invasion of the rights of others" is not afforded the cloak of protection provided by the First Amendment.

. . .

It is therefore our conclusion that under all of the circumstances herein presented that appellant's suspension was not violative of his First and Fourteenth Amendment rights and that the judgment below was proper.

Affirmed.

WILLIAM E. MILLER, Circuit Judge (dissenting).

. . .

The evidence in this case clearly brings it within the ambit of *Tinker v. Des Moines Independent Community School District*. It is my firm conviction that the Principal in suspending the student simply over-reacted and was motivated by the kind of "undifferentiated fear or apprehension of disturbance" which the court in *Tinker* held to be insufficient to overcome the right to freedom of expression. True enough, in this case the Principal was aware of the disturbances which had occurred during the prior school year, but he failed to take into account, in acting so hastily and precipitately, the following differentiating factors which appear to me to be of controlling significance:

1. The protests of the previous year were against a group of school symbols which by long usage and custom, if not by express official sanction, carried the impact of official sanction, whereas the wearing of the small sleeve insignia in this case by a single student could in no way represent an official ruling or have the appearance of doing so.

2. In the early part of the 1970–71 school year (in September) a football game was played by the school team when some students imprudently and in violation of the school's code of conduct waved Confederate flags, with no resulting protests or outbreaks of violence, indicating a lessening of racial tension at the school.

3. In the interim between school years, the Board of Education, acting upon the recommendation of a citizens committee which had made an intensive study of the events of 1969–70, mandated the discontinuance at Brainerd of the song "Dixie" and the Confederate Flag as school symbols, but retained the designation of "Rebels" for the school's athletic teams. If such continued use officially of a term equally as suggestive of the Confederacy as the flag caused no disruption, it is difficult to conceive how the wearing of a confederate flag insignia could be seriously taken as disruptive.

4. There was no finding by the Committee that the wearing of confederate symbols on clothing by individual students as matters of personal choice had contributed to the previous trouble or that it should be prohibited for the future.

5. The complaints received by the Principal concerning this student's display of the Confederate Flag on his sleeve were, at best, minimal if not trivial.

6. As of the time this student was suspended there had been no acts of violence at the school and no significant threats of disruption, despite the continued "official" use of the team name "Rebels" and the events at the opening football game. There was every reason to believe that the official steps taken by the School Board in abolishing the school song and flag had satisfied the demands of those who protested the year before.

7. The nature of the "symbolism" in this case (entitled under *Tinker* to the same reverence as "pure speech") is of significance: It was small; it was worn as a part of an article of clothing; and it had no inherent qualities for causing disruption or disturbance.

8. The emblem was worn by the student in a quiet, peaceful and dignified manner with no untoward gestures or remarks.

9. The Principal conducted no substantial inquiry to ascertain the true facts as to whether the wearing of the insignia would lead to further trouble.

The fact is that despite the racial strife of the year before the circumstances were altogether different in the school year beginning in the fall of 1970, and there is no substantial basis to support the Principal's apprehension and fear that a small emblem worn by a single student on the sleeve of his jacket, which was merely symbolic of one of the historic facts of American life, would activate anew the kind of turmoil which had previously existed and which had been caused by entirely different circumstances. After all, it should be emphasized, the school symbols which were discontinued, such as the song "Dixie" and the Confederate Flag, at least bore the appearance of officialdom and could hardly be compared with the personal choice of a single student to decorate his jacket with a harmless emblem of the Confederate Flag.

In *Melton*, the Court found that the interference threatened by Melton's Confederate flag insignia was material and substantial under the *Tinker* standard. *Melton* is a court of appeals case that was appealed to the Supreme Court through a petition for a *writ of certiorari*, which the Court issues to direct a lower court to deliver a case for review. The Supreme Court has discretion to choose the cases it wishes to hear. When the Court declines to hear a case, as it did in *Melton*, it "denies certiorari," or, in the vernacular, "denies cert." The Court denies cert in more than 99 percent of the cases in which it is sought. It is extremely difficult to get a case taken up by the Supreme Court.

> Although it is hard to get a case heard before the Supreme Court, it is relatively easy to go hear someone else's Supreme Court case being argued. Arguments are open to the public, so you may want to organize a class trip to Washington to see one; it is an unforgettable experience.
>
> The Supreme Court is in session between October and April and accommodates about fifty spectators on a first-come-first-served basis. Groups of thirty or more should write at least one month in advance to:
>
> Office of the Marshall
> Supreme Court of the United States of America
> 1 First Street N.E.
> Washington, D.C. 20543

EXERCISE 2.6. The student in *Melton* was sent home from school because the principal anticipated that the emblem on his jacket might cause "material and substantial interference" at school. Based on the earlier events surrounding the Confederate flag at Brainerd, do you think that this was indeed the right decision? Or did Judge Miller, in dissent, successfully prove his point that this was an overreaction on the part of the school? Should a school have to wait for a disruption to occur before it limits students' rights? Why or why not? Discuss whether or not the court came to the correct decision.

EXERCISE 2.7. Some people see the Confederate battle flag as a symbol of slavery, secession from the Union, and white supremacy. Others see it as a symbol of regional and historic pride. Can the same symbol mean different things to different people? What if someone wore a Confederate flag emblem to your school? What kind of effect do you think it would have? What message would he or she be sending?

EXERCISE 2.8. Do you think that racist and sexist symbols enjoy less First Amendment protection than other speech? Does the Fourteenth Amendment principle of Equal Protection give government more power to censor racist expression? Why or why not? If you were a principal or teacher, would you allow Confederate flags to be worn as part of student clothing in your classroom? Does the fact that the United States fought a war against the Confederacy in which hundreds of thousands of Americans died make any difference?

FOR THE CLASS

TINKER ARMBANDS—WITH A TWIST. On Friday, November 14, 1997, in Champlin City, the Champlin High School principal, Mr. Sanford, announced that "interracial couples will not be permitted to attend the Holiday Dance." Champlin High is a public school.

Heather Hammer had planned to attend with her boyfriend, Shane Jackson, a white student. Heather's father is African-American. Her mother, who died when Heather was nine, was white. Heather made an appointment with Mr. Sanford in order to ask permission to attend the dance with Shane.

Heather entered Mr. Sanford's office at 8:00 a.m. Monday morning, November 17. She explained to him that regardless of the race of her dance date, she might be violating the new rule since she was both black and white. Heather was left speechless when Mr. Sanford told her: "Heather, I am sorry, but unfortunately this school cannot be forced to pay the cost for the mistake of two foolish people. You're black and that's that."

By the time Heather got home that afternoon she was distraught. She told her father the entire story. Heather had never seen her father as angry as he was that afternoon. He telephoned Suzanne Simon, chair of the Champlin County School Board, who called an emergency meeting for the next evening. The Board met with a large and boisterous crowd in the audience.

Heather was relieved when the school board voted to require Mr. Sanford to retract his ban on interracial dating, which he grudgingly did the next day. By the time the retraction was made, every student knew what had happened to Heather. Everyone had an opinion about the actions and the words of the principal.

The following Monday students talked about these events and began organizing to express their sentiments. Seventeen African-American students and one white student, Shane, wore to school black armbands with a small white "X" on the outside of the band to symbolize what they saw, in the words of one student, as "the militant anti-racism of Malcolm X."

The next day, twenty-two white students wore T-shirts emblazoned with the Confederate flag and the logo, "The South Shall Rise Again." While yelling back and forth by various students in the hallways often became loud and many students were obviously upset by the tensions (which mirrored tensions in the town over a racially motivated killing), there were no violent altercations between students inside or outside of school.

As the tensions increased, Mr. Sanford announced his new policy that "no student is to come to school wearing a Malcolm X armband or a Confederate flag T-shirt, or any other item of clothing intended to deliver a racial message." The following day, Stacy Clarke, Devon Jenkins, and five other students wore Confederate flag T-shirts and eight students, including Heather and Shane, wore Malcolm X armbands. All fifteen students were suspended for two days. Every student appealed the decision of suspension and asked that the disciplinary action be removed from their records, but every suspension was upheld by the School Board.

The cases have made it to the Supreme Court and will be heard together. Should the suspensions of Hammer, Jackson, and the other students who wore Malcolm X armbands be upheld or reversed? Should the suspensions of the students who wore Confederate flag T-shirts be upheld or reversed?

Select nine students to act as Supreme Court justices and six more to act as attorneys arguing for each of the three sides in the case: two to represent Hammer, Jackson, and the "X" armband-wearing students; two to represent Clarke, Jenkins, and the Confederate T-shirt–wearing students; and two to represent the Champlin County School Board, which upheld the principal's discipline of all the students. The students acting as counsel should compose oral arguments in defense of their clients. The students acting as Supreme Court justices should discuss the case, vote on a decision, and compose opinions following oral argument as to why they are upholding or reversing the discipline. (Concurring and dissenting opinions are, of course, allowed.)

BAN ON BLUE JEANS. In a Greenwich, Connecticut, local newspaper, a report appears on Friday that annual "National Coming Out Day" is the following Thursday, May 5. The story states that gays and lesbians and their supporters will wear blue jeans to show their support for gay rights. The Greenwich school board learns that many high school students intend to wear blue jeans (which are ordinarily allowed) and that another group of students plans to wear buttons that say "God Made Adam and Eve, Not Adam and Steve" provided by a local conservative group. The school board announces that "any student who wears blue jeans to school on May 5 or wears a button expressing an opinion about homosexuality will be sent home for the rest of the day." Can the school board do this under Supreme Court case law?

Divide the class into two groups, then take turns making arguments on both sides. Do you think the school board dealt well with the expected expression from students? How would you have handled it if you were on the school board?

A Hirsute Lawsuit: Do Boys Have the Right to Wear Long Hair?

According to *Tinker,* students can choose their own dress as long as their choices do not threaten "material" and "substantial" disruption to school activities. In *Karr v. Schmidt* (1972), the Fifth Circuit considered a claim that a student's hairstyle represents a symbolic and expressive choice that deserves First Amendment protection. The plaintiff was Chesley Karr, a sixteen-year-old boy at Coronado High School in El Paso, Texas, who was not allowed to enroll in his junior year of high school because he had grown his hair long and refused to cut it despite his school's repeated demands that he do so.

Chesley argued that his hairstyle was deeply personal and integrally related to his sense of style and personal values. He went to federal court and challenged the "boy hair" provisions in the following dress code:

> The matter of student grooming is of utmost concern to parents who realize the importance of seeing that children are properly attired when they leave for school each day. Also, student behavior is influenced by proper dress and grooming. Consequently, student grooming is the proper concern of school administrators and teachers. In order to help ensure proper acceptable behavior on the part of the students, it becomes necessary to establish certain guidelines to aid parents and students in selecting the proper attire for the school year. Schools also recognize that parents are basically responsible for their children's dress and general appearance. The role of the school is one of guidance for pupils in an effort for total education and the development of proper attitudes. Student dress will be considered acceptable if it does not violate any of the three following principles: 1. Clothing worn is not to be suggestive or indecent. 2. Clothing and general appearance is not to be of the type that would cause a disturbance or interfere with the instructional program. 3. Clothing and general appearance is to be such as not to constitute a health or safety hazard. Guidelines for dress and grooming are:
>
> . . .
>
> FOR BOYS
> Hair may be blocked, but is not to hang over the ears or the top of the collar of a standard dress shirt and must not obstruct vision. No artificial means to conceal the length of the hair is to be permitted; i.e., ponytails, buns, wigs, combs, or straps.
>
> . . .
>
> Cleanliness of body and clothing is expected of all students at all times. No child shall be admitted to school or shall be allowed to continue in school who fails to conform to the proper standards of dress.

Chesley won a First Amendment and Equal Protection victory in federal district court in Texas. The court found that "the presence and enforcement of the haircut rule causes far more disruption of the classroom instructional process than the hair it seeks to prohibit."

The district court rejected the different reasons offered by the school to support the rule against long hair. For example, the school argued that the rule was necessary to guarantee cleanliness, but the district court found that the length of a student's hair is unrelated to "habits of personal hygiene." That is, a person can have long hair that is clean or short hair that is dirty.

The district court also rejected the claim that long hair creates a safety hazard in science laboratories; if true, the court said, this would mean that the rule should apply to girls as well as boys. The court also found that, even though fights occurred between long- and short-haired students, the proper course of action for the school board was to "[teach] tolerance" and stop the fighting rather than interfere with personal liberty.

However, when the school system appealed this judgment, the Fifth Circuit Court of Appeals reversed and found in the school's favor. According to this holding, personal decisions about hair length are not protected by the First Amendment. Schools can actually make boys cut their hair. What do you think of the reasoning in the following decision? Would it come out the same way today?

— —

KARR

v.

SCHMIDT

United States Court of Appeals
Fifth Circuit
April 28, 1972.

LEWIS R. MORGAN, Circuit Judge.

. . .

III

. . . Is there a constitutionally protected right to wear one's hair in a public high school in the length and style that suits the wearer? We hold that no such right is to be found within the plain meaning of the Constitution.

. . .

A. The First Amendment.—The most frequently asserted basis for a constitutional right to wear long hair lies in the First Amendment. It is argued that the wearing of long hair is symbolic speech by which the wearer conveys his individuality, his rejection of conventional values, and the like. Accordingly, it is argued that the wearing of hair is subject to the protection of the First Amendment. . . .

We find considerable difficulty, however, with the First Amendment approach to this question. First, we think it doubtful that the wearing of long hair has sufficient communicative content to entitle it to the protection of the First Amendment. . . . For some, no doubt, the wearing of long hair is intended to convey a discrete message to the world. But for many, the wearing of long hair is simply a matter of personal taste or the result of peer group influence.[5] Appellee Karr, for example, has brought this suit not because his hair conveys a message but "because I like my hair long." Surely if we are to have workable rules of constitutional law, the validity of the regulation cannot turn on the plaintiff's subjective motivation in wearing his hair long.

For these reasons, we think it inappropriate that the protection of the First Amendment be extended to the wearing of long hair. Moreover, it is our belief that the Supreme Court's decision in *Tinker* supports this view. In *Tinker,* three students were suspended for wearing to school black armbands to publicize their objection to [Vietnam] hostilities. The court concluded that the wearing of armbands under such circumstances was closely akin to pure speech and thus fell within the ambit of the First Amendment. The court, however, clearly distinguished the case which we have here of hair and grooming regulations. It observed:

"The problem posed by the present case does not relate to regulation of the length of skirts or the type of clothing, to hair style, or deportment. . . . Our problem involves direct, primary First Amendment rights akin to pure speech."

The conclusion is inescapable that this paragraph was intended to delimit the outer reach of the court's holding. We read this language as indicating that the right to style one's hair as one pleases in the public schools does not inherit the protection of the First Amendment.

. . .

In this case, it is evident from the record that the school authorities seek only to accomplish legitimate objectives in promulgating the hair regulation here in question. The record nowhere suggests that their goals are other than the elimination of classroom distraction, the avoidance of violence between long and short haired students, the elimination of potential health hazards, and the elimination of safety hazards resulting from long hair in the science labs.

. . .

Reversed.

. . . Circuit Judges, join, dissenting.

Hair styles change. A high school boy if he chooses should be able to wear his hair as Yul Brynner does or as Joe Namath does without fear of being deprived of an education

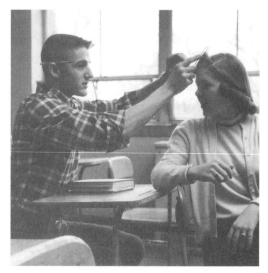

Hairstyles change, as seen from these 1999, 1957, and 1970 photographs. Should schools have power to regulate hairstyle, or does the First Amendment right of expression cover not only what is in your head but what is on it?

by a majority of school board members who grew up at a time the crew-cut was fashionable.

Individual rights never seem important to those who tolerate their infringement. Yet the Bill of Rights and the Fourteenth Amendment were designed to limit the reach of majority control over fundamental personal rights. Many young men and boys regard long hair as an expression of affinity with their peers and disapproval of the older generations' handling of the Vietnam War and current social problems. Some may wear their hair long because the girls like it long. Either way, the right to wear one's hair as one pleases is a fundamental right implicit "within the commodious concept of liberty, embracing freedoms great and small."

. . .

I

. . .

To me the right to wear one's hair as one pleases, although unspecified in our Bill of Rights, is a "fundamental" right protected by the Due Process Clause. Hair is a purely personal matter—a matter of personal style which for centuries has been one aspect of the manner in which we hold ourselves out to the rest of the world. Like other elements of costume, hair is a symbol: of elegance, of efficiency, of affinity and association, of nonconformity and rejection of traditional values. A person shorn of the freedom to vary the length and style of his hair is forced against his will to hold himself out symbolically as a person holding ideas contrary, perhaps, to ideas he holds most dear. Forced dress, including forced hair style, humiliates the unwilling complier, forces him to submerge his individuality in the "undistracting" mass, and in general, smacks of the exaltation of organization over member, unit over component, and state over individual. I always thought this country does not condone such repression.

. . .

I ask: What is the important state interest that permits a public school board to deny an education to a boy whose hair is acceptably long to his parents but too long to suit a majority of the School Board of El Paso, Texas?

I submit that under the First and Fourteenth Amendments, if a student wishes to show his disestablishmentarianism by wearing long hair or has the whim to wear long hair, antidisestablishmentarians on public school boards have no constitutional authority to prevent it.

EXERCISE 2.9. What statement are you making (if any) with your hairstyle? Are you making it consciously or unconsciously? What do the style, color, and cut of your hair express about you? The French semiologist Roland Barthes argued that people inevitably make statements with their clothing and hairstyle, and there is no way around it. Do you agree?

EXERCISE 2.10. If a public high school can ban *long* hair for boys because it may cause fights between long- and short-haired students, can it ban *short* hair for girls by the same rationale? Can a school with a feminist agenda require boys to grow long hair and girls to have short hair to "change outmoded sexist stereotypes"?

EXERCISE 2.11. Write a one- or two-page essay explaining why hair length and style *should* or *should not* be protected by the First Amendment. Should the same rules hold for both boys and girls?

Double Entendres and Double Standards: Lewd and Suggestive Language in a Student Government Campaign Speech

One of the things that makes people most nervous about free speech in school is the undeniable fact that teenagers frequently talk about sex and sexuality, sometimes in irreverent and crude ways. In *Bethel School District v. Fraser* (1986), the Supreme Court's anxiety about adolescent sexual innuendo led to a major retreat from its earlier free speech decision in *Tinker*.

The case began when Matthew Fraser, a popular student and known "cutup" at Bethel High School in Pierce County, Washington, gave a nominating speech for a fellow student running for a student government position. The theme of the speech was a sophomoric sexual metaphor that included the following sentences:

> I know a man who is firm—he's firm in his pants, he's firm in his shirt, his character is firm—but most . . . of all, his belief in you, the students of Bethel, is firm . . . . Jeff Kuhlman is a man who takes his point and pounds it in. If necessary, he'll take an issue and nail it to the wall. He doesn't attack things in spurts—he drives hard, pushing and pushing until finally—he succeeds. . . . Jeff is a man who will go to the very end—even the climax, for each and every one of you. . . . So vote for Jeff for A.S.B. vice-president—he'll never come between you and the best our high school can be.

The Court found that the school did nothing wrong in disciplining Fraser for this speech. What is the Court's reasoning? How would you have decided this case?

JUSTICE WARREN E. BURGER (1907–1995) was born on Constitution Day (September 17) in St. Paul, Minnesota, where he went to high school, college, and night law school at the St. Paul College of Law (now the William Mitchell College of Law). After a career at the Justice Department and service as a judge on the U.S. Court of Appeals for the District of Columbia Circuit, Burger was appointed to the Supreme Court by President Richard Nixon in 1969. Burger remained on the Court until 1986, when he left to devote himself fully to the Commission on the Bicentennial of the Constitution, a post from which he argued for pervasive constitutional education in American schools and colleges.

HIGHLIGHTS

➤ In high school, Burger was president of the student council, a reporter on the student newspaper, and a well-rounded athlete. He was forced to turn down a partial scholarship to Princeton because his family could not afford to pay the difference. Burger married Elvera Stromberg, who was a schoolteacher, and future Supreme Court justice Harry Blackmun was best man at his wedding.

➤ As Chief Justice, Burger shrunk the time allotted to Supreme Court litigants from two hours per case to one hour per case.

➤ The Chief Justice is the presiding officer of the Supreme Court who votes in every case along with the other justices. When he is part of the majority, he assigns the task of writing opinions to the other justices. He is also the chief administrative officer of the federal judicial branch.

BETHEL SCHOOL DISTRICT NO. 403
v.
FRASER

Supreme Court of the United States
Argued March 3, 1986.
Decided July 7, 1986.

Chief Justice BURGER delivered the opinion of the Court.

We granted certiorari to decide whether the First Amendment prevents a school district from disciplining a high school student for giving a lewd speech at a school assembly.

I

A

On April 26, 1983, respondent Matthew N. Fraser, a student at Bethel High School in Pierce County, Washington, delivered a speech nominating a fellow student for student elective office. Approximately 600 high school students, many of whom were 14-year-olds, attended the assembly. Students were required to attend the assembly or to report to the study hall. The assembly was part of a school-sponsored educational program in self-government. . . . During the entire speech, Fraser referred to his candidate in terms of an elaborate, graphic, and explicit sexual metaphor.

Two of Fraser's teachers, with whom he discussed the contents of his speech in advance, informed him that the speech was "inappropriate and that he probably should not deliver it," and that his delivery of the speech might have "severe consequences."

During Fraser's delivery of the speech, a school counselor observed the reaction of students to the speech. Some students hooted and yelled; some by gestures graphically simulated the sexual activities pointedly alluded to in respondent's speech. Other students appeared to be bewildered and embarrassed by the speech. One teacher reported that on the day following the speech, she found it necessary to forgo a portion of the scheduled class lesson in order to discuss the speech with the class.

A Bethel High School disciplinary rule prohibiting the use of obscene language in the school provides:

"Conduct which materially and substantially interferes with the educational process is prohibited, including the use of obscene, profane language or gestures."

The morning after the assembly, the Assistant Principal called Fraser into her office and notified him that the school considered his speech to have been a violation of this rule. Fraser was presented with copies of five letters submitted by teachers, describing his con-

Matthew Fraser stands in front of Bethel High School, which suspended him for his sexually suggestive nomination speech for a fellow student in 1983. The Court found that the school acted within its powers to discipline Fraser because he gave his saucy speech at a school-sponsored event.

duct at the assembly; he was given a chance to explain his conduct, and he admitted to having given the speech described and that he deliberately used sexual innuendo in the speech. Fraser was then informed that he would be suspended for three days, and that his name would be removed from the list of candidates for graduation speaker at the school's commencement exercises.

Fraser sought review of this disciplinary action through the School District's grievance procedures. The hearing officer determined that the speech given by respondent was "indecent, lewd, and offensive to the modesty and decency of many of the students and faculty in attendance at the assembly." The examiner determined that the speech fell within the ordinary meaning of "obscene," as used in the disruptive-conduct rule, and affirmed the discipline in its entirety. Fraser served two days of his suspension, and was allowed to return to school on the third day.

B

. . . [Fraser] alleged a violation of his First Amendment right to freedom of speech and sought both injunctive relief and monetary damages. . . . The District Court held that the school's sanctions violated respondent's right to freedom of speech under the First Amendment to the United States Constitution, that the school's disruptive-conduct rule is unconstitutionally vague and overbroad, and that the removal of respondent's name from the graduation speaker's list violated the Due Process Clause of the Fourteenth Amendment because the disciplinary rule makes no mention of such removal as a possible sanction. The District Court awarded [Fraser] $278 in damages, $12,750 in litigation costs and attorney's fees, and enjoined the School District from preventing [him] from speaking at the commencement ceremonies. [Fraser], who had been elected graduation speaker by a write-in vote of his classmates, delivered a speech at the commencement ceremonies on June 8, 1983.

The Court of Appeals for the Ninth Circuit affirmed the judgment of the District Court, holding that [Fraser's] speech was indistinguishable from the protest armband in *Tinker v. Des Moines Independent Community School Dist.* . . .

We granted certiorari. We reverse.

II

. . . The Court of Appeals . . . appears to have proceeded on the theory that the use of lewd and obscene speech in order to make what the speaker considered to be a point in a nominating speech for a fellow student was essentially the same as the wearing of an armband in *Tinker* as a form of protest or the expression of a political position.

The marked distinction between the political "message" of the armbands in *Tinker* and the sexual content of respondent's speech in this case seems to have been given little weight by the Court of Appeals. In upholding the students' right to engage in a nondisruptive, passive expression of a political viewpoint in *Tinker,* this Court was careful to note that the case did "not concern speech or action that intrudes upon the work of the schools or the rights of other students."

. . . [W]e turn to consider the level of First Amendment protection accorded to Fraser's utterances and actions before an official high school assembly attended by 600 students.

III

. . .

. . . The undoubted freedom to advocate unpopular and controversial views in schools and classrooms must be balanced against the society's countervailing interest in teaching students the boundaries of socially appropriate behavior. Even the most heated political discourse in a democratic society requires consideration for the personal sensibilities of the other participants and audiences.

In our Nation's legislative halls, where some of the most vigorous political debates in our society are carried on, there are rules prohibiting the use of expressions offensive to other participants in the debate. Senators have been censured for abusive language directed at other Senators. . . . Can it be that what is proscribed in the halls of Congress is beyond the reach of school officials to regulate?

The First Amendment guarantees wide freedom in matters of adult public discourse. A sharply divided Court upheld the right to express an antidraft viewpoint in a public place, albeit in terms highly offensive to most citizens. It does not follow, however, that simply because the use of an offensive form of expression may not be prohibited to adults making what the speaker considers a political point, the same latitude must be permitted to children in a public school. . . .

Surely it is a highly appropriate function of public school education to prohibit the use of vulgar and offensive terms in public discourse. . . . The determination of what manner of speech in the classroom or in school assembly is inappropriate properly rests with the school board.

. . .

The pervasive sexual innuendo in Fraser's speech was plainly offensive to both teachers and students—indeed to any mature person. By glorifying male sexuality, and in its verbal content, the speech was acutely insulting to teenage girl students. The speech could well be seriously damaging to its less mature audience, many of whom were only 14 years old and on the threshold of awareness of human sexuality. Some students were reported as bewildered by the speech and the reaction of mimicry it provoked.

. . .

We hold that petitioner School District acted entirely within its permissible authority in imposing sanctions upon Fraser in response to his offensively lewd and indecent speech. Unlike the sanctions imposed on the students wearing armbands in *Tinker,* the penalties imposed in this case were unrelated to any political viewpoint. The First Amendment does not prevent the school officials from determining that to permit a vulgar and lewd speech such as respondent's would undermine the school's basic educational mission. A high school assembly or classroom is no place for a sexually explicit monologue directed towards an unsuspecting audience of teenage students. Accordingly, it was perfectly appropriate for the school to disassociate itself to make the point to the pupils that vulgar speech and lewd conduct is wholly inconsistent with the "fundamental values" of public school education. . . .

. . .

Reversed.

Justice MARSHALL, dissenting.

. . . I dissent from the Court's decision . . . because in my view the School District failed to demonstrate that respondent's remarks were indeed disruptive. The District Court and Court of Appeals conscientiously applied *Tin-*

JUSTICE THURGOOD MARSHALL (1908–1994), the first African-American Supreme Court justice, was born in Baltimore, Maryland, which he later described as "the most segregated city in the United States." He graduated from a segregated high school and went north to all-black Lincoln University in Pennsylvania. He could not go to law school in Maryland because the state school was for whites only, so he rose before dawn every morning and commuted to Howard Law School in Washington, D.C., where he studied under Dean Charles Hamilton Houston, the architect of the legal strategy to end Jim Crow segregation. Marshall's distinguished career as a civil rights lawyer led to his appointment as Solicitor General of the United States, a position from which he argued eighteen cases before the Supreme Court, and later as a federal appeals court judge. President Lyndon Johnson appointed Marshall to the Supreme Court in 1967, and he remained there until 1991.

HIGHLIGHTS

➤ As head of the NAACP Legal Defense Fund, Marshall argued along with other civil rights attorneys for the plaintiff black children in *Brown v. Board of Education,* the landmark case that discredited the doctrine of separate but equal and ended legalized apartheid in America.

ker v. Des Moines Independent Community School Dist. and concluded that the School District had not demonstrated any disruption of the educational process. I recognize that the school administration must be given wide latitude to determine what forms of conduct are inconsistent with the school's educational mission; nevertheless, where speech is involved, we may not unquestioningly accept a teacher's or administrator's assertion that certain pure speech interfered with education. . . .

EXERCISE 2.12. The *Fraser* Court found that schools could censor and punish students for "lewd, indecent or offensive" speech. While reaffirming that high school students have First Amendment rights, it held that such rights are not equal to the rights of adult citizens. After all, grown-ups do have the right to make lewd, indecent, and offensive remarks in public. (Think about "Saturday Night Live," Howard Stern, Beavis and Butthead, and other raunchy comedies or comedians on TV and radio.)

What exactly was wrong with Matthew's nominating speech? If you were the principal of Bethel High School, how would you have handled it? Do you think that suspension is an effective and appropriate response? What else could be done?

EXERCISE 2.13. Chief Justice Burger drew out a gender dimension to the legal conflict and wrote, "By glorifying male sexuality, and in its verbal content, the speech was acutely insulting to teenage girl students." Do you agree with this point? Was it more insulting to girls than to boys? Should girls (must girls) in high school be protected from the hyperactive sexual imaginations of teenage boys?

FOR THE CLASS

WHEN DO TEENAGERS GET THEIR POETIC LICENSE? Amy Feathertail was taking an elective in the second semester of her junior year at Palmetto High, a public "magnet" school for students who excel in language and writing. The class was about poetic interpretation and composition.

The school's mission statement requires each student in poetry class to compose a poem of publishable quality to be included in a book produced by the school at the end of the school year. The book was to be sold and the profits given to the school's magnet program. Each student was also to present his or her poem at a pre-graduation ceremony. While the presentation of the poem is not a requirement for graduation, it is the only opportunity students have to qualify for a statewide poetry competition. The winner of the state competition earns a $10,000 scholarship for college.

Amy composed a poem dedicated to young women in the United States and focused on what she perceived as the failure of society to celebrate and nourish female sexuality. The poem reads as follows:

Silence
We were to be as side-by-side
no matter as to the way we became
but after Woodhull and Steinem and Hillary Clinton
we are still submerged, bewildered, repressed:
We need the other to continue
to love, to care, to know eternity, to explore the day and the night
but we get treated as three-fifths human,
neither allowed to think creative thoughts that change
things and
relationships
nor permitted to feel
passion, urgent love, mad lust
the indecent naked longings for connection
that are man's birthright.
(They don't share anything, even things they must share.)
No one of us would know the subtle beauty of life
were we to be the same as you, driven animals, conquerors of nature,
but can we not even be ourselves?
We know no Self, no Mind, no Sex as we might want it;
We know only the place that you made for us.

The poem was enthusiastically approved by Amy's teacher, Mr. Metzloff, who said it showed "real intensity of emotion, precision of thought, and control of language." Mr. Metzloff approved publication of the poem in the school's book but, after reading it, Principal Hartner refused to allow Amy to present it to the assembly, saying that it was "lewd and indecently suggestive, inappropriate for the many younger students who will see it and a poor reflection on our academic program."

When the book was published, the school sold 1,093 copies. Of these, seven were returned because the individual purchasers were offended by Amy's poem.

In not having been permitted to recite her poem, Amy was denied the opportunity to compete for the state poetry competition and scholarship. She sues in court, alleging that her First Amendment rights were violated and asking for damages up to $10,000. Both sides agree that it would be better for all parties concerned to engage in mediation and negotiation rather than go through a protracted court battle.

Select one student to play the role of the professional *mediator*—that is, a neutral party charged with bringing the opposing sides to agreement by suggesting solutions and fostering productive negotiation. The mediator will hear from both the principal and from Amy about the decision not to allow her to present her poem to the high school community. Students appearing for the principal should explain why he did what he did and on what legal foundation he bases his decision. Students appearing for Amy should explain why they think this kind of censorship violates the First Amendment and why her poem should have been allowed into the competition. What is the mediator's decision? Were Amy's rights violated and, if so, does she get any money for her injuries? How much? Can you think of any other creative ways to work out the situation?

Coed Naked Civil Liberties: Do It to the First Amendment

Although *Fraser* gave schools authority to censor and punish "lewd, indecent and offensive" student speech, many states have given student speakers the same free speech rights that adults enjoy. The Supreme Court sets a basic floor for constitutional rights—not a ceiling on them—and the state legislatures and state courts can always decide to offer citizens (adults and minors) *more* rights and liberties under state law than they enjoy directly under the U.S. Constitution.

Consider the Student Free Expression Act passed by the Massachusetts legislature in 1974:

> The rights of students to freedom of expression in the public schools of the Commonwealth shall not be abridged, provided that such right shall not cause any disruption or disorder within the school. Freedom of expression shall include without limitation the rights and responsibilities of students, collectively and in-

After Jeffrey Pyle (left) was sent home for wearing a suggestive T-shirt, he and his brother Jonathan (right) challenged their school's rapidly evolving dress code by designing and wearing a series of sexually provocative and politically pointed T-shirts to class. The Pyle brothers are both in law school now.

dividually, (a) to express their views through speech and symbols, (b) to write, publish, and disseminate their views. . . .

In a very interesting case, *Pyle v. School Committee of South Hadley* (1996), the Supreme Judicial Court of Massachusetts interpreted this statute to allow students at South Hadley High School in Western Massachusetts to wear T-shirts with funny sexual subtexts that may be offensive to other students.

The *Pyle* case started when high school senior Jeffrey Pyle wore a shirt to gym class that his mother had given him bearing this message: "Coed Naked Band. Do It to the Rhythm." The shirt featured an illustration of closely inter-twined musical instruments. He was told not to wear it again, but he did and was promptly sent home for violating the school's dress code, which made it a vio-lation to wear a message that would "harass, threaten, intimidate, or demean an individual or group of individuals because of sex, color, race, religion, handicap, national origin or sexual orientation."

Jeffrey and his brother Jon were outraged and won the support of their mother and father (a professor of constitutional law at Mount Holyoke College) in an ir-reverent campaign they embarked upon to test the limits of the school's policy. The boys began to wear T-shirts of the same general type to school, including:

See Dick Drink/See Dick Drive/See Dick Die/Don't Be a Dick
Coed Naked Gerbils [Front] Some People Will Censor Anything [Back]
Coed Naked Civil Liberties [Front] Do It to the First Amendment [Back]
Legalize It [with a drawing of a marijuana plant]
A Century of Women On Top/Smith College Centennial/1875–1975
Boring Teacher-Approved Non-Suggestive T-Shirt
Coed Naked Censorship [Front] They Do It in South Hadley [Back]

The Pyle brothers were disciplined for violating a provision of a new, hastily adopted dress code prohibiting students from wearing clothing that "has com-ments, pictures, slogans, or designs that are obscene, profane, lewd or vulgar."

On July 25, 1996, the Massachusetts Supreme Judicial Court upheld the Pyle brothers' claim that state law absolutely protected the expression of their mes-sage, even if considered "vulgar" by some, so long as that expression causes no material disruption of the educational program. "The statute is unambiguous," the court held, "and must be construed as written. . . . *Our Legislature is free to grant greater rights to the citizens of this Commonwealth than would otherwise be pro-tected under the United States Constitution.*" The court thus stuck very closely to the *Tinker* standard and proclaimed broad free speech rights for students in Massa-chusetts.

EXERCISE 2.14. Many teachers and students saw Jeffrey Pyle's first T-shirt ("Coed Naked Band/ Do It to the Rhythm") as sexist or sexually harassing. Do you agree? Why or why not? Should students be allowed to wear sexist T-shirts? T-shirts with pictures of nude women (or men)?

EXERCISE 2.15. Should people have a right to wear "offensive" clothing? How do we know what "offensive" is? Who defines it? What do you find offensive? What do you wear that other people find offensive? (The late comedian Lenny Bruce once said, "My parents came to America to be offensive.")

EXERCISE 2.16. No student actually complained to the school administration about any of the Pyle brothers' T-shirts. Is that relevant in trying to decide whether such T-shirts are really "disruptive"? How does *Tinker* approach this problem?

EXERCISE 2.17. Did the Pyle brothers make a mountain out of a mole hill? Or did they do the right thing by standing up for their rights? What would you have done?

FOR THE CLASS

DRAFT A DRESS CODE. Break the class up into groups of three. Each group should write a dress code for your school that deals with both general standards of dress and specific standards for "message clothing." Come back together as a class. Read the various codes and compare their virtues and flaws in a class discussion. See if you can come up with a dress code for the school that achieves unanimous support in your class.

Although *Tinker* suggested that students might be treated like adult citizens in terms of the right to speak, the *Fraser* decision signaled the Court's second thoughts about relatively unrestrained expression in public schools. In Chapter 3, we will examine cases dealing with the rights of student newspaper reporters and the like. There, we will see how the Supreme Court in the 1980s turned away from broad student rights, substantially limiting the reach of *Tinker,* and upheld broad powers of school authorities to censor and regulate student expression in school.

Thought Control or Quality Control: *Board of Education v. Pico* and the Problem of Library Book Removal

The First Amendment protects not only the right to speak but also the right to receive information. Citizens have a right to information even when the government thinks the information in question may be dangerous and prefers to suppress its availability. In the public school context, the principle of free access to information loses some of its clarity because the Supreme Court has recognized that a school system controls its curriculum, its libraries, and the selection of textbooks. Yet, the general control over information exercised by the school system is not unlimited. For example, school officials cannot ban specific library books for political reasons. Consider the events that culminated in *Board of Education v. Pico*, a 1982 case that established this principle.

After several members of the Island Trees Board of Education went to a conference of the conservative Parents of New York United (PONYU), they returned home with a list of books that they considered for various reasons "objectionable" and "improper fare." The list of dangerous books included a number that were already in the Island Trees school libraries, among them the following:

> *Slaughterhouse-five*, by Kurt Vonnegut, Jr.
> *The Naked Ape*, by Desmond Morris
> *Down These Mean Streets*, by Piri Thomas
> *Best Short Stories of Negro Writers*, edited by Langston Hughes
> *Go Ask Alice*, by anonymous
> *Laughing Boy*, by Oliver LaFarge
> *Black Boy*, by Richard Wright
> *A Hero Ain't Nothin' but a Sandwich*, by Alice Childress
> *Soul on Ice*, by Eldridge Cleaver
> *A Reader for Writers*, edited by Jerome Archer
> *The Fixer*, by Bernard Malamud

Because these books had been described as "anti-American, anti-Christian, anti-Semitic, and just plain filthy," the Board of Education ordered public school librarians to deliver the books to the Board so they could be examined. The Board then formed a parent/teacher Book Review Committee to advise it on which books should be taken out of the libraries and which kept in the stacks. The Committee recommended the removal of only two books, but the Board went ahead without any further explanation and removed nine of the books from the public school libraries, making one other book available only with parental consent.

When a group of students brought a suit alleging violation of their First Amendment rights, the District Court threw the suit out and held for the Board of Education, finding that it had only targeted books that were "vulgar." But a panel of the Second Circuit—and then a closely divided Supreme Court (5–4)—found that the students had a right to go to trial in the case to show that the books were removed as part of an official effort at thought control rather than in an attempt to regulate student access to vulgar materials.

There was no majority opinion in *Board of Education v. Pico*, but Justice Brennan announced the judgment of the Supreme Court in an opinion that was joined in full by Justices Marshall and Stevens and in part by Justice Blackmun. Essentially, Justice Brennan found that this case was special because it did not involve textbooks but library books, and did not involve selection of books in the first instance but ad hoc removal of books that were already selected and purchased. Justice Brennan wrote:

> [We] think that the First Amendment rights of students may be directly and sharply implicated by the removal of the books from the shelves of a school library. . . . [W]e have held that in a variety of contexts "the Constitution protects the right to receive information and ideas." *Stanley v. Georgia.* [W]e do not deny that local school boards have a substantial legitimate role to play in the determination of school library content. [But] that discretion may not be exercised in a narrowly partisan or political manner. If a Democratic school board, motivated by party affiliation, ordered the removal of all books written by or in favor of Republicans, few would doubt that the order violated the constitutional rights of students denied access to those books. The same conclusion would surely apply if an all-white school board, motivated by racial animus, decided to remove all books authored by blacks or advocating racial equality or integration. Our Constitution does not permit the official suppression of ideas.

Justice Rehnquist vigorously dissented from the Court's decision. He wrote:

> I can cheerfully concede [that a Democratic school board could not, for political reasons, remove all books by or in favor of Republicans, and that an all-white school board, motivated by racial animus, could not remove all books authored by blacks or advocating racial equality], but as in so many other cases the extreme examples are seldom the ones that arise in the real world of constitutional litigation. In this case the facts taken most favorably to respondents suggest that nothing of this sort happened. The nine books removed undoubtedly did contain "ideas," but in the light of the excerpts from them . . ., it is apparent that eight of them contained demonstrable amounts of vulgarity and profanity and the ninth contained nothing that could be considered partisan or political.

EXERCISE 2.18. Do you agree with the implication that the Island Trees Board of Education could have refused to purchase these books in the first place? If not, does that mean the Board had a *constitutional obligation* to order these books? Does it have a constitutional obligation to order new copies when these become too beat-up to use? Or does the decision simply stand for the proposition that books cannot be kept out of libraries for the wrong reasons? What are the right reasons to deny books a place in the library? Should children have access to any books that adults can obtain?

EXERCISE 2.19. There have been frequent efforts to get Mark Twain's classic *Huckleberry Finn* removed from high school curricula and libraries because of its alleged racism and frequent use of the word "nigger." Using your school library and the Internet, research the debate over *Huckleberry Finn* and write a two-to-three-page paper about various perspectives expressed on this subject. Do you think that Twain's book should be removed from the schools? If not, how should it be taught, specifically with respect to its language, which is undoubtedly experienced as demeaning and painful by many students? Is school the right place to learn how to participate in a civil discourse when one is feeling injured and insulted?

FOR THE CLASS

LITERATURE AND VULGARITY IN THE HIGH SCHOOL LIBRARY. Do you agree with the premise, apparently shared by justices in both the majority and the dissent in *Pico*, that it is fine to remove books from the library when they are vulgar? Literature, films, and art described as "vulgar" are generally protected under the First Amendment. But should the general rules apply in the school setting? Are there dangers to having vulgar literature in a school library? Are there dangers to removing vulgar literature from a school library? Assume that there is a proposal in your school district to remove from the high school curriculum and the school libraries the eleven books at issue in *Pico* on the grounds that they are all vulgar. Transform yourselves into members of the school board and debate whether or not the books should indeed be removed. Can you speak about what the books say? Take a vote.

Notes

1. "The text is as follows: . . . 'Therefore, be it RESOLVED, That the West Virginia Board of Education does hereby recognize and order that the commonly accepted salute to the Flag of the United States—the right hand is placed upon the breast and the following pledge repeated in unison: "I pledge allegiance to the Flag of the United States of America and to the Republic for which it stands; one Nation, indivisible, with liberty and justice for all"—now becomes a regular part of the program of activities in the public schools, supported in whole or in part by public funds, and that all teachers as defined by law in West Virginia and pupils in such schools shall be required to participate in the salute honoring the Nation represented by the Flag; provided, however, that refusal to salute the Flag be regarded as an act of insubordination, and shall be dealt with accordingly.' "

2. "The Nation may raise armies and compel citizens to give military service. It follows, of course, that those subject to military discipline are under many duties and may not claim many freedoms that we hold inviolable as to those in civilian life."

3. "The only suggestions of fear of disorder in the report are these: 'A former student of one of our high schools was killed in Vietnam. Some of his friends are still in school and it was felt that if any kind of a demonstration existed, it might evolve into something which would be difficult to control.'"

"Students at one of the high schools were heard to say they would wear arm bands of other colors if the black bands prevailed."

"Moreover, the testimony of school authorities at trial indicates that it was not fear of disruption that motivated the regulation prohibiting the armbands; and regulation was directed against 'the principle of the demonstration' itself. School authorities simply felt that 'the schools are no place for demonstrations,' and if the students 'didn't like the way our elected officials were handling things, it should be handled with the ballot box and not in the halls of our public schools.'"

4. "Relevant portions of the code provided as follows: a) 'Also, provocative symbols on clothing will not be allowed.' b) Re: Brainerd High School . . . year 1970–71 SYMBOLS: According to the Board of Education, July 8th, 1970, meeting the status of symbols for Brainerd High School is as follows: The Confederate Flag and Confederate Soldier cannot be used as symbols for any public school in Chattanooga, therefore, all displays of the Flag and Soldier are removed from the school premises and cannot be used in any display where Brainerd is involved. SONG DIXIE: The song 'Dixie' can no longer be used as a fight or pep song at Pep Meetings, Athletic contests or other school functions. It may be played in concert when other music of similar kind composes the program."

5. "As one commentator has suggested, the wearing of long hair may well convey nothing more than contempt for traditional notions of good grooming."

Read On

Abraham, Henry J., and Barbara Perry. *Freedom and the Court: Civil Rights and Liberties in the United States*. New York: Oxford University Press, 1998.

Bosmajian, Haig. *The Freedom Not to Speak*. New York: New York University Press, 1999.

Fish, Stanley. *There's No Such Thing as Free Speech and It's a Good Thing Too*. New York: Oxford University Press, 1994.

Johnson, John W. *The Struggle for Student Rights:* Tinker v. Des Moines *and the 1960's*. Lawrence: University Press of Kansas, 1997.

Yudof, Mark G., David L. Kirp, and Betsy Levin. *Educational Policy and the Law*. 3d ed. St. Paul, Minn.: West Publishing, 1992.

For Further Information

Student Press Law Center (703) 807-1904

American Civil Liberties Union at *www.aclu.org*

First Amendment Center at *www.freedomforum.org/first/welcome.asp*

ALL THE NEWS THE SCHOOL SEES FIT TO PRINT: FREEDOM OF THE STUDENT PRESS

3

"Congress shall make no law . . . abridging the freedom of speech, or of the press. . . ."
THE FIRST AMENDMENT

"Were it left to me to decide whether we should have a government without newspapers, or newspapers without a government, I should not hesitate a moment to choose the latter."
THOMAS JEFFERSON

From the beginning of the Republic, Americans have prided themselves on a tradition of spirited and robust journalism. In the twentieth century, the press achieved landmark victories when the Supreme Court handed down decisions declaring that media should be free from government censorship. The Court has come to a constitutional understanding that a free press in a democracy is vital to holding government accountable. For the Americans of the twenty-first century, freedom of the press is sacred under the First Amendment.

In the public school setting, however, the student press does not enjoy this kind of autonomy. Although the *Tinker* case implied that student writers and editors might have a right to publish anything that would not materially disrupt school functions, the Court in *Hazelwood School District v. Kuhlmeier* (1988) developed a much narrower understanding of the rights of student journalists working on school-sponsored newspapers, magazines, and yearbooks.

As you read *Hazelwood* and the cases that follow, consider whether student journalists should have the same rights as adult journalists. Has the Supreme Court struck the right balance between the rights of students and the interest that school systems have in regulating the content of materials that go out under their name? How does the flowering of the Internet affect this issue?

POINTS TO PONDER

How does the basic First Amendment liberty of freedom of the press apply to student publications?

- Should school officials have the authority to review, regulate, and censor the content of school-sponsored student publications?
- Should school officials have the authority to censor student publications produced outside of school but distributed on school property?
- Should school officials have the authority to punish students for critical statements that other students make about them and circulate on the Internet on personal websites run from home?

Freedom of the Student Press in Official School-Sponsored Activities

When a school sponsors an activity in which students express themselves, how much control can it exert over the students' expression? In the following landmark case, a school principal censored two articles in the school's student newspaper because he felt that they dealt inappropriately with sensitive themes related to sex and family. The students tried to invoke their *Tinker* rights, asserting that their articles were educationally sound and would not cause "substantial" or "material" disruption of the school program.

But the Court found that *Tinker* was the wrong standard to use when the school is *itself* sponsoring and promoting the activity, which was the school newspaper. The Court asked only whether the censorship is "reasonably related to legitimate pedagogical concerns." This is a much easier standard for schools to meet. Read the following case and think about how *Bethel v. Fraser* was a bridge to this decision. Do you think that the Court went too far in allowing principals and teachers to act as censors, or do you agree that when the school's name is itself implicated, the school should basically get to pick and choose what is published?

HAZELWOOD SCHOOL DISTRICT
v.
KUHLMEIER

Supreme Court of the United States
Argued Oct. 13, 1987.
Decided Jan. 13, 1988.

Justice WHITE delivered the opinion of the Court.

This case concerns the extent to which educators may exercise editorial control over the contents of a high school newspaper produced as part of the school's journalism curriculum.

I

. . . [T]hree former Hazelwood East students who were staff members of Spectrum, the school newspaper . . . contend that school officials violated their First Amendment rights by deleting two pages of articles from the May 13, 1983, issue of Spectrum. Spectrum was written and edited by the Journalism II class at Hazelwood East. The newspaper was published every three weeks or so during the 1982–1983 school year. More than 4,500 copies of the newspaper were distributed during that year to students, school personnel, and members of the community.

. . .

The practice at Hazelwood East during the spring 1983 semester was for the journalism teacher to submit page proofs of each Spectrum issue to Principal Reynolds for his review prior to publication. On May 10, Emerson delivered the proofs of the May 13 edition to Reynolds, who objected to two of the articles scheduled to appear in that edition. One of the stories described three Hazelwood East students' experiences with pregnancy; the other discussed the impact of divorce on students at the school.

Reynolds was concerned that, although the pregnancy story used false names "to keep the identity of these girls a secret," the pregnant students still might be identifiable from the text. He also believed that the article's references to sexual activity and birth control were inappropriate for some of the younger students at the school. In addition, Reynolds was concerned that a student identified by name in the divorce story had complained that her father "wasn't spending enough time with my mom, my sister and I" prior to the divorce, "was always out of town on business or out late playing cards with the guys," and "always argued about everything" with her mother. Reynolds believed that the student's parents should have been given an opportunity to respond to these remarks or to consent to their publication. He was unaware that Emerson had deleted the student's name from the final version of the article.

Reynolds believed that there was no time to make the necessary changes in the stories

Robert Reynolds, principal of Hazelwood East High, stands in front of his school in January 1988 holding a copy of *Spectrum,* the student newspaper that was censored in this case. In *Hazelwood* the Court gave school authorities broad new powers to regulate the content of school-sponsored newspapers and yearbooks for "reasonable" pedagogical purposes.

before the scheduled press run and that the newspaper would not appear before the end of the school year if printing were delayed to any significant extent. He concluded that his only options under the circumstances were to publish a four-page newspaper instead of the planned six-page newspaper, eliminating the two pages on which the offending stories appeared, or to publish no newspaper at all. Accordingly, he directed Emerson to withhold from publication the two pages containing the stories on pregnancy and divorce. He informed his superiors of the decision, and they concurred.

. . .

II

Students in the public schools do not "shed their constitutional rights to freedom of speech or expression at the schoolhouse gate." *Tinker.* They cannot be punished merely for expressing their personal views on the school premises—whether "in the cafeteria, or on the playing field, or on the campus during the authorized hours,"—unless school authorities have reason to believe that such expression will "substantially interfere with the work of the school or impinge upon the rights of other students."

We have nonetheless recognized that the First Amendment rights of students in the public schools "are not automatically coextensive with the rights of adults in other settings," and must be "applied in light of the special characteristics of the school environment." *Tinker.* A school need not tolerate student speech that is inconsistent with its "basic educational mission," even though the government could not censor similar speech outside the school. Accordingly, we held in *Fraser* that a student could be disciplined for having delivered a speech that was "sexually explicit" but not legally obscene at an official school assembly, because the school was entitled to "disassociate itself" from the speech in a manner that would demonstrate to others that such vulgarity is "wholly inconsistent with the 'fundamental values' of public school education." We thus recognized that "[t]he determination of what manner of speech in the classroom or in school assembly is inappropriate properly rests with the school board," rather than with the federal courts. . . .

. . .

The question whether the First Amendment requires a school to tolerate particular student speech—the question that we addressed in *Tinker*—is different from the question whether the First Amendment requires a school affirmatively to promote particular student speech. The former question addresses educators' ability to silence a student's personal expression that happens to occur on the school premises. The latter question concerns educators' authority over school-sponsored publications, theatrical productions, and other expressive activities that students, parents, and members of the public might reasonably perceive to bear the imprimatur of the school. These activities may fairly be characterized as part of the school curriculum, whether or not they occur in a traditional classroom setting, so long as they are supervised by faculty members and designed to impart particular knowledge or skills to student participants and audiences.

Educators are entitled to exercise greater control over this second form of student expression to assure that participants learn whatever lessons the activity is designed to teach, that readers or listeners are not exposed to material that may be inappropriate for their level of maturity, and that the views of the individual speaker are not erroneously attributed to the school. Hence, a school may in its capacity as publisher of a school newspaper or producer of a school play "disassociate itself," not only from speech that would "substantially interfere with [its] work . . . or impinge upon the rights of other students," *Tinker*, but also from speech that is, for example, ungrammatical, poorly written, inadequately researched, biased or prejudiced, vulgar or profane, or unsuitable for immature audiences. A school must be able to set high standards for the student speech that is disseminated under its auspices—standards that may be higher than those demanded by some newspaper publishers or theatrical producers in the "real" world—and may refuse to disseminate student speech that does not meet those standards. In addition, a school must be able to take into account the emotional maturity of the intended audience in determining whether to disseminate student speech on potentially sensitive topics, which might range from the existence of Santa Claus in an elementary school setting to the particulars of teenage sexual activity in a high school setting. A school must also retain the authority to refuse to sponsor student speech that might reasonably be perceived to advocate drug or alcohol use, irresponsible sex, or conduct otherwise inconsistent with "the shared values of a civilized social order," or to associate the school with any position other than neutrality on matters of political controversy. . . .

Accordingly, we conclude that the standard articulated in *Tinker* for determining when a school may punish student expression need not also be the standard for determining when a school may refuse to lend its name and resources to the dissemination of student expression. Instead, we hold that educators do not offend the First Amendment by exercising editorial control over the style and content of student speech in school-sponsored expressive activities so long as their actions are reasonably related to legitimate pedagogical concerns.

. . .

We also conclude that Principal Reynolds acted reasonably in requiring the deletion from the May 13 issue of Spectrum of the pregnancy article, the divorce article, and the remaining articles that were to appear on the same pages of the newspaper. The initial paragraph of the pregnancy article declared that "[a]ll names have been changed to keep the identity of these girls a secret." The principal concluded that the students' anonymity was not adequately protected, however, given the other identifying information in the article and the small number of pregnant students at the school. . . . In addition, he could reasonably have been concerned that the article was not sufficiently sensitive to the privacy interests of the students' boyfriends and parents, who were discussed in the article but who were given no opportunity to consent to its publication or to offer a response. The article did not contain graphic accounts of sexual activity. The girls did comment in the article, however, concerning their sexual histories and their use or nonuse of birth control. It was not unreasonable for the principal to have concluded that such frank talk was inappropriate in a school-sponsored publication distributed to 14-year-old freshmen and presumably taken home to be read by students' even younger brothers and sisters.

The student who was quoted by name in the version of the divorce article seen by Principal Reynolds made comments sharply critical of her father. The principal could reasonably have concluded that an individual publicly identified as an inattentive parent—indeed, as one who chose "playing cards with the guys" over home and family—was entitled to an opportunity to defend himself as a matter of journalistic fairness. These concerns were shared by both of Spectrum's faculty advisers for the 1982–1983 school year, who testified that they would not have allowed the article to be printed without deletion of the student's name.

. . .

In sum, we cannot reject as unreasonable Principal Reynolds' conclusion that neither the pregnancy article nor the divorce article was suitable for publication in Spectrum. Reynolds could reasonably have concluded that the students who had written and edited these articles had not sufficiently mastered those portions of the Journalism II curriculum that pertained to the treatment of controversial issues and personal attacks, the need to protect the privacy of individuals whose most intimate concerns are to be revealed in the newspaper, and "the legal, moral, and ethical restrictions imposed upon journalists within

[a] school community" that includes adolescent subjects and readers. Finally, we conclude that the principal's decision to delete two pages of Spectrum, rather than to delete only the offending articles or to require that they be modified, was reasonable under the circumstances as he understood them. Accordingly, no violation of First Amendment rights occurred.

Reversed.

Justice BRENNAN, with whom Justice MARSHALL and Justice BLACKMUN join, dissenting.

When the young men and women of Hazelwood East High School registered for Journalism II, they expected a civics lesson. Spectrum, the newspaper they were to publish, "was not just a class exercise in which students learned to prepare papers and hone writing skills, it was a . . . forum established to give students an opportunity to express their views while gaining an appreciation of their rights and responsibilities under the First Amendment to the United States Constitution. . . ." [T]he student journalists published a Statement of Policy—tacitly approved each year by school authorities—announcing their expectation that "Spectrum, as a student-press publication, accepts all rights implied by the First Amendment. . . . Only speech that 'materially and substantially interferes with the requirements of appropriate discipline' can be found unacceptable and therefore prohibited." The school board itself affirmatively guaranteed the students of Journalism II an atmosphere conducive to fostering such an appreciation and exercising the full panoply of rights associated with a free student press. "School sponsored student publications," it vowed, "will not restrict free expression or diverse viewpoints within the rules of responsible journalism."

. . .

In my view the principal broke more than just a promise. He violated the First Amendment's prohibitions against censorship of any student expression that neither disrupts classwork nor invades the rights of others, and against any censorship that is not narrowly tailored to serve its purpose.

I

. . .

Free student expression undoubtedly sometimes interferes with the effectiveness of the school's pedagogical functions. Some brands of student expression do so by directly preventing the school from pursuing its pedagogical mission: The young polemic who stands on a soapbox during calculus class to deliver an eloquent political diatribe interferes with the legitimate teaching of calculus. And the student who delivers a lewd endorsement of a student-government candidate might so extremely distract an impressionable high school audience as to interfere with the orderly operation of the school. Other student speech, however, frustrates the school's legitimate pedagogical purposes merely by expressing a message that conflicts with the school's, without directly interfering with the school's expression of its message: A student who responds to a political science teacher's question with the retort, "socialism is good," subverts the school's inculcation of the message that capitalism is better. Even the maverick who sits in class passively sporting a symbol of protest against a government policy, *Tinker*, or the gossip who sits in the student commons swapping stories of sexual escapade could readily muddle a clear official message condoning the government policy or condemning teenage sex. Likewise, the student newspaper that, like Spectrum, conveys a moral position at odds with the school's official stance might subvert the administration's legitimate inculcation of its own perception of community values.

If mere incompatibility with the school's pedagogical message were a constitutionally sufficient justification for the suppression of student speech, school officials could censor each of the students or student organizations in the foregoing hypotheticals, converting our public schools into "enclaves of totalitarianism," that "strangle the free mind at its source," *Barnette*. The First Amendment permits no such blanket censorship authority. While the "constitutional rights of students in public school are not automatically coextensive with the rights of adults in other settings," *Fraser*, students in the public schools do not "shed their constitutional rights to freedom of speech or expression at the schoolhouse gate," *Tinker*. Just as the public on the street corner must, in the interest of fostering "enlightened opinion," tolerate speech that "tempt[s] [the listener] to throw [the speaker] off the street," public educators must accommodate some student expression even if it offends them or offers views or values that contradict those the school wishes to inculcate.

In *Tinker*, this Court struck the balance. We held that official censorship of student expression—there the suspension of several students until they removed their armbands protesting the Vietnam war—is unconstitutional unless the speech "materially disrupts classwork or involves substantial disorder or invasion of the rights of others. . . ."

. . .

II

. . .

A

The Court is certainly correct that the First Amendment permits educators "to assure that participants learn whatever lessons the activity is designed to teach. . . ." That is, however, the essence of the *Tinker* test, not an excuse to abandon it. Under *Tinker*, school officials may censor only such student speech as would "materially disrup[t]" a legitimate curricular function. Manifestly, student speech is more likely to disrupt a curricular function when it arises in the context of a curricular activity—one that "is designed to teach" something—than when it arises in the context of a noncurricular activity. Thus, under *Tinker*, the school may constitutionally punish the budding political orator if he disrupts calculus class but not if he holds his tongue for the cafeteria. That is not because some more stringent standard applies in the curricular context. (After all, this Court applied the same standard whether the students in *Tinker* wore their armbands to the "classroom" or the "cafeteria.") It is because student speech in the noncurricular context is less likely to disrupt materially any legitimate pedagogical purpose.

I fully agree with the Court that the First Amendment should afford an educator the prerogative not to sponsor the publication of a newspaper article that is "ungrammatical, poorly written, inadequately researched, biased or prejudiced," or that falls short of the "high standards for . . . student speech that is disseminated under [the school's] auspices. . . ." But we need not abandon *Tinker* to reach that conclusion; we need only apply it. The enumerated criteria reflect the skills that the curricular newspaper "is designed to teach." The educator may, under *Tinker*, constitutionally "censor" poor grammar, writing, or research because to reward such expression would "materially disrup[t]" the newspaper's curricular purpose.

. . .

B

The Court's second excuse for deviating from precedent is the school's interest in shielding an impressionable high school audience from material whose substance is "unsuitable for immature audiences." Specifically, the majority decrees that we must afford educators authority to shield high school students from exposure to "potentially sensitive topics" (like "the particulars of teenage sexual activity") or unacceptable social viewpoints (like the advocacy of "irresponsible se[x] or conduct otherwise inconsistent with 'the shared values of a civilized social order'") through school-sponsored student activities.

Tinker teaches us that the state educator's undeniable, and undeniably vital, mandate to inculcate moral and political values is not a general warrant to act as "thought police" stifling discussion of all but state-approved topics and advocacy of all but the official position. Otherwise educators could transform students into "closed-circuit recipients of only that which the State chooses to communicate," *Tinker*, and cast a perverse and impermissible "pall of orthodoxy over the classroom.". . . Thus, the State cannot constitutionally prohibit its high school students from recounting in the locker room "the particulars of [their] teenage sexual activity," nor even from advocating "irresponsible se[x]" or other presumed abominations of "the shared values of a civilized social order." Even in its capacity as educator the State may not assume an Orwellian "guardianship of the public mind."

The mere fact of school sponsorship does not, as the Court suggests, license such thought control in the high school, whether through school suppression of disfavored viewpoints or through official assessment of topic sensitivity. The former would constitute unabashed and unconstitutional viewpoint discrimination. . . . Just as a school board may not purge its state-funded library of all books that "'offen[d] [its] social, political and moral tastes,'" school officials may not, out of like motivation, discriminatorily excise objectionable ideas from a student publication. The State's prerogative to dissolve the student newspaper entirely (or to limit its subject matter) no more entitles it to dictate which viewpoints students may express on its pages, than the State's prerogative to close down the schoolhouse entitles it to prohibit the nondisruptive expression of antiwar sentiment within its gates.

. . .

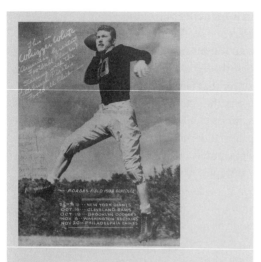

The author of this opinion, **JUSTICE BYRON R. WHITE**, was born in Fort Collins, Colorado, in 1917, and went to Wellington High School and the University of Colorado, where he earned varsity letters in football, basketball, and baseball and graduated as class valedictorian in 1938. After playing for the Pittsburgh Steelers for one year, "Whizzer" White went to Oxford on a Rhodes Scholarship, where he met George Bernard Shaw and John F. Kennedy, son of the American Ambassador. White left Oxford early for Yale Law School because of the onset of World War II. Before finishing law school, he played for the Detroit Lions and served in the Navy, where he would meet Kennedy again, before finally returning to Yale Law School after the war. In 1962, after White had served in the Kennedy Justice Department, President Kennedy appointed him to the Court. He served until 1993, making him one of the longest-serving justices in history.

HIGHLIGHTS

➤ In 1938, in his senior year of college, White was selected for Phi Beta Kappa and two days later scored all of Colorado's points in a 17–7 win over the Utah football team, a feat that included a 97-yard touchdown on a punt return. A stand-out athlete, he made the All-American team that year as a halfback.

C

. . .

. . . Dissociative means short of censorship are available to the school. It could, for example, require the student activity to publish a disclaimer, such as the "Statement of Policy" that Spectrum published each school year announcing that "[a]ll . . . editorials appearing in this newspaper reflect the opinions of the Spectrum staff, which are not necessarily shared by the administrators or faculty of Hazelwood East," or it could simply issue its own response clarifying the official position on the matter and explaining why the student position is wrong. Yet, without so much as acknowledging the less oppressive alternatives, the Court approves of brutal censorship.

. . .

IV

The Court opens its analysis in this case by purporting to reaffirm *Tinker's* time-tested proposition that public school students "do not 'shed their constitutional rights to freedom of speech or expression at the schoolhouse gate.'" That is an ironic introduction to an opinion that denudes high school students of much of the First Amendment protection that *Tinker* itself prescribed. Instead of "teach[ing] children to respect the diversity of ideas that is fundamental to the American system," and "that our Constitution is a living reality, not parchment preserved under glass," the Court today "teach[es] youth to discount important principles of our government as mere platitudes." *Barnette.* The young men and women of Hazelwood East expected a civics lesson, but not the one the Court teaches them today.

I dissent.

EXERCISE 3.1. Consider the Court's outcomes in *Tinker, Fraser,* and *Hazelwood.* How have the Court's holdings changed? Is the Court expanding or restricting the free speech rights of students?

EXERCISE 3.2. Draw (by hand or with a computer) a Venn diagram that reflects what kinds of student speech are protected by the First Amendment in *Tinker* and *Hazelwood* and what kinds are not. Does this help you to conceptualize legal categories?

EXERCISE 3.3. What was wrong with the student-written articles that Hazelwood East censored? Do you think that such articles are appropriate or important for students to write and read? If you were the principal, would you have censored the articles? Why or why not?

EXERCISE 3.4. Should school be a place where only teachers and administrators transmit knowledge and messages to students or a place where students also bring knowledge in and circulate their own messages to fellow students and teachers? How does *West Virginia v. Barnette* answer this question? How about *Hazelwood*? What image does Justice White have of high school students? What image does Justice Brennan have?

EXERCISE 3.5. Can school authorities at Hazelwood East censor articles that speak respectfully of the decision of high school students to go through with their pregnancies and have babies, but publish articles that condemn this decision and urge pregnant students to have abortions? Can school authorities censor one side in a political controversy, like the pro-choice side or the pro-life side in the abortion debate? Generally, the First Amendment requires government to be *viewpoint-neutral*, that is, scrupulously evenhanded among all sides in a political debate. Does *Hazelwood* respect that principle?

FOR THE CLASS

DRAFTING AN EDITORIAL POLICY FOR YOUR SCHOOL NEWSPAPER. The principal of your school has just appointed your class a school task force to come up with an editorial policy for your school newspaper that both respects students' First Amendment rights and prevents embarrassment of the school community and its members. Write a policy explaining what the newspaper will publish and what it will not. Do you leave it wide open? Are there categories of expression forbidden, such as obscene, libelous, dangerous, or disruptive speech? What will be the process for defining such categories? Do you attach a disclaimer? Do you forbid only articles that will materially and substantially disrupt school? Do you appoint faculty advisors who have free rein to censor articles for both grammatical and substantive reasons? Does the principal get final say? Bring your policies to class and discuss them as a task force, trying to find consensus for a final recommendation to the principal. Can you agree on the exact wording of a policy?

Squelching Debate: The Blair Witch-Hunt Project

In October of 1996, an interesting sequence of events took place at Blair High School in Montgomery County, Maryland. At Blair, there is an honors class that permits students to produce television news shows, commentaries, debates, and roundtable talk shows under the supervision of a teacher. They receive academic credit for their work. The TV news shows produced in the high school's studio are broadcast on the Montgomery County Public Schools' local cable channel, Channel 60.

The students have a monthly show called "Shades of Gray," which has been on Channel 60 for many years. In October 1996, the students planned and produced a debate format talk show on the subject of whether gays and lesbians should be allowed to enter into marriage. Two conservative adult guests appeared to oppose gay marriage and two liberal adult guests came to speak in favor of it. The show was taped; the teacher who oversees the class, Christopher Lloyd, praised the students' work, and the show was all set to air on Channel 60.

At that point, however, officials in the school system who run the cable channel decided to preview the tape, which was not their ordinary practice. They notified Mr. Lloyd and the students that their show would not be broadcast because it was "inappropriate" for the station. A series of meetings and phone calls ensued in which the students tried to get the school authorities to explain what was wrong with their debate show on gay marriage. On October 23, 1996, the program director for Channel 60, Barbara Wood, sent an e-mail explaining the decision:

> We felt that the gentleman who was a guest on the show [Dr. Frank Kameny] brought up the issue of religion and God in a very heated and controversial manner. . . . We both felt it would be inappropriate to air the program for that reason alone.

The school authorities apparently reacted negatively to the following segment of the show. It began when the student host asked a question about the basis of the guests' views about the issue. One of the conservative guests, Ms. Paula Govers, press secretary for Concerned Women for America, introduced religion into the discussion:

> Govers: The Concerned Women for America believes that marriage is an institution sanctioned by God, licensed by the state, specifically between one man and one woman, and specifically for the purpose of procreation and should be a covenant between two people that should be a lifetime commitment.

This comment prompted the liberal guests, Dr. Frank Kameny, of the Washington, D.C. Gay and Lesbian Activists Alliance, and Judith Schaeffer, of People for the American Way, to respond:

KAMENY: Paula, you said that the First Amendment guarantees us freedom of religion, and we all have our own views of God. My God gave us homosexuality as a blessing given to us by our creator God to be enjoyed to its fullest—exultantly, exuberantly, joyously. My God sanctifies same-sex marriage even if your God does not, and we are both American citizens and both Gods deserve equal recognition from our—not your—our government.

SCHAEFFER: That's exactly what the First Amendment requires. The government cannot legislate religious beliefs.

KAMENY: If you don't want to enter into a same-sex marriage, don't. But don't tell us just because your God doesn't sanctify it, my God is to be ignored.

GOVERS: Dr. Kameny, you said that your God does sanctify these unions. So your religious beliefs would say it's a good thing and our religious beliefs would say it's not. Why does your view get to trump ours?

KAMENY: It does not. If you believe that, you have an absolute right not to enter into a same-sex marriage.

KRIS ARDIZONNE [the other conservative guest and legal director of the Eagle Forum]: But my taxpayer dollars go to pay for the institution of marriage. And we don't believe in it.

KAMENY: And so do the tax dollars of gay people go to pay for marriage as well. . . .

Although the students' teacher and the principal of Blair High School saw this exchange of views as spirited and enlightening, the Montgomery County Public Schools officials thought it was inappropriate for the mostly adult audience of Channel 60.

The Blair students went to the Mongtomery County Board of Education to appeal the decision of the Superintendent of the schools to censor broadcast of the show. They made the following three arguments:

1. *The decision not to air the show violated the school system's own policy on student expression.* The student's guide to Rights and Responsibilities in Montgomery County Public School states: "School-sponsored publications such as newspapers, literary magazines, and yearbooks will be encouraged. . . . Students have the right to decide on the contents of these publications, as long as the contents meet specific guidelines." The guidelines disallow only four categories of material: material that threatens the health and safety of student (such as use of illegal drugs), material that is obscene, material that is libelous, and material that causes, or is reasonably expected to cause, substantial disruption of school activities. The students argued that the censored show fell into none of these four categories.

2. *The decision to censor violated the First Amendment by discriminating against a speaker because of his religious views.* The students quoted the Supreme Court's 1995 decision in *Rosenberger v. University of Virginia*, which struck down the University of Virginia's practice of subsidizing student journals that had secular points of view but declining to subsidize those that had a religious point of view. The Court stated: "The government must abstain from regulating speech when the specific motivating ideology, or the opinion or perspective of the speaker, is the rationale for the restriction." The students argued that the school system was objecting to "the gentleman who was a guest on the show" who "brought up the issue of religion and God in a very heated and controversial manner."

3. *Because the educators in this case—the media teacher and the Blair principal—both fa-*

vored broadcast of the show, the school system could not use to its advantage the Hazelwood Court's finding that educators can censor when "their actions are reasonably related to legitimate pedagogical concerns." The pedagogues in this case were *opposed* to censorship.

The students never had to go to court because the school board voted 4–3 to reverse the superintendent and to air the show six times. The principal, Philip Gainous, subsequently won an award from the Freedom Forum in Virginia for standing up for the First Amendment rights of his students, and many of the students have since gone on to study media and broadcasting in college. Their case has given much force to arguments of students in other schools that they should have the same rights on video and television productions that they have in newspapers and yearbooks. Students in Montgomery County subsequently lobbied their school board to pass a set of guidelines on student speech that incorporates basic First Amendment ideas.

FOR THE CLASS

THE BLAIR WITCH-HUNT PROJECT: DIFFERING PERSPECTIVES. If this case had gone to court, who do you think would have won the case? Could the school system have used *Hazelwood* to its advantage? Why or why not? Divide into teams and argue it from both perspectives. What was wrong with the broadcast from the school system's perspective?

Underground Newspapers

Although the *Hazelwood* Court has given school systems greater latitude to censor school newspapers, many schools have written and stood by policies that codify the old *Tinker* standard, which is much more friendly to student expression. Still, a great number of school systems have used *Hazelwood* to reject and censor student writings for school newspapers deemed offensive, subversive, mischievous, insubordinate, or inappropriate.

This response—along with the rise of the Internet and desktop publishing—has led to the return of so-called "underground newspapers," unofficial student-written, student-published newspapers or "'zines" where the students express themselves in an uninhibited way. These newspapers are often a fountain of creativity and irreverence.

The cases concerned with underground newspapers stay true to the *Tinker* standard: school authorities cannot censor unofficial student speech unless education and school operations are in danger of being disrupted. Is this standard too soft?

Consider the following Seventh Circuit case from 1970. Two students at Joliet Central High School in Illinois wrote a response to an official "Principal's Report to Parents" sent home with students. They were expelled for doing so, and appealed their expulsion as a violation of the First Amendment. What follows is the written response that got them into trouble:

MY REPLY

Recently, we students at Joliet Central were subjected to a pamphlet called "Bits Of Steel." This occurrence took place a few weeks before the Christmas vacation. The reason why I have not expressed my opinions on this pamphlet before now is simple: being familiar with the J-HI Journal at Central, I knew that they would not print my views on the subject.

In my critique of this pamphlet I shall try to follow the same order in which the articles were presented.

The pamphlet started with a message from the principal, David Ross. This is logical because the entire pamphlet is supposed to be "The Principal's Report to Parents." In this article Ross states why the pamphlet was put out and the purpose it is supposed to accomplish, namely, the improvement of communication between parents and administration. He has to be kidding. Surely, he realizes that a great majority of these pamphlets are thrown away by the students, and in this case that is how it should have been. I urge all students in the future to either refuse to accept or destroy upon acceptance all propaganda that Central's administration publishes.

The second article told about the Human Relations committee which we have here at Central. It told why the committee was assembled and what its purpose is. It also listed the members of the committee who attend school here at Central. All-in-all this was probably the best article in the whole pamphlet, but never fear the administration defeated its own purpose in the next article which was a racial breakdown of the Central campus. As far as I could see this article served no practical purpose. By any chance did the administration feel that such a breakdown would improve racial relations? I think not. This article had such statements as: Spanish American students were included with the white students. Well, wasn't that nice of the administration. In other words, the only difference noted was whether the student was white or Negro.

This was followed by an article called "Did you Know?" This was, supposedly, to inform the parents of certain activities. Intertwined throughout it were numerous rules that the parents were to see their children obeyed. Quite ridiculous.

Next came an article on attendance. There's not much I can say about this one. It simply told the haggard parents the utterly idiotic and asinine procedure that they must go through to assure that their children will be excused for their absences.

Questions from the parents was the next in the line of articles. This consisted of a set of three questions written by the administration and then answered by the administration. The first question was designed to inform the reader about the background of the new superintendent. The second was about the paperbacks which were placed in the dean's office. They state that the books were put there "so that your sons and daughters may read while they wait. The hope is that no moment for learning will be lost." Boy, this is a laugh. Our whole system of education with all its arbitrary rules and schedules seems dedicated to nothing but wasting time. The last question concerned the Wednesday Que-ins. It was followed by a quote: "Sometimes we, parents and schoolmen, must seem cruel in order to be kind to the children placed in our care." Do you think that the administration is trying to tell us something about the true purpose of the Wednesday Que-ins?

The next gem we came across was from our beloved senior dean. Our senior dean seems to feel that the only duty of a dean or parent is to be the administrator of some type of punishment. A dean should help or try to understand a student instead of merely punishing him. Our senior dean makes several interesting statements such as, "Proper attitudes must be part of our lives and the lives of our children." I believe that a person should be allowed to mold his own attitudes toward life, as long as they are not radically anti-social, without extensive interference from persons on the outside, especially those who are unqualified in such fields. Another interesting statement that he makes is, "Therefore let us not cheat our children, our precious gifts from God, by neglecting to discipline them." It is my opinion that a statement such as this is the product of a sick mind. Our senior dean because of his position of authority over a large group of young adults poses a threat to our community. Should a mind whose only thought revolves around an act of discipline be allowed to exert influence over the young minds of our community? I think not. I would urge the Board of Education to request that this dean amend his thinking or resign. The man in the dean's position must be qualified to the extent that his concern is to help the students rather than discipline or punish them. This pamphlet also contained an article from the freshman dean. I should like to say that Dean Engers, in his article, shows a great deal of promise. He appears to be genuinely interested in the problems of the students entrusted to him. All I can say to him is to keep up the good work. The last thing of any interest in the pamphlet was about the despicable and disgusting detention policy at Central. I think most students feel the same way as I about this policy. Therefore I will not even go into it. In the whole pamphlet I could see only one really bright side. We were not subjected to an article written by Mr. Diekelman.

Senior Editor
Grass High

EXERCISE 3.6. Before you read the actual decision in this case, write your own opinion of one to two pages applying the *Tinker* standard to the students' document. Does their expulsion violate the First Amendment? Why or why not? Explain your analysis, using the *Tinker* test.

SCOVILLE
v.
BOARD OF EDUCATION OF JOLIET TOWNSHIP
HIGH SCHOOL NO. 204

United States Court of Appeals
Seventh Circuit
April 1, 1970.

KILEY, Circuit Judge.

The plaintiffs, minors, were expelled from high school after writing, off the school premises, a publication which was distributed in school and which contained, among other things, material critical of school policies and authorities. This civil rights action was brought for declaratory judgment, injunctive relief, and damages, alleging violation of First and Fourteenth Amendment rights, as well as an unconstitutional application of an Illinois statute. . . .

The plaintiffs are Raymond Scoville and Arthur Breen, students at Joliet Central High School, one of three high schools administered by the defendant Board of Education. Scoville was editor and publisher, and Breen senior editor, of the publication "Grass High." They wrote the pertinent material. "Grass High" is a publication of fourteen pages containing poetry, essays, movie and record reviews, and a critical editorial. Sixty copies were distributed to faculty and students at a price of fifteen cents per copy.

On January 18, 1968, three days after "Grass High" was sold in the school, the dean advised plaintiffs that they could not take their fall semester examinations. Four days thereafter plaintiffs were suspended for a period of five days. Nine days after that Scoville was removed as editor of the school paper, and both he and Breen were deprived of further participation in school debating activities.

The dean then sent a report to the superintendent of the high schools with a recommendation of expulsion for the remainder of the school year. The superintendent wrote the parents of plaintiffs that he would present the report, together with the recommendation, to the Board of Education at its next meeting. He invited the parents to be present. Scoville's mother wrote a letter to the Board expressing plaintiffs' sorrow for the trouble they had caused, stating that they had learned a lesson, that they were worried and upset about possible interruption in their education and that the parents thought the boys had already been adequately punished. Neither plaintiffs nor their parents attended the Board meeting. The Board expelled plaintiffs from the day classes for the second semester . . . upon a determination that they were guilty of "gross disobedience [and] misconduct." The Board permitted them to attend, on a probationary basis, a day class in physics, and night school at Joliet Central. The suit before us followed.

. . . At no time, either before the Board of Education or in the district court, was the expulsion of the plaintiffs justified on grounds other than the objectionable content of the publication. The Board has not objected to the place, time or manner of distribution. The court found and it is not disputed that plaintiffs' conduct did not cause any commotion or disruption of classes.

No charge was made that the publication was libelous, and the district court felt it unnecessary to consider whether the language in "Grass High" labeled as "inappropriate and indecent" by the Board could be suppressed as obscene. The court thought that the interest in maintaining its school system outweighed the private interest of the plaintiffs in writing and publishing "Grass High." The basis of the court's decision was an editorial entitled "My Reply" . . . which—after criticizing the school's pamphlet, "Bits of Steel," addressed to parents—urged the students not to accept "in the future," for delivery to parents, any "propaganda" issued by the school, and to destroy it if accepted.

I

Plaintiffs contend that the expulsion order violated their First and Fourteenth Amendment freedoms. The same cases are cited by plaintiffs and defendants in support of their arguments on this contention. The authoritative decision, pertinent to the important issue before us, is *Tinker v. Des Moines School District*. *Tinker* is a high school "arm band" case, but its rule is admittedly dispositive of the case before us.

The *Tinker* rule narrows the question before us to whether the writing of "Grass High" and its sale in school to sixty students and faculty members could "reasonably have led [the Board] to forecast substantial disruption of or material interference with school activities . . . or intru[sion] into the school affairs or the lives of others," *Tinker*. We hold that the district court erred in deciding that the complaint "on its face" disclosed a clear and present danger justifying defendants' "forecast" of the harmful consequences referred to in the *Tinker* rule.

Tinker announces the principles which underlie our holding: High school students are persons entitled to First and Fourteenth Amendment protections. States and school officials have "comprehensive authority" to prescribe and control conduct in the schools through reasonable rules consistent with fundamental constitutional safeguards. Where rules infringe upon freedom of expression, the school officials have the burden of showing justification.

Plaintiffs' freedom of expression was infringed by the Board's action, and defendants had the burden of showing that the action was taken upon a reasonable forecast of a substantial disruption of school activity.

. . .

The "Grass High" editorial imputing a "sick mind" to the dean reflects a disrespectful and tasteless attitude toward authority. Yet does that imputation to sixty students and faculty members, without more, justify a "forecast" of substantial disruption or material interference with the school policies or invade the rights of others? We think not. The reference undoubtedly offended and displeased the dean. But mere "expressions of [the students'] feelings with which [school officials] do not wish to contend" is not the showing required by the *Tinker* test to justify expulsion.

Finally, there is the "Grass High" random statement, "Oral sex may prevent tooth decay." This attempt to amuse comes as a shock to an older generation. But today's students in high school are not insulated from the shocking but legally accepted language used by demonstrators and protesters in streets and on campuses and by authors of best-selling modern literature. A hearing might even disclose that high school libraries contain literature which would lead students to believe the statement made in "Grass High" was unobjectionable.

We believe the discussion above makes it clear, on the basis of the admitted facts and exhibits, that the Board could not have reasonably forecast that the publication and distribution of this paper to the students would substantially disrupt or materially interfere with school procedures.

Reversed and remanded.

CASTLE, Senior Circuit Judge (dissenting).

. . .

. . . In my view, plaintiffs' advocacy of disregard of the school's procedure carried with it an inherent threat to the effective operation of a method the school authorities had a right to utilize for the purpose of communicating with the parents of students.
I would affirm the judgment of the District Court.

EXERCISE 3.7. The Court of Appeals in this case determined that the actions of the school board and Joliet Central High School violated the students' First Amendment rights. Because the publication could not have reasonably substantially disrupted or materially interfered with school activities, the board's actions were not justified under *Tinker*. Do you think the court in 1970 would have ruled for the students if "My Reply" were printed as an editorial in the official school newspaper? (Remember that this was pre-*Hazelwood*.) What about if it were printed today as part of an underground newspaper? Should the result be the same?

EXERCISE 3.8. A group of fellow students asks your advice. They want to publish a student newspaper to talk about what they see as sexism and homophobia in your school. Should they join the school newspaper, form their own paper, go on the Internet and create a website, or do something else? Should they meet with school authorities? What advice do you give them to protect their rights and their careers as students?

Cyber-Censors: The Coming Conflicts Over Internet Homepages

As we launch a new century strongly defined by the Internet and other new technologies, new free speech issues are surfacing across the country in high schools. What happens if a student posts stinging criticism of his school and teachers on an Internet homepage and then school authorities retaliate by suspending and punishing him academically?

Although no such case has made it to the Supreme Court yet, several lower courts have ruled on this kind of situation. In *Brandon Beussink v. Woodland R-IV School District* (1998), the United States District Court for the Eastern District of Missouri reversed Woodland High School's disciplinary action against Brandon Beussink, who was at the time a high school junior. Brandon had posted material "highly critical" of the school administration and "used vulgar language to convey his opinion regarding the teachers, the principal and the school's own homepage."

Although Brandon designed his homepage at home and did not intend for it to be accessed at school, he did show it to a friend, Amanda Brown. Later, after the two friends had a falling out, Amanda decided to get back at Brandon by showing his homepage to the school's computer teacher, who promptly reported it to the school principal, Yancy Poorman. Mr. Poorman said that he became "upset" by its contents and immediately suspended Brandon from school for five days. Then, as his anger apparently swelled, he "reconsidered" and suspended Brandon for ten days. Because of the school's absenteeism policy, this suspension would have resulted in Brandon's flunking all of his junior year classes.

Brandon went to court and won an injunction against his discipline on First Amendment grounds. The court found that Brandon's personal webpage caused no disruption in his classes—unlike the suspension itself—and that any fear of disruption was unreasonable. Stated District Judge Sippel: "Disliking or being upset by the content of a student's speech is not an acceptable justification for limiting student speech under *Tinker*."

EXERCISE 3.9. Did Judge Sippel make the right decision? Does it seem right to you that school authorities should have no more authority to punish student speech on the Internet than outside of school in an underground or national magazine? If you were the high school principal in this case, how would you have reacted to Brandon's Internet messages? Would there have been a better way to change such negative dynamics? Can the Internet become a positive force for communication among students, teachers, and administrators in high schools? How?

Read On

Hentoff, Nat. *Free Speech for Me—But Not for Thee*. New York: HarperCollins, 1992.

Levy, Leonard. *Emergence of a Free Press*. New York: Oxford University Press, 1985.

For Further Information

The Freedom Forum at *www.freedomforum.org*

Electronic Frontier Foundation at (212) 888-7811 or *www.eff.org*

Student Press Law Center at (703) 807-1904.

4 SHOULD PUBLIC SCHOOLS GET RELIGION? STRIKING THE RIGHT CHURCH-STATE BALANCE ON CAMPUS

"Congress shall make no law respecting an establishment of religion, or prohibiting the free exercise thereof. . . ." THE FIRST AMENDMENT

"As long as there are math tests, there will be prayer in the public schools." REV. JESSE JACKSON

Reverend Jackson's humorous comment points up what is really at stake in many of the conflicts over religion in public schools. The fact is that nothing today stops public school students from prayerfully meditating or saying quiet prayers on their own while at school. The major constitutional issue is *organized* school prayer, where teachers and administrators get involved in leading or encouraging prayer.

When it comes to religion, the First Amendment has two separate commands: government may not "establish" a religion, nor may it prohibit the "free exercise" of religion. Thus, government may neither sponsor or endorse a religion of its own nor deliberately interfere with citizens' freedom to practice their own faiths.

The Framers thought that these two constitutional principles respecting church and state—the Establishment Clause and the Free Exercise Clause—reinforce one another and stand best when they stand together. But sometimes the two principles come into conflict, or at least many people think that they do. Many Americans feel that if we do everything we can to drive religion from the public square, we will then be violating the free exercise of religious citizens and impoverishing our public life. Others believe that if we allow religion into public spaces and activities, we will invite sectarian conflict, hard feelings, and manipulation of religious sentiment by government leaders. What do you think?

POINTS TO PONDER

How do the First Amendment's religion clauses affect public school students?

- Should school officials be able to establish a morning prayer for all students?
- Should nondenominational prayers be allowed during official school functions?
- Should public school officials be allowed to post the Ten Commandments?
- Should religious beliefs ever excuse students from completing their state-required schooling?

Freedom from Establishment of Religion at School

Religion and schools are a controversial mix, and a large part of the Supreme Court's treatment of religious issues has taken place in the school environment. For example, the Court has considered the constitutionality of public reimbursement of parochial school parents for purchasing supplies for their children (allowed when part of a general program for all parents), whether or not public schools should allow religious student groups to meet at school (allowed when secular student groups are permitted to meet as well), and whether or not organized school prayer and a display of the Ten Commandments are constitutionally permissible (they are not, as we shall see). The general operating principle is that public school authorities may not endorse or promote religion on campus, but also may not deliberately exclude or discriminate against religious students and their families.

Since the Supreme Court decided *Engel v. Vitale* in 1962, it has been unconstitutional for school authorities to lead students in organized school prayer. Many politicians vehemently disagree with this holding and blame it for the nation's perceived moral demise. Some even link it to disasters like the 1999 Columbine High School killings in Littleton, Colorado. Others think the ban on organized school prayer is critical to maintaining Thomas Jefferson's "wall of separation" between church and state. Do you agree with the following decision that school-led prayers violate the Establishment Clause?

JUSTICE HUGO L. BLACK (1886–1971) wrote the majority opinion for this decision. He was the last of eight children born to a storekeeper and farmer in Clay County, Alabama. Skipping college, he went to the University of Alabama Law School, where he graduated with honors. After a distinguished career as a progressive reformer in public life, including stints as a judge, prosecutor, and U.S. senator, Black was appointed to the Supreme Court by President Franklin Delano Roosevelt in 1937. He served thirty-one years.

HIGHLIGHTS

➤ Justice Black attended medical school for one year at age seventeen.

➤ As a county prosecuting attorney in Alabama, he ran a successful grand jury investigation of the Bessamer, Alabama, police department, which was known for its barbaric torture chamber. Despite his own brief membership in the Ku Klux Klan, Black's passionate concern for human rights later became a hallmark of his jurisprudence.

ENGEL
v.
VITALE

Supreme Court of the United States
Argued April 3, 1962.
Decided June 25, 1962.

Justice BLACK delivered the opinion of the Court.

The respondent Board of Education of Union Free School District No. 9, New Hyde Park, New York, acting in its official capacity under state law, directed the School District's principal to cause the following prayer to be said aloud by each class in the presence of a teacher at the beginning of each school day:

"Almighty God, we acknowledge our dependence upon Thee, and we beg Thy blessings upon us, our parents, our teachers and our Country."

This daily procedure was adopted on the recommendation of the State Board of Regents, a governmental agency created by the State Constitution to which the New York Legislature has granted broad supervisory, executive, and legislative powers over the State's public school system. These state officials composed the prayer which they recommended and published as a part of their "Statement on Moral and Spiritual Training in the Schools," saying: "We believe that this Statement will be subscribed to by all men and women of good will, and we call upon all of them to aid in giving life to our program."

. . . [T]he parents of ten pupils brought this action in a New York State Court insisting that use of this official prayer in the public schools was contrary to the beliefs, religions, or religious practices of both themselves and their children. Among other things, these parents challenged the constitutionality of . . . the School District's regulation ordering the recitation of this particular prayer on the ground that these actions of official governmental agencies violate that part of the First Amendment of the Federal Constitution which commands that

Students in a San Antonio, Texas, classroom bow their heads in prayer in June 1962. Ever since the Court decided *Engel v. Vitale* it has been unconstitutional for public school officials to conduct organized prayers of any kind in the classroom.

"Congress shall make no law respecting an establishment of religion.". . . The New York Court of Appeals, over the dissents of Judges Dye and Fuld, sustained an order of the lower state courts which had upheld the power of New York to use the Regents' prayer as a part of the daily procedures of its public schools so long as the schools did not compel any pupil to join in the prayer over his or his parents' objection. We granted certiorari to review this important decision involving rights protected by the First and Fourteenth Amendments.

We think that by using its public school system to encourage recitation of the Regents' prayer, the State of New York has adopted a practice wholly inconsistent with the Establishment Clause. There can, of course, be no doubt that New York's program of daily classroom invocation of God's blessings as prescribed in the Regents' prayer is a religious activity. It is a solemn avowal of divine faith and supplication for the blessings of the Almighty. . . .

The petitioners contend among other things that the state laws requiring or permitting use of the Regents' prayer must be struck down as a violation of the Establishment Clause because that prayer was composed by governmental officials as a part of a governmental program to further religious beliefs. For this reason, petitioners argue, the State's use of the Regents' prayer in its public school system breaches the constitutional wall of separation between Church and State. We agree with that contention since we think that the constitutional prohibition against laws respecting an establishment of religion must at least mean that in this country it is no part of the business of government to compose official prayers for any group of the American people to recite as a part of a religious program carried on by government.

. . .The First Amendment was added to the Constitution to stand as a guarantee that neither the power nor the prestige of the Federal Government would be used to control, support or influence the kinds of prayer the American people can say that the people's religions must not be subjected to the pressures of government for change each time a new political administration is elected to office. Under that Amendment's prohibition against governmental establishment of religion, as reinforced by the provisions of the Fourteenth Amendment, government in this country, be it state or federal, is without power to prescribe by law any particular form of prayer which is to be used as an official prayer in carrying on any program of governmentally sponsored religious activity.

There can be no doubt that New York's state prayer program officially establishes the religious beliefs embodied in the Regents' prayer. The respondents' argument to the contrary, which is largely based upon the contention that the Regents' prayer is "non-denominational" and the fact that the program, as modified and approved by state courts, does not require all pupils to recite the prayer but permits those who wish to do so to remain silent or be excused from the room, ignores the essential nature of the program's constitutional defects. Neither the fact that the prayer may be denominationally neutral nor the fact that its observance on the part of the students is voluntary can serve to free it from the limitations of the Establishment Clause, as it might from the Free Exercise Clause, of the First Amendment, both of which are operative against the States by virtue of the Fourteenth Amendment.

Although these two clauses may in certain instances overlap, they forbid two quite different kinds of governmental encroachment upon religious freedom. The Establishment Clause . . . does not depend upon any showing of direct governmental compulsion and is violated by the enactment of laws which establish an official religion whether those laws operate directly to coerce nonobserving individuals or not. . . . When the power, prestige and financial support of government is placed behind a particular religious belief, the indirect coercive pressure upon religious minorities to conform to the prevailing officially approved religion is plain. But the purposes underlying the Establishment Clause go much further than that. Its first and most immediate purpose rested on the belief that a union of government and religion tends to destroy government and to degrade religion. . . . The Establishment Clause thus stands as an expression of principle on the part of the Founders of our Constitution that religion is too personal, too sacred, too holy, to permit its "unhallowed perversion" by a civil magistrate. Another purpose of the Establishment Clause rested upon an awareness of the historical fact that governmentally established religions and religious persecutions go hand in hand. The Founders knew that only a few years after the Book of Common Prayer became the only accepted form of religious services in the established Church of England, an Act of Uniformity was passed to compel all Englishmen to attend those services and to make it a criminal offense to conduct or attend religious gatherings of any other kind. . . .

It has been argued that to apply the Constitution in such a way as to prohibit state laws respecting an establishment of religious services in public schools is to indicate a hostility toward religion or toward prayer. Nothing, of course, could be more wrong. . . . It is neither sacrilegious nor antireligious to say that each separate government in this country should stay out of the business of writing or sanctioning official prayers and leave that purely religious function to the people themselves and to those the people choose to look to for religious guidance.

It is true that New York's establishment of its Regents' prayer as an officially approved religious doctrine of that State does not amount to a total establishment of one particular religious sect to the exclusion of all others that, indeed, the governmental endorsement of that prayer seems relatively insignificant when compared to the governmental encroachments upon religion which were commonplace 200 years ago. To those who may subscribe to the view that because the Regents' official prayer is so brief and general there can be no danger to religious freedom in its governmental establishment, however, it may be appropriate to say in the words of James Madison, the author of the First Amendment:

"It is proper to take alarm at the first experiment on our liberties. . . . Who does not see that the same authority which can establish Christianity, in exclusion of all other Religions, may establish with the same ease any particular sect of Christians, in exclusion of all other Sects? That the same authority which can force a citizen to contribute three pence only of his property for the support of any one establishment, may force him to conform to any other establishment in all cases whatsoever?"

The judgment of the Court of Appeals of New York is reversed and the cause remanded for further proceedings not inconsistent with this opinion.

Reversed and remanded.

Justice STEWART, dissenting.

A local school board in New York has provided that those pupils who wish to do so may join in a brief prayer at the beginning of each school day, acknowledging their dependence upon God and asking His blessing upon them and upon their parents, their teachers, and their country. The Court today decides that in permitting this brief nondenominational prayer the school board has violated the Constitution of the United States. I think this decision is wrong.

The Court does not hold, nor could it, that New York has interfered with the free exercise of anybody's religion. For the state courts have made clear that those who object to reciting the prayer must be entirely free of

JUSTICE POTTER STEWART (1915–1985) was born in Jackson, Michigan, on January 23, 1915. He went to prep school at Hotchkiss. Upon graduation from Yale University, Stewart went to Cambridge, England, on a Henry Fellowship and, one year later, entered Yale Law School. Stewart served active duty in the Navy, practiced privately, and was a judge on the United States Court of Appeals for the Sixth Circuit before President Dwight Eisenhower appointed him justice in 1958. He served until 1981.

HIGHLIGHTS

➢   During World War II, Stewart served as a deck officer on oil tankers.

➢   On the Court, Justice Stewart was well known for his pithy and witty statements in opinions. About obscenity, he said: "I shall not today further attempt to define the kinds of material I understand to be embraced within that shorthand description; and perhaps I could never succeed in intelligibly doing so. But I know it when I see it." In a capital punishment case, he wrote that arbitrary imposition of the death penalty is "cruel and unusual in the way that being struck by lightning is cruel and unusual."

any compulsion to do so, including any "embarrassments and pressures." But the Court says that in permitting school children to say this simple prayer, the New York authorities have established "an official religion."

With all respect, I think the Court has misapplied a great constitutional principle. I cannot see how an "official religion" is established by letting those who want to say a prayer say it. On the contrary, I think that to deny the wish of these school children to join in reciting this prayer is to deny them the opportunity of sharing in the spiritual heritage of our Nation.

. . .

I dissent.

EXERCISE 4.1. Imagine that your class had to recite these same words in unison every morning: "Almighty God, we acknowledge our dependence upon Thee, and we beg Thy blessings upon us, our parents, our teachers and our Country." How would that make you feel? Who might it make feel uncomfortable? Are there religious students who might be turned off to the form or content of this prayer? (One writer of atheist leanings, the *Nation* magazine's Katha Pollitt, said she is tempted to favor prayer in the public schools because she is sure that it will turn all the students against religion!)

EXERCISE 4.2. The Court ruled in *Engel v. Vitale* that schools could not organize moments of prayer. In a later decision, *Wallace v. Jaffree* (1985), it allowed general "moments of silence" for meditation and reflection. Some object that this policy is a dressed-up form of group prayer while others argue that it favors Transcendental Meditation and other spiritual practices over traditional religion. Does the Court's decision in *Wallace* seem to you like a good place to draw the line?

Saying a Benediction for Invocation

Even after *Engel v. Vitale,* many local school system officials and teachers continued to lead students in group prayer at official ceremonial events, such as graduations and homecoming games. Then, in 1992, the Supreme Court handed down its decision in *Lee v. Weisman,* which held that public school officials could not invite clergy members to open graduation with an invocation prayer or close it with a benediction. Do you think that the Court was pushing things too far with this decision, as Justice Scalia suggests, or is this ruling necessary to allow all students, regardless of religious belief, to enjoy "one of life's most significant occasions," as Justice Kennedy argues?

LEE
v.
WEISMAN

Supreme Court of the United States
Argued Nov. 6, 1991.
Decided June 24, 1992.

Justice KENNEDY delivered the opinion of the Court.

School principals in the public school system of the city of Providence, Rhode Island, are permitted to invite members of the clergy to offer invocation and benediction prayers as part of the formal graduation ceremonies for middle schools and for high schools. The question before us is whether including clerical members who offer prayers as part of the official school graduation ceremony is consistent with the Religion Clauses of the First Amendment, provisions the Fourteenth Amendment makes applicable with full force to the States and their school districts.

I

A

Deborah Weisman graduated from Nathan Bishop Middle School, a public school in Providence, at a formal ceremony in June 1989. She was about 14 years old. For many years it has been the policy of the Providence School Committee and the Superintendent of Schools to permit principals to invite members of the clergy to give invocations and benedictions at middle school and high school graduations. Many, but not all, of the principals elected to include prayers as part of the graduation ceremonies. Acting for himself and his daughter, Deborah's father, Daniel Weisman, objected to any prayers at Deborah's middle school graduation, but to no avail. The school principal, petitioner Robert E. Lee, invited a rabbi to deliver prayers at the graduation exercises for Deborah's class. Rabbi Leslie Gutterman, of the Temple Beth El in Providence, accepted.

It has been the custom of Providence school officials to provide invited clergy with a pamphlet entitled "Guidelines for Civic Occasions," prepared by the National Conference of Christians and Jews. The Guidelines recommend that public prayers at nonsectarian civic ceremonies be composed with "inclusiveness and sensitivity," though they acknowledge that "[p]rayer of any kind may be inappropriate on some civic occasions." The principal gave Rabbi Gutterman the pamphlet before the graduation and advised him the invocation and benediction should be nonsectarian.

Rabbi Gutterman's prayers were as follows:

"INVOCATION
"God of the Free, Hope of the Brave:
"For the legacy of America where diversity is celebrated and the rights of mi-

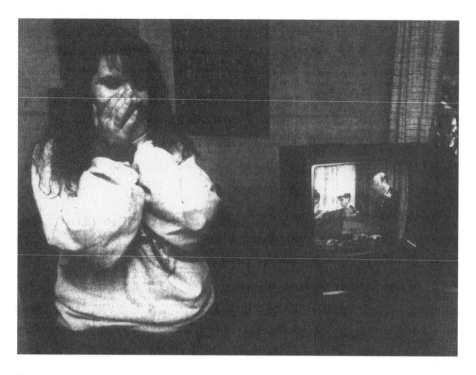

Deborah Weisman reacts with astonishment at seeing herself on television in June 1992. Her case led the Supreme Court to forbid public schools to invite clergy members to give religious invocations or benedictions at graduation ceremonies.

norities are protected, we thank You. May these young men and women grow up to enrich it.

"For the liberty of America, we thank You. May these new graduates grow up to guard it.

"For the political process of America in which all its citizens may participate, for its court system where all may seek justice we thank You. May those we honor this morning always turn to it in trust.

"For the destiny of America we thank You. May the graduates of Nathan Bishop Middle School so live that they might help to share it.

"May our aspirations for our country and for these young people, who are our hope for the future, be richly fulfilled.

AMEN"

"BENEDICTION

"O God, we are grateful to You for having endowed us with the capacity for learning which we have celebrated on this joyous commencement.

"Happy families give thanks for seeing their children achieve an important milestone. Send Your blessings upon the teachers and administrators who helped prepare them.

"The graduates now need strength and guidance for the future, help them to understand that we are not complete with academic knowledge alone. We must each strive to fulfill what You require of us all: To do justly, to love mercy, to walk humbly.

"We give thanks to You, Lord, for keeping us alive, sustaining us and allowing us to reach this special, happy occasion.

AMEN"

. . .

The school board . . . argued that these short prayers and others like them at graduation exercises are of profound meaning to many students and parents throughout this country who consider that due respect and acknowledgment for divine guidance and for the deepest spiritual aspirations of our people ought to be expressed at an event as important in life as a graduation. We assume this to be so in addressing the difficult case now before us, for the significance of the prayers lies also at the heart of Daniel and Deborah Weisman's case.

B

. . .

The case was submitted on stipulated facts. The District Court held that petitioners' practice of including invocations and benedictions in public school graduations violated the Establishment Clause of the First Amendment, and it enjoined petitioners from continuing the practice. The court applied the three-part Establishment Clause test set forth in *Lemon v. Kurtzman*. Under that test as described in our past cases, to satisfy the Establishment Clause a governmental practice must (1) reflect a clearly secular purpose; (2) have a primary effect that neither advances nor inhibits religion; and (3) avoid excessive government entanglement with religion. The District Court held that petitioners' actions violated the second part of the test. . . . The court determined that the practice of including invocations and benedictions, even so-called nonsectarian ones, in public school graduations creates an identification of governmental power with religious practice, endorses religion, and violates the Establishment Clause. . . .

On appeal, the United States Court of Appeals for the First Circuit affirmed. . . . We granted certiorari, . . . and now affirm.

II

These dominant facts mark and control the confines of our decision: State officials direct the performance of a formal religious exercise at promotional and graduation ceremonies for secondary schools. Even for those students who object to the religious exercise, their attendance and participation in the state-sponsored religious activity are in a fair and real sense obligatory, though the school district does not require attendance as a condition for receipt of the diploma.

. . . The government involvement with religious activity in this case is pervasive, to the point of creating a state-sponsored and state-directed religious exercise in a public school. Conducting this formal religious observance conflicts with settled rules pertaining to prayer exercises for students, and that suffices to determine the question before us.

The principle that government may accommodate the free exercise of religion does not supersede the fundamental limitations imposed by the Establishment Clause. It is beyond dispute that, at a minimum, the Constitution guarantees that government may not coerce anyone to support or participate in religion or its exercise. . . . The State's involvement in the school prayers challenged today violates these central principles.

. . .

The State's role did not end with the decision to include a prayer and with the choice of a clergyman. Principal Lee provided Rabbi Gutterman with a copy of the "Guidelines for Civic Occasions," and advised him that his prayers should be nonsectarian. Through these means the principal directed and controlled the content of the prayers. . . .

Petitioners argue, and we find nothing in the case to refute it, that the directions for the content of the prayers were a good-faith attempt by the school to ensure that the sectarianism which is so often the flashpoint for religious animosity be removed from the graduation ceremony. The concern is understandable, as a prayer which uses ideas or images identified with a particular religion may foster a different sort of sectarian rivalry than an invocation or benediction in terms more neutral. The school's explanation, however, does not resolve the dilemma caused by its participation. The question is not the good faith of the school in attempting to make the prayer acceptable to most persons, but the legitimacy of its undertaking that enterprise at all when the object is to produce a prayer to be used in a formal religious exercise which students, for all practical purposes, are obliged to attend.

. . .

The degree of school involvement here made it clear that the graduation prayers bore the imprint of the State and thus put school-age children who objected in an untenable position. We turn our attention now to consider the position of the students, both those who desired the prayer and she who did not.

To endure the speech of false ideas or offensive content and then to counter it is part of learning how to live in a pluralistic society, a society which insists upon open discourse towards the end of a tolerant citizenry. And tolerance presupposes some mutuality of obligation. It is argued that our constitutional vision of a free society requires confidence in our own ability to accept or reject ideas of which we do not approve, and that prayer at a high school graduation does nothing more than offer a choice. By the time they are seniors, high school students no doubt have been required to attend classes and assemblies and to complete assignments exposing them to ideas they find distasteful or immoral or absurd or all of these. Against this background, students may consider it an odd measure of justice to be subjected during the course of their educations to ideas deemed offensive and irreligious, but to be denied a brief, formal prayer ceremony that the school offers in return. This argument cannot prevail, however. It overlooks a fundamental dynamic of the Constitution. The First Amendment protects speech and religion by quite different mechanisms. Speech is protected by ensuring its full expression even when the government participates, for the very object of some of our most important speech is to persuade the government to adopt an idea as its own. The method for protecting freedom of worship and freedom of conscience in religious matters is quite the reverse. In religious debate or expression the government is not a prime participant, for the Framers deemed religious establishment antithetical to the freedom of all. The Free Exercise Clause embraces a freedom of conscience and worship that has close parallels in the speech provisions of the First Amendment, but the Establishment Clause is a specific prohibition on forms of state intervention in religious affairs with no precise counterpart in the speech provisions. The explanation lies in the lesson of history that was and is the inspiration for the Establishment Clause, the lesson that in the hands of government what might begin as a tolerant expression of religious views may end in a policy to indoctrinate and coerce. A state-created orthodoxy puts at grave risk that freedom of belief and conscience which are the sole assurance that religious faith is real, not imposed.

The lessons of the First Amendment are as urgent in the modern world as in the 18th century when it was written. One timeless lesson is that if citizens are subjected to state-sponsored religious exercises, the State disavows its own duty to guard and respect that sphere of inviolable conscience and belief which is the mark of a free people. To compromise that principle today would be to deny our own tradition and forfeit our standing to urge others to secure the protections of that tradition for themselves.

As we have observed before, there are heightened concerns with protecting freedom of conscience from subtle coercive pressure in the elementary and secondary public schools. . . . What to most believers may seem nothing more than a reasonable request that the nonbeliever respect their religious practices, in a school context may appear to the nonbeliever or dissenter to be an attempt to employ the machinery of the State to enforce a religious orthodoxy.

Rabbi Leslie Gutterman, left, leads a prayer at the Nathan Bishop Middle School graduation in 1989. At right are principal Robert E. Lee and school board member Bruce Lundlun. The Court's decision in *Lee v. Weisman* has fueled the long-running controversy over prayer in schools.

We need not look beyond the circumstances of this case to see the phenomenon at work. The undeniable fact is that the school district's supervision and control of a high school graduation ceremony places public pressure, as well as peer pressure, on attending students to stand as a group or, at least, maintain respectful silence during the invocation and benediction. . . . There can be no doubt that for many, if not most, of the students at the graduation, the act of standing or remaining silent was an expression of participation in the rabbi's prayer. That was the very point of the religious exercise. It is of little comfort to a dissenter, then, to be told that for her the act of standing or remaining in silence signifies mere respect, rather than participation. What matters is that, given our social conventions, a reasonable dissenter in this milieu could believe that the group exercise signified her own participation or approval of it.

Finding no violation under these circumstances would place objectors in the dilemma of participating, with all that implies, or protesting. We do not address whether that choice is acceptable if the affected citizens are mature adults, but we think the State may not, consistent with the Establishment Clause, place primary and secondary school children in this position. Research in psychology supports the common assumption that adolescents are often susceptible to pressure from their peers towards conformity, and that the influence is strongest in matters of social convention. To recognize that the choice imposed by the State constitutes an unacceptable constraint only acknowledges that the government may no more use social pressure to enforce orthodoxy than it may use more direct means.

. . .

There was a stipulation in the District Court that attendance at graduation and promotional ceremonies is voluntary. . . . The argument lacks all persuasion. . . . Everyone knows that in our society and in our culture high school graduation is one of life's most significant occasions. . . .

The importance of the event is the point the school district and the United States rely upon to argue that a formal prayer ought to be permitted, but it becomes one of the principal reasons why their argument must fail. Their contention . . . is that the prayers are an essential part of these ceremonies because for many persons an occasion of this significance lacks meaning if there is no recognition, however brief, that human achievements cannot be understood apart from their spiritual essence. We think the Government's position that this interest suffices to force students to choose between compliance or forfeiture demonstrates fundamental inconsistency in its argumentation. It fails to acknowledge that what for many of Deborah's classmates and their parents was a spiritual imperative was for Daniel and Deborah Weisman religious conformance compelled by the State. . . . The Constitution forbids the State to exact religious conformity from a student as the price of attending her own high school graduation. This is the calculus the Constitution commands.

. . .

We do not hold that every state action implicating religion is invalid if one or a few citizens find it offensive. People may take offense at all manner of religious as well as nonreligious messages, but offense alone does not in every case show a violation. We know too that sometimes to endure social isolation or even anger may be the price of conscience or nonconformity. But, by any reading of our cases, the conformity required of the student in this case was too high an exaction to withstand the test of the Establishment Clause. The prayer exercises in this case are especially improper because the State has in every practical sense compelled attendance and participation in an explicit religious exercise at an event of singular importance to every student, one the objecting student had no real alternative to avoid.

. . .

. . . We recognize that, at graduation time and throughout the course of the educational process, there will be instances when religious values, religious practices, and religious persons will have some interaction with the public schools and their students. But these matters, often questions of accommodation of religion, are not before us. The sole question presented is whether a religious exercise may be conducted at a graduation ceremony in circumstances where, as we have found, young graduates who object are induced to conform. No holding by this Court suggests that a school can persuade or compel a student to participate in a religious exercise. That is being done here, and it is forbidden by the Establishment Clause of the First Amendment.

For the reasons we have stated, the judgment of the Court of Appeals is *Affirmed.*

Justice SCALIA, with whom The Chief Justice, Justice WHITE, and Justice THOMAS join, dissenting.

. . .

. . . In holding that the Establishment Clause prohibits invocations and benedictions at public school graduation ceremonies, the Court—with nary a mention that it is doing so—lays waste a tradition that is as old as public school graduation ceremonies themselves, and that is a component of an even more longstanding American tradition of nonsectarian prayer to God at public celebrations generally. . . .

I

. . .

The history and tradition of our Nation are replete with public ceremonies featuring prayers of thanksgiving and petition. . . .

From our Nation's origin, prayer has been a prominent part of governmental ceremonies and proclamations. The Declaration of Independence, the document marking our birth as a separate people, "appealed to the Supreme Judge of the world for the rectitude of our intentions" and avowed "a firm reliance on the protection of divine Providence." In his first inaugural address, after swearing his oath of office on a Bible, George Washington deliberately made a prayer a part of his first official act as President:

"[I]t would be peculiarly improper to omit in this first official act my fervent supplications to that Almighty Being who rules over the universe, who presides in the councils of nations, and whose providential aids can supply every human defect, that His benediction may consecrate to the liberties and happiness of the people of the United States a Government instituted by themselves for these essential purposes."

Such supplications have been a characteristic feature of inaugural addresses ever since. . . .

. . .

II

. . . The Court's argument that state officials have "coerced" students to take part in the invocation and benediction at graduation ceremonies is, not to put too fine a point on it, incoherent.

The Court identifies two "dominant facts" that it says dictate its ruling that invocations and benedictions at public school graduation ceremonies violate the Establishment Clause. Neither of them is in any relevant sense true.

A

The Court declares that students' "attendance and participation in the [invocation and benediction] are in a fair and real sense obligatory." But what exactly is this "fair and real sense"? According to the Court, students at graduation who want "to avoid the fact or appearance of participation" in the invocation and benediction are *psychologically* obligated by "public pressure, as well as peer pressure, . . . to stand as a group or, at least, maintain respectful silence" during those prayers. This assertion—*the very linchpin of the Court's opinion*—is almost as intriguing for what it does not say as for what it says. It does not say, for example, that students are psychologically coerced to bow their heads, place their hands in a Dürer-like prayer position, pay attention to the prayers, utter "Amen," or in fact pray. (Perhaps further intensive psychological research remains to be done on these matters.) It claims only that students are psychologically coerced "to stand . . . *or*, at least, maintain respectful silence." Both halves of this disjunctive (*both* of which must amount to the fact or appearance of participation in prayer if the Court's analysis is to survive on its own terms) merit particular attention.

To begin with the latter: The Court's notion that a student who simply sits in "respectful silence" during the invocation and benediction (when all others are standing) has somehow joined or would somehow be perceived as having joined in the prayers is nothing short of ludicrous. We indeed live in a vulgar age. But surely "our social conventions" have not coarsened to the point that anyone who does not stand on his chair and shout obscenities can reasonably be deemed to have assented to everything said in his presence. Since the Court does not dispute that students exposed to prayer at graduation ceremonies retain (despite "subtle coercive pressures") the free will to sit, there is absolutely no basis for the Court's decision. It is fanciful enough to say that "a reasonable dissenter," standing head erect in a class of bowed heads, "could believe that the group exercise signified her own participation or approval of it." It is beyond the absurd to say that she could entertain such a belief while pointedly declining to rise.

But let us assume the very worst, that the nonparticipating graduate is "subtly coerced" . . . to stand! Even that half of the disjunctive does not remotely establish a "participation" (or an "appearance of participation") in a religious exercise. The Court acknowledges that "in our culture standing . . . can signify adherence to a view or simple respect for the views of others." (Much more often the latter than the former, I think, except perhaps in the proverbial town meeting, where one votes by standing.) But if it is a permissible inference that one who is standing is doing so simply out of respect for the prayers of others that are in progress, then how can it possibly be said that a "reasonable dissenter . . . could believe that the group exercise signified her own participation or approval"? Quite obviously, it cannot. I may add, moreover, that maintaining respect for the religious observances of others is a fundamental civic virtue that government (including the public schools) can and should cultivate so that even if it were the case that the displaying of such respect might be mistaken for taking part in the prayer, I would deny that the dissenter's interest in avoiding *even the false appearance of participation* constitutionally trumps the government's interest in fostering respect for religion generally.

The opinion manifests that the Court itself has not given careful consideration to its test of psychological coercion. For if it had, how could it observe, with no hint of concern or disapproval, that students stood for the Pledge of Allegiance, which immediately preceded Rabbi Gutterman's invocation? . . .

I also find it odd that the Court concludes that high school graduates may not be subjected to this supposed psychological coercion, yet refrains from addressing whether "mature adults" may. I had thought that the reason graduation from high school is regarded as so significant an event is that it is generally associated with transition from adolescence to young adulthood. Many graduating seniors, of course, are old enough to vote. Why, then, does the Court treat them as though they were first-graders? Will we soon have a jurisprudence that distinguishes between mature and immature adults?

B

The other "dominant fac[t]" identified by the Court is that "[s]tate officials direct the performance of a formal religious exercise" at school graduation ceremonies. "Direct[ing] the performance of a formal religious exercise" has a sound of liturgy to it, summoning up images of the principal directing acolytes where to carry the cross, or showing the rabbi where to unroll the Torah. . . . All the record shows is that principals of the Providence public schools, acting within their delegated authority, have invited clergy to deliver invocations and benedictions at graduations; and that Principal Lee invited Rabbi Gutterman, provided him a two-page pamphlet, prepared by the National Conference of Christians and Jews, giving general advice on inclusive prayer for civic occasions, and advised him that his prayers at graduation should be nonsectarian. How these facts can fairly be transformed into the charges that Principal Lee "directed and controlled the content of [Rabbi Gutterman's] prayer," . . . is difficult to fathom. The Court identifies nothing in the record remotely suggesting that school officials have ever drafted, edited, screened, or censored graduation prayers, or that Rabbi Gutterman was a mouthpiece of the school officials.

These distortions of the record are, of course, not harmless error: without them the Court's solemn assertion that the school officials could reasonably be perceived to be "enforcing a religious orthodoxy," would ring as hollow as it ought.

III

The deeper flaw in the Court's opinion does not lie in its wrong answer to the question whether there was state-induced "peer-pressure" coercion; it lies, rather, in the Court's making violation of the Establishment Clause hinge on such a precious question. The coercion that was a hallmark of historical establishments of religion was coercion of religious orthodoxy and of financial support *by force of law and threat of penalty.* . . .

. . .

Thus, while I have no quarrel with the Court's general proposition that the Establishment Clause "guarantees that government may not coerce anyone to support or participate in religion or its exercise," I see no warrant for expanding the concept of coercion beyond acts backed by threat of penalty. . . .

. . . [T]here is nothing in the record to indicate that failure of attending students to take part in the invocation or benediction was subject to any penalty or discipline. . . .

The Court relies on our "school prayer" cases . . . [b]ut whatever the merit of those cases, they do not support, much less compel, the Court's psycho-journey. . . . [W]e have made clear our understanding that school prayer occurs within a framework in which legal coercion to attend school (i.e., coercion under threat of penalty) provides the ultimate backdrop. . . . Voluntary prayer at graduation—a one-time ceremony at which parents, friends, and relatives are present—can hardly be thought to raise the same concerns.

IV

. . .

. . . Given the odd basis for the Court's decision, invocations and benedictions will be able to be given at public school graduations next June, as they have for the past century and a half, so long as school authorities make clear that anyone who abstains from screaming in protest does not necessarily participate in the prayers. All that is seemingly needed is an announcement, or perhaps a written insertion at the beginning of the graduation program, to the effect that, while all are asked to rise for the invocation and benediction, none is compelled to join in them, nor will be assumed, by rising, to have done so. That obvious fact recited, the graduates and their parents may proceed to thank God, as Americans have always done, for the blessings He has generously bestowed on them and on their country.

. . .

The narrow context of the present case involves a community's celebration of one of the milestones in its young citizens' lives, and it is a bold step for this Court to seek to banish from that occasion, and from thousands of similar celebrations throughout this land, the expression of gratitude to God that a majority of the community wishes to make. The issue before us today is not the abstract philosophical question whether the alternative of frustrating this desire of a religious majority is to be preferred over the alternative of imposing "psychological coercion," or a feeling of exclusion, upon nonbelievers. Rather, the question is *whether a mandatory choice in favor of the former has been imposed by the United States Constitution.* As the age-old practices of our people show, the answer to that question is not at all in doubt.

I must add one final observation: The Founders of our Republic knew the fearsome potential of sectarian religious belief to generate civil dissension and civil strife. And they also knew that nothing, absolutely nothing, is so inclined to foster among religious believers of various faiths a toleration—no, an affection—for one another than voluntarily joining in prayer together, to the God whom they all worship and seek. Needless to say, no one should be compelled to do that, but it is a shame to deprive our public culture of the opportunity, and indeed the encouragement, for people to do it voluntarily. The Baptist or Catholic who heard and joined in the simple and inspiring prayers of Rabbi Gutterman on this official and patriotic occasion was inoculated from religious bigotry and prejudice in a manner that cannot be replicated. To deprive our society of that important unifying mechanism, in order to spare the nonbeliever what seems to me the minimal inconvenience of standing or even sitting in respectful nonparticipation, is as senseless in policy as it is unsupported in law.

For the foregoing reasons, I dissent.

EXERCISE 4.3. The valedictorian of your high school graduating class, Suzie Smith, was chosen (as usual) by virtue of her grade point average. She is a devout Moslem who has written her valedictorian address about the importance in her life of Mohammed and why she thinks students who abuse drugs and alcohol or belong to gangs need to discover Mohammed in their personal lives. She wants to finish by inviting her fellow graduates to come with her to her mosque before they leave for college or work. The principal is nervous about letting her give such a speech, but students in the past have always been allowed to speak about the topic of their choice and are usually edited for length, clarity, and style only. The principal does not want to be sued by non-Moslem parents, but she also does not want to be sued by Suzie and her family.

Knowing that you are taking this class, the principal asks your advice on how to handle the situation without violating the Establishment Clause or Suzie's free speech and Free Exercise rights. How will you advise the principal to act in this majority Christian community? (What if Suzie were a Methodist? A Jehovah's Witness? A Catholic? A Hare Krishna? A Hindu? A follower of Rev. Sun Myung Moon? Does it change your views?) Discuss the problem with your classmates and come up with what you think is sound legal and policy advice for the principal.

INTERVIEWING THE JUSTICES. Select two students to play the anchors of an evening television news talk show like *Nightline*. The anchors have garnered an unusual assignment: they will be interviewing the nine Supreme Court justices about their opinions in *Lee v. Weisman*. Select one set of students to play Justice Kennedy (who wrote the Court's majority opinion) and the four justices who agreed with him. Select a second set of students to play Justice Scalia (who wrote the dissenting opinion) and the three justices who dissented alongside him. Try to get to the bottom of the views of each justice. Why did those who sided with the majority think that a graduation benediction violated the Establishment Clause? How did they think that such prayers affected students and their families? And why did the dissenters object to the majority's decision? What standard does Justice Scalia think is appropriate to consider whether graduation prayers are allowable? How does he think students and their families experience such prayers? The news anchors should bring on additional guests, played by other students in the class, to play teachers and students who discuss their own thoughts about the case. (This exercise is for fun and learning; in reality, Supreme Court justices almost never discuss their opinions in public, and certainly never in a format like this.)

Government Aid to Private Religious Schools: When Does It Cross the Line?

It is clear that government cannot give tax dollars to religious schools for the purposes of teaching religion or for supporting the school's academic program generally. This kind of subsidy is precisely what the First Amendment forbids. The First Amendment guarantees that government will not establish religions or tax the public to support them.

Yet many public services are rendered to private religion, and they pose no constitutional problem. For example, if a church is on fire, the fire department can put the fire out without violating the First Amendment. Police officers can help churches, mosques, and synagogues if they have been vandalized or burglarized. Cities can provide sewage and garbage collection. None of these forms of public aid is invalid because they are part of neutral and universal government services that do not bolster a specifically religious mission of the churches.

In the following case, the Court considers the constitutionality of a New Jersey township's policy of reimbursing parents for the cost of sending their children to private school, including private religious school, on public buses. The plaintiffs attacking the policy argued that it was designed to make parochial school cheaper and to indirectly subsidize religious schools. The township argued that it was part of a universal policy to pay for all kids, whether in public or private school, to get to school safely and on time. What do you think? What does the Court decide?

—————

EVERSON
v.
BOARD OF EDUCATION OF THE TOWNSHIP OF EWING

Supreme Court of the United States
Argued Nov. 20, 1946.
Decided Feb. 10, 1947.

Justice BLACK delivered the opinion of the Court.

A New Jersey statute authorizes its local school districts to make rules and contracts for the transportation of children to and from schools. The appellee, a township board of education, acting pursuant to this statute, authorized reimbursement to parents of money expended by them for the bus transportation of their children on regular busses operated by the public transportation system. Part of this money was for the payment of transportation of some children in the community to Catholic parochial schools. These church schools give their students, in addition to secular education, regular religious instruction conforming to the religious tenets and modes of worship of the Catholic Faith. . . .

. . .

. . . The New Jersey statute is challenged as a "law respecting an establishment of religion." The First Amendment, as made applicable to the states by the Fourteenth, commands that a state "shall make no law respecting an establishment of religion, or prohibiting the free exercise thereof. . . ." These words of the First Amendment reflected in the minds of early Americans a vivid mental picture of conditions and practices which they fervently wished to stamp out in order to preserve liberty for themselves and for their posterity. Doubtless their goal has not been entirely reached; but so far has the Nation moved toward it that the expression "law respecting an establishment of religion," probably does not so vividly remind present-day Americans of the evils, fears, and political problems that caused that expression to be written into our Bill of Rights. . . .

. . .

The "establishment of religion" clause of the First Amendment means at least this: Neither a state nor the Federal Government can set up a church. Neither can pass laws which aid one religion, aid all religions, or prefer one religion over another. Neither can force nor influence a person to go to or to remain away from church against his will or force him to profess a belief or disbelief in any religion. No person can be punished for entertaining or professing religious beliefs or disbeliefs, for church attendance or non-attendance. No tax in any amount, large or small, can be levied to support any religious activities or institutions, whatever they may be called, or whatever form they may adopt to teach or practice religion. . . .

We must consider the New Jersey statute in accordance with the foregoing limitations imposed by the First Amendment. . . . New Jersey cannot consistently with the "establishment of religion" clause of the First Amendment contribute tax-raised funds to the support of an institution which teaches the tenets and faith of any church. On the other hand, other language of the amendment commands that New Jersey cannot hamper its citizens in the free exercise of their own religion. . . . While we do not mean to intimate that a state could not provide transportation only to children attending public schools, we must be careful, in protecting the citizens of New Jersey against state-established churches, to be sure that we do not inadvertently prohibit New Jersey from extending its general state law benefits to all its citizens without regard to their religious belief. Measured by these standards, we cannot say that the First Amendment prohibits New Jersey from spending tax-raised funds to pay the bus fares of parochial school pupils as a part of a general program under which it pays the fares of pupils attending public and other schools. . . . That Amendment requires the state to be a neutral in its relations with groups of religious believers and non-believers; it does not require the state to be their adversary. State power is no more to be used so as to handicap religions than it is to favor them.

. . .

The First Amendment has erected a wall between church and state. That wall must be kept high and impregnable. We could not approve the slightest breach. New Jersey has not breached it here.

Affirmed.

Justice RUTLEDGE, with whom Justice FRANKFURTER, Justice JACKSON and Justice BURTON agree, dissenting.

. . .

I

Not simply an established church, but any law respecting an establishment of religion is forbidden. The Amendment was broadly but not loosely phrased. It is the compact and exact summation of its author's views formed during his long struggle for religious freedom. . . .

. . .

A young girl travels alone to religious school by public bus. Bus transportation plays a role in a number of constitutional controversies relating to schools.

III

. . .

Does New Jersey's action furnish support for religion by use of the taxing power? Certainly it does, if the test remains undiluted as Jefferson and Madison made it, that money taken by taxation from one is not to be used or given to support another's religious training or belief, or indeed one's own. . . .

The funds used here were raised by taxation. The Court does not dispute, nor could it, that their use does in fact give aid and encouragement to religious instruction. It only concludes that this aid is not "support" in law. . . . Here parents pay money to send their children to parochial schools and funds raised by taxation are used to reimburse them. This not only helps the children to get to school and the parents to send them. It aids them in a substantial way to get the very thing which they are sent to the particular school to secure, namely, religious training and teaching.

. . .

New Jersey's action therefore exactly fits the type of exaction and the kind of evil at which Madison and Jefferson struck. Under the test they framed it cannot be said that the cost of transportation is no part of the cost of education or of the religious instruction given. . . .

. . . Payment of transportation is no more, nor is it any the less essential to education, whether religious or secular, than payment for tuitions, for teachers' salaries, for buildings, equipment and necessary materials. Nor is it any the less directly related, in a school giving religious instruction, to the primary religious objective all those essential items of cost are intended to achieve. No rational line can be drawn between payment for such larger, but not more necessary, items and payment for transportation. . . .[1]

EXERCISE 4.4. *Everson* may have been an easy case since the city buses simply got the children to the schoolhouse door; government action did not actually follow students inside the religious schools. What would you think about a local policy of reimbursing all parents of children in public or private school for the cost of any schoolbooks they buy, including both secular and religious books? What would you think about a city policy, designed to make teaching a more attractive option for talented college graduates, that gave teachers a 10 percent bonus for working in the city at public or private schools, including religious schools?

EXERCISE 4.5. Do you think a school voucher policy that gives parents tuition vouchers redeemable at public, private, or religious schools is constitutional under the Establishment Clause? Several such programs have already been attacked by critics, but most have passed constitutional muster on the grounds that it is the parents, not the government, who dictate the allocation of money to religious schools. Do you agree with this rationale, or do you think school vouchers are simply a clever way to channel public money directly into the coffers of religious institutions?

In addition to money, there are other resources that the government can share—constitutionally or unconstitutionally—with religious schools: specifically, teachers, time, and use of school facilities.

In the next two cases, the Court considers the legitimacy of "released time" programs in which students are released from regular class activities in order that they may take religious classes. The first program, which took place in Illinois, was struck down, but the one considered in the second case was upheld. What was the difference between the two according to the Court?

MCCOLLUM

v.

BOARD OF EDUCATION OF SCHOOL DISTRICT NO. 71

Supreme Court of the United States
Argued Dec. 8, 1947.
Decided March 8, 1948.

Justice BLACK delivered the opinion of the Court.

. . .

Appellant's petition . . . alleged that religious teachers, employed by private religious groups, were permitted to come weekly into the school buildings during the regular hours set apart for secular teaching, and then and there for a period of thirty minutes substitute their religious teaching for the secular education provided under the compulsory education law. The petitioner charged that this joint public-school religious-group program violated the First and Fourteenth Amendments to the United States Constitution. . . .

. . .

The foregoing facts, . . . show the use of tax-supported property for religious instruction and the close cooperation between the school authorities and the religious council in promoting religious education. The operation of the State's compulsory education system thus assists and is integrated with the program of religious instruction carried on by separate religious sects. . . . This is beyond all question a utilization of the tax-established and tax-supported public school system to aid religious groups to spread their faith. And it falls squarely under the ban of the First Amendment (made applicable to the States by the Fourteenth) as we interpreted it in *Everson v. Board of Education.* There we said: "Neither a state nor the Federal Government can set up a church. Neither can pass laws which aid one religion, aid all religions, or prefer one religion over another. Neither can force or influence a person to go to or to remain away from church against his will or force him to profess a belief or disbelief in any religion. No person can be punished for entertaining or professing religious beliefs or disbeliefs, for church attendance or non-attendance. No tax in any amount, large or small, can be levied to support any religious activities or institutions, whatever they may be called, or whatever form they may adopt to teach or practice religion. Neither a state nor the Federal Government can, openly or secretly, participate in the affairs of any religious organizations or groups and vice versa. In the words of Jefferson, the clause against establishment of religion by law was intended to erect 'a wall of separation between church and State.'"

To hold that a state cannot consistently with the First and Fourteenth Amendments utilize its public school system to aid any or all religious faiths or sects in the dissemination of their doctrines and ideals does not, as counsel urge, manifest a governmental hostility to religion or religious teachings. A manifestation of such hostility would be at war with our national tradition as embodied in the First Amendment's guaranty of the free exercise of religion. For the First Amendment rests upon the premise that both religion and government can best work to achieve their lofty aims if each is left free from the other within its respective sphere. Or, as we said in the *Everson* case, the First Amendment has erected a wall between Church and State which must be kept high and impregnable.

Here not only are the State's tax-supported public school buildings used for the dissemination of religious doctrines. The State also affords sectarian groups an invaluable aid in that it helps to provide pupils for their religious classes through use of the State's compulsory public school machinery. This is not separation of Church and State.

. . .

Reversed and remanded.

Justice FRANKFURTER delivered the following opinion, in which Justice JACKSON, Justice RUTLEDGE and Justice BURTON join [concurring].

. . . Illinois has here authorized the commingling of sectarian with secular instruction in the public schools. The Constitution of the United States forbids this.

. . .

Of course, "released time" as a generalized conception, undefined by differentiating particularities, is not an issue for Constitutional adjudication. Local programs differ from each other in many and crucial respects. Some "released time" classes are under separate denominational auspices, others are conducted jointly by several denominations, often embracing all the religious affiliations of a community. Some classes in religion teach a limited sectarianism; others emphasize democracy, unity and spiritual values not anchored in a particular creed. Insofar as these are manifestations merely of the free exercise of religion, they are quite outside the scope of judicial concern, except insofar as the Court may be called upon to protect the right of religious freedom. It is only when challenge is made to the share that the public schools have in the execution of a particular "released time" program that close judicial scrutiny is demanded of the exact relation between the religious instruction and the public educational system in the specific situation before the Court. . . .

. . .

We do not consider, as indeed we could not, school programs not before us which, though colloquially characterized as "released time," present situations differing in aspects that may well be constitutionally crucial. Different forms which "released time" has taken during more than thirty years of growth include programs which, like that before us, could not withstand the test of the Constitution; others may be found unexceptionable. . . . We find that the basic Constitutional principle of absolute Separation was violated when the State of Illinois, speaking through its Supreme Court, sustained the school authorities of Champaign in sponsoring and effectively furthering religious beliefs by its educational arrangement.

. . . The public school is at once the symbol of our democracy and the most pervasive means for promoting our common destiny. In no activity of the State is it more vital to keep out divisive forces than in its schools, to avoid confusing, not to say fusing, what the Constitution sought to keep strictly apart. "The great American principle of eternal separation"—Elihu Root's phrase bears repetition—is one of the vital reliances of our Constitutional system for assuring unities among our people stronger than our diversities. It is the Court's duty to enforce this principle in its full integrity.

ZORACH
v.
CLAUSON

Supreme Court of the United States
Argued Jan. 31–Feb. 1, 1952.
Decided April 28, 1952.

Justice DOUGLAS delivered the opinion of the Court.

New York City has a program which permits its public schools to release students during the school day so that they may leave the school buildings and school grounds and go to religious centers for religious instruction or devotional exercises. A student is released on written request of his parents. Those not released stay in the classrooms. The churches make weekly reports to the schools, sending a list of children who have been released from public school but who have not reported for religious instruction.

This "released time" program involves neither religious instruction in public school classrooms nor the expenditure of public funds. All costs, including the application blanks, are paid by the religious organizations. The case is therefore unlike *McCollum.* . . .

Appellants, who are taxpayers and residents of New York City and whose children attend its public schools, challenge the present law, contending it is in essence not different from the one involved in the *McCollum* case. Their argument, stated elaborately in various ways, reduces itself to this: the weight and influence of the school is put behind a program for religious instruction; public school teachers police it, keeping tab on students who are released; the classroom activities come to a halt while the students who are released for religious instruction are on leave; the school is a crutch on which the churches are leaning for support in their religious training; without the cooperation of the schools this "released time" program, like the one in the *McCollum* case, would be futile and ineffective. . . .

It takes obtuse reasoning to inject any issue of the "free exercise" of religion into the present case. No one is forced to go to the religious classroom and no religious exercise or instruction is brought to the classrooms of the public schools. A student need not take religious instruction. He is left to his own desires as to the manner or time of his religious devotions, if any.

There is a suggestion that the system involves the use of coercion to get public school students into religious classrooms. There is no evidence in the record before us that supports that conclusion. The present record indeed tells us that the school authorities are neutral in this regard and do no more than release students whose parents so request. If in fact coercion were used, if it were established that any one or more teachers were using their office to persuade or force students to take the religious instruction, a wholly different case would be presented. Hence we put aside that claim of coercion both as respects the "free exercise" of religion and "an establishment of religion" within the meaning of the First Amendment.

. . .

We would have to press the concept of separation of Church and State to these extremes to condemn the present law on constitutional grounds. The nullification of this law would have wide and profound effects. . . .

. . . The government must be neutral when it comes to competition between sects. It may not thrust any sect on any person. It may not make a religious observance compulsory. It may not coerce anyone to attend church, to observe a religious holiday, or to take religious instruction. But it can close its doors or suspend its operations as to those who want to repair to their religious sanctuary for worship or instruction. No more than that is undertaken here.

. . .

In the *McCollum* case the classrooms were used for religious instruction and the force of the public school was used to promote that instruction. Here, as we have said, the public schools do no more than accommodate their schedules to a program of outside religious instruction. We follow the *McCollum* case. But we cannot expand it to cover the present released time program unless separation of Church and State means that public institutions can make no adjustments of their schedules to accommodate the religious needs of the people. We cannot read into the Bill of Rights such a philosophy of hostility to religion.

Justice BLACK, dissenting.

. . .

I see no significant difference between the invalid Illinois system and that of New York here sustained. Except for the use of the school buildings in Illinois, there is no difference between the systems which I consider even worthy of mention. In the New York program,

A second-grade teacher at Oklahoma Elementary School in Jefferson County looks at a copy of the Ten Commandments posted on a classroom wall. The Court in *Stone v. Graham* found that, under the Establishment Clause, states may not display the Ten Commandments in classrooms.

as in that of Illinois, the school authorities release some of the children on the condition that they attend the religious classes, get reports on whether they attend, and hold the other children in the school building until the religious hour is over. As we attempted to make categorically clear, the *McCollum* decision would have been the same if the religious classes had not been held in the school buildings. . . .

. . .

. . . The First Amendment was therefore to insure that no one powerful sect or combination of sects could use political or governmental power to punish dissenters whom they could not convert to their faith. Now as then, it is only by wholly isolating the state from the religious sphere and compelling it to be completely neutral, that the freedom of each and every denomination and of all nonbelievers can be maintained. It is this neutrality the Court abandons today when it treats New York's coercive system as a program which merely "encourages religious instruction or cooperates with religious authorities." The abandonment is all the more dangerous to liberty because of the Court's legal exaltation of the orthodox and its derogation of unbelievers.

Under our system of religious freedom, people have gone to their religious sanctuaries not because they feared the law but because they loved their God. . . . The spiritual mind of man has thus been free to believe, disbelieve, or doubt, without repression, great or small, by the heavy hand of government. Statutes authorizing such repression have been stricken. Before today, our judicial opinions have refrained from drawing invidious distinctions between those who believe in no religion and those who do believe. The First

Amendment has lost much if the religious follower and the atheist are no longer to be judicially regarded as entitled to equal justice under law.

Justice FRANKFURTER, dissenting.

. . .

The result in the *McCollum* case was based on principles that received unanimous acceptance by this Court, barring only a single vote. I agree with Mr. Justice BLACK that those principles are disregarded in reaching the result in this case. Happily they are not disavowed by the Court. From this I draw the hope that in future variations of the problem which are bound to come here, these principles may again be honored in the observance.

The First Amendment and the Ten Commandments

We know that schools shape the educational experience of students not only by the words spoken in the classroom but also by the various signs and messages displayed in the students' physical environment. Can a state require public school teachers to put up a display of the Ten Commandments in their classrooms? Consider the following landmark case, in which the Court said no.

A *per curiam* opinion is one handed down by the entire Court (or a majority of it) in which no single justice is given attribution for authorship. Do you prefer to know who writes the decision? Is that information important or distracting?

—

STONE

v.

GRAHAM

Supreme Court of the United States
Decided Nov. 17, 1980.

PER CURIAM.
A Kentucky statute requires the posting of a copy of the Ten Commandments, purchased with private contributions, on the wall of each public classroom in the State.
 . . . We conclude that Kentucky's statute requiring the posting of the Ten Command-

ments in public schoolrooms had no secular legislative purpose, and is therefore unconstitutional.

The Commonwealth [of Kentucky] insists that the statute in question serves a secular legislative purpose, observing that the legislature required the following notation in small print at the bottom of each display of the Ten Commandments: "The secular application of the Ten Commandments is clearly seen in its adoption as the fundamental legal code of Western Civilization and the Common Law of the United States."

The trial court found the "avowed" purpose of the statute to be secular, even as it labeled the statutory declaration "self-serving." Under this Court's rulings, however, such an "avowed" secular purpose is not sufficient to avoid conflict with the First Amendment. In *Abington School District v. Schempp* this Court held unconstitutional the daily reading of Bible verses and the Lord's Prayer in the public schools, despite the school district's assertion of such secular purposes as "the promotion of moral values, the contradiction to the materialistic trends of our times, the perpetuation of our institutions and the teaching of literature."

The pre-eminent purpose for posting the Ten Commandments on schoolroom walls is plainly religious in nature. The Ten Commandments are undeniably a sacred text in the Jewish and Christian faiths, and no legislative recitation of a supposed secular purpose can blind us to that fact. The Commandments do not confine themselves to arguably secular matters, such as honoring one's parents, killing or murder, adultery, stealing, false witness, and covetousness. Rather, the first part of the Commandments concerns the religious duties of believers: worshipping the Lord God alone, avoiding idolatry, not using the Lord's name in vain, and observing the Sabbath Day.

This is not a case in which the Ten Commandments are integrated into the school curriculum, where the Bible may constitutionally be used in an appropriate study of history, civilization, ethics, comparative religion, or the like. Posting of religious texts on the wall serves no such educational function. If the posted copies of the Ten Commandments are to have any effect at all, it will be to induce the schoolchildren to read, meditate upon, perhaps to venerate and obey, the Commandments. However desirable this might be as a matter of private devotion, it is not a permissible state objective under the Establishment Clause.

It does not matter that the posted copies of the Ten Commandments are financed by voluntary private contributions, for the mere posting of the copies under the auspices of the legislature provides the "official support of the State . . . Government" that the Establishment Clause prohibits. Nor is it significant that the Bible verses involved in this case are merely posted on the wall, rather than read aloud . . . for "it is no defense to urge that the religious practices here may be relatively minor encroachments on the First Amendment." [T]he judgment below is reversed.

It is so ordered.

Justice REHNQUIST, dissenting.

. . . The Court's summary rejection of a secular purpose articulated by the legislature and confirmed by the state court is without precedent in Establishment Clause jurisprudence. This Court regularly looks to legislative articulations of a statute's purpose in Establishment Clause cases and accords such pronouncements the deference they are due. . . . The fact that the asserted secular purpose may overlap with what some may see as a religious objective does not render it unconstitutional. As this Court stated in *McGowan v. Maryland*, in upholding the validity of Sunday closing laws, "the present purpose and effect of most of [these laws] is to provide a uniform day of rest for all citizens; the fact that this day is Sunday, a day of particular significance for the dominant Christian sects, does not bar the state from achieving its secular goals."

. . .

The Establishment Clause does not require that the public sector be insulated from all things which may have a religious significance or origin. This Court has recognized that "religion has been closely identified with our history and government," and that "[t]he history of man is inseparable from the history of religion. . . ." Kentucky has decided to make students aware of this fact by demonstrating the secular impact of the Ten Commandments.

EXERCISE 4.6. If a teacher cannot post the Ten Commandments in the classroom, can she integrate a recitation of the Ten Commandments into a teaching unit on the tale of Exodus in a literature class on the Bible? Can a public high school even offer a course on the Bible and teach about its various books and chapters so long as the material is presented from a literary perspective? Why or why not? What is the difference between posting the Ten Commandments in the front of the room and teaching about the Bible in a literature class? Is there a danger of offending religious students by teaching the Bible as literature rather than the revealed word of God?

EXERCISE 4.7. After a controversy in early 1997 involving an Alabama state court judge who posted the Ten Commandments in his courtroom and was forced to take them down by a federal district court, there was a move in Congress to express support for the judge. In a Resolution passed on March 5, 1997, the U.S. House of Representatives voted 295–125 to express its sense that the "Ten Commandments are a declaration of the fundamental principles that are the cornerstones of a fair and just society" and that the "public display in government offices and courthouses of the Ten Commandments should be permitted." No one ever sued to claim that this Resolution violated the Establishment Clause, but do you think it did, following the logic of *Stone v. Graham*? On the one hand, the Resolution was nonbinding and had no real effect, and thus it could be argued that it did not coerce anyone to do anything. On the other hand, it seemed to constitute an official symbolic endorsement of religion. Do you think the House Resolution praising the Ten Commandments was constitutional? If the House of Representatives can endorse the Ten Commandments, why not Jesus Christ our Savior? (It is true that both houses of Congress employ chaplains and open their sessions with prayer, but the Supreme Court has allowed these practices on the grounds that they are historically recognized.)

EXERCISE 4.8. Even for those who think that posting the Ten Commandments is a good idea and should be allowed under the First Amendment, there is a major problem: which version should be displayed? There are multiple versions of the Ten Commandments, with different wordings and orderings used by different churches and religions. For example, here are the Ten Commandments according to the Russian Orthodox Church of Washington, D.C.[2]

1. "Thou shalt have no other gods before Me."
2. "Thou shalt not make unto thee any graven image, or any likeness of any thing that is in heaven above, or that is in the earth beneath, or that is in the water under the earth: thou shalt not bow down thyself to them, nor serve them."
3. "Thou shalt not take the name of the Lord thy God in vain."
4. "Remember the Sabbath day, to keep it holy. Six days shalt thou labor and do all thy work: but the seventh day is the Sabbath of the Lord thy God."
5. "Honor thy father and thy mother: that thy days may be long upon the land which the Lord thy God giveth thee."
6. "Thou shalt not kill."
7. "Thou shalt not commit adultery."
8. "Thou shalt not steal."
9. "Thou shalt not bear false witness against thy neighbor."
10. "Thou shalt not covet thy neighbor's house, thou shalt not covet thy neighbor's wife, nor his manservant, nor his maidservant, nor his ox, nor his ass, nor any thing that is thy neighbor's."

Contrast this version with the translation of the Commandments that hung on the wall of Alabama state court judge Roy Moore's courtroom.[3]

1. "You shall have no other gods before me"
2. "You shall not take the name of the Lord your God in vain"
3. "You shall not make unto yourself any graven image"
4. "Remember the sabbath day, to keep it holy"
5. "Honor your father and your mother: that your days may be long"
6. "You shall not kill"
7. "You shall not commit adultery"
8. "You shall not steal"
9. "You shall not bear false witness against your neighbour"
10. "You shall not covet."

Does the sheer variety in Ten Commandments presentations reinforce the sense that government should not be meddling in religion?

TALK SHOW DEBATE. On June 17, 1999, in the wake of continuing public concern about the April 20 massacre at Columbine High School in Littleton, Colorado, the U.S. House of Representatives passed a law purporting to give states the power to post the Ten Commandments in public buildings, including public schools. One representative, criticizing the Court's decision in *Stone v. Graham*, said that, had the Ten Commandments been posted on the wall at Columbine High, the massacre never would have happened. Do you agree? Set up a TV-style talk show in which a moderator has several guests on either side of the issue and discuss.

DRAFT A SCHOOL BOARD POLICY ON HOLIDAY PROGRAMS. During the Christmas/Hannukah/Kwanza period, public and secular private schools confront the complexities of how to properly observe a religiously saturated holiday season. No school wants to be the grinch that steals the joy of the holiday season, but how do you put on holiday programs that do not cross the line? After all, many religions—Judaism, Islam, Hinduism—do not celebrate Christmas at all, and even some that do, like the Greek Orthodox or Serbian Orthodox, celebrate Christmas at a different time altogether. In recognition of these facts, the Supreme Court has disallowed Christmas nativity scenes in public places, including schools. Yet, many public schools have students sing songs and perform skits in holiday shows that celebrate Christmas because Christianity is (in many places) the majority religion. Should schools be required to offer a sampling of religious traditions so that every child's tradition is represented? What about atheist families that object to any religious overtones in official school programs? Should there be no mention of Christmas, Hannukah, or Kwanza? Turn your class into a school board to discuss this problem. Vote on a system-wide policy for appropriate holiday programs and decorations.

The Free Exercise Rights of Religious Americans

As we have seen, one significant issue that courts face in this area is the extent to which schools can make religion a part of the educational experience of students. But another is the extent to which parents can use religion to keep their kids *out* of school. In this famous decision about the Free Exercise of religion, the Court upheld the right of Amish families to stop sending their children to school after the eighth grade. As you read this decision, ask yourself whether the holding applies broadly to people and children of *all* faiths, or whether there were unique, compelling facts about the Amish community that justified this constitutional exemption. Everyone loves the Amish, but how far does the logic of this case really go?

WISCONSIN
v.
YODER

Supreme Court of the United States
Argued Dec. 8, 1971.
Decided May 15, 1972.

Chief Justice BURGER delivered the opinion of the Court.

. . .

Respondents Jonas Yoder and Wallace Miller are members of the Old Order Amish religion, and respondent Adin Yutzy is a member of the Conservative Amish Mennonite Church. They and their families are residents of Green County, Wisconsin. Wisconsin's compulsory school-attendance law required them to cause their children to attend public or private school until reaching age 16 but the respondents declined to send their children, ages 14 and 15, to public school after they complete the eighth grade. The children were not enrolled in any private school, or within any recognized exception to the compulsory-attendance law, and they are conceded to be subject to the Wisconsin statute.

. . . [R]espondents were charged, tried, and convicted of violating the compulsory-attendance law in Green County Court and were fined the sum of $5 each. Respondents

In *Wisconsin v. Yoder* the Court upheld the right of Amish families to take their children out of school after the eighth grade.

defended on the ground that the application of the compulsory-attendance law violated their rights under the First and Fourteenth Amendments. The trial testimony showed that respondents believed, in accordance with the tenets of Old Order Amish communities generally, that their children's attendance at high school, public or private, was contrary to the Amish religion and way of life. They believed that by sending their children to high school, they would not only expose themselves to the danger of the censure of the church community, but . . . also endanger their own salvation and that of their children. The State stipulated that respondents' religious beliefs were sincere.

. . .

A related feature of Old Order Amish communities is their devotion to a life in harmony with nature and the soil, as exemplified by the simple life of the early Christian era that continued in America during much of our early national life. Amish beliefs require members of the community to make their living by farming or closely related activities. . . .

Amish objection to formal education beyond the eighth grade is firmly grounded in these central religious concepts. They object to the high school, and higher education generally, because the values they teach are in marked variance with Amish values and the Amish way of life; they view secondary school education as an impermissible exposure of their children to a "worldly" influence in conflict with their beliefs. The high school tends to emphasize intellectual and scientific accomplishments, self-distinction, competitiveness, worldly success, and social life with other students. Amish society emphasizes informal learning through doing; a life of "goodness," rather than a life of intellect; wisdom, rather than technical knowledge, community welfare, rather than competition; and separation from, rather than integration with, contemporary worldly society.

Formal high school education beyond the eighth grade is contrary to Amish beliefs, not only because it places Amish children in an environment hostile to Amish beliefs with increasing emphasis on competition in class work and sports and with pressure to conform to the styles, manners, and ways of the peer group, but also because it takes them away from their community, physically and emotionally, during the crucial and formative adolescent period of life. During this period, the children must acquire Amish attitudes favoring manual work and self-reliance and the specific skills needed to perform the adult role of an Amish farmer or housewife. They must learn to enjoy physical labor. Once a child has learned basic reading, writing, and elementary mathematics, these traits, skills, and attitudes admittedly fall within the category of those best learned through example and "doing" rather than in a classroom. And, at this time in life, the Amish child must also grow in his faith and his relationship to the Amish community if he is to be prepared to accept the heavy obligations imposed by adult baptism. In short, high school attendance with teachers who are not of the Amish faith and may even be hostile to it interposes a serious barrier to the integration of the Amish child into the Amish religious community. Dr. John Hostetler, one of the experts on Amish society, testified that the modern high school is not equipped, in curriculum or social environment, to impart the values promoted by Amish society.

. . .

. . . The testimony of Dr. Donald A. Erickson, an expert witness on education, also showed that the Amish succeed in preparing their high school age children to be productive members of the Amish community. He described their system of learning through doing the skills directly relevant to their adult roles in the Amish community as "ideal" and perhaps superior to ordinary high school education. The evidence also showed that the Amish have an excellent record as law-abiding and generally self-sufficient members of society.

. . .

I

There is no doubt as to the power of a State, having a high responsibility for education of its citizens, to impose reasonable regulations for the control and duration of basic education. . . . [A] State's interest in universal education, however highly we rank it, is not totally free from a balancing process when it impinges on fundamental rights and interests, such as those specifically protected by the Free Exercise Clause of the First Amendment, and the traditional interest of parents with respect to the religious upbringing of their children. . . .

It follows that in order for Wisconsin to compel school attendance beyond the eighth grade against a claim that such attendance interferes with the practice of a legitimate religious belief, it must appear either that the State does not deny the free exercise of religious belief by its requirement, or that there is a state interest of sufficient magnitude to override the interest claiming protection under the Free Exercise Clause. . . .

The essence of all that has been said and written on the subject is that only those interests of the highest order and those not otherwise served can overbalance legitimate claims to the free exercise of religion. . . .

II

We come then to the quality of the claims of the respondents concerning the alleged encroachment of Wisconsin's compulsory school-attendance statute on their rights and the rights of their children to the free exercise of the religious beliefs they and their forbears have adhered to for almost three centuries. In evaluating those claims we must be careful to determine whether the Amish religious faith and their mode of life are, as they claim, inseparable and interdependent. A way of life, however virtuous and admirable, may not be interposed as a barrier to reasonable state regulation of education if it is based on purely secular considerations; to have the protection of the Religion Clauses, the claims must be rooted in religious belief. . . . Thus, if the Amish asserted their claims because of their subjective evaluation and rejection of the contemporary secular values accepted by the majority, much as Thoreau rejected the social values of his time and isolated himself at Walden Pond, their claims would not rest on a religious basis. Thoreau's choice was philosophical and personal rather than religious, and such belief does not rise to the demands of the Religion Clauses [of the First Amendment].

. . . [T]he record in this case abundantly supports the claim that the traditional way of life of the Amish is not merely a matter of personal preference, but one of deep religious conviction, shared by an organized group, and intimately related to daily living. That the

Old Order Amish daily life and religious practice stem from their faith is shown by the fact that it is in response to their literal interpretation of the Biblical injunction from the Epistle of Paul to the Romans, "be not conformed to this world . . . ." This command is fundamental to the Amish faith. Moreover, for the Old Order Amish, religion is not simply a matter of theocratic belief. As the expert witnesses explained, the Old Order Amish religion pervades and determines virtually their entire way of life, regulating it with the detail of the Talmudic diet through the strictly enforced rules of the church community.

. . .

The impact of the compulsory-attendance law on respondents' practice of the Amish religion is not only severe, but inescapable, for the Wisconsin law affirmatively compels them, under threat of criminal sanction, to perform acts undeniably at odds with fundamental tenets of their religious beliefs. Nor is the impact of the compulsory-attendance law confined to grave interference with important Amish religious tenets from a subjective point of view. It carries with it precisely the kind of objective danger to the free exercise of religion that the First Amendment was designed to prevent. As the record shows, compulsory school attendance to age 16 for Amish children carries with it a very real threat of undermining the Amish community and religious practice as they exist today; they must either abandon belief and be assimilated into society at large, or be forced to migrate to some other and more tolerant region.

In sum, the unchallenged testimony of acknowledged experts in education and religious history, almost 300 years of consistent practice, and strong evidence of a sustained faith pervading and regulating respondents' entire mode of life support the claim that enforcement of the State's requirement of compulsory formal education after the eighth grade would gravely endanger if not destroy the free exercise of respondents' religious beliefs.

III

. . .

We turn, then, to the State's broader contention that its interest in its system of compulsory education is so compelling that even the established religious practices of the Amish must give way. Where fundamental claims of religious freedom are at stake, however, we cannot accept such a sweeping claim; despite its admitted validity in the generality of cases, we must searchingly examine the interests that the State seeks to promote by its requirement for compulsory education to age 16, and the impediment to those objectives that would flow from recognizing the claimed Amish exemption.

The State advances two primary arguments in support of its system of compulsory education. It notes . . . that some degree of education is necessary to prepare citizens to participate effectively and intelligently in our open political system if we are to preserve freedom and independence. Further, education prepares individuals to be self-reliant and self-sufficient participants in society. We accept these propositions.

However, the evidence adduced by the Amish in this case is persuasively to the effect that an additional one or two years of formal high school for Amish children in place of their long-established program of informal vocational education would do little to serve those interests. . . . It is one thing to say that compulsory education for a year or two beyond the eighth grade may be necessary when its goal is the preparation of the child for life in modern society as the majority live, but it is quite another if the goal of education be viewed as the preparation of the child for life in the separated agrarian community that is the keystone of the Amish faith.

. . . No one can question the State's duty to protect children from ignorance but this argument does not square with the facts disclosed in the record. Whatever their idiosyncrasies as seen by the majority, this record strongly shows that the Amish community has been a highly successful social unit within our society, even if apart from the conventional "mainstream." Its members are productive and very law-abiding members of society; they reject public welfare in any of its usual modern forms. . . .

. . .

The State, however, supports its interest in providing an additional one or two years of compulsory high school education to Amish children because of the possibility that some such children will choose to leave the Amish community, and that if this occurs they will be ill-equipped for life. The State argues that if Amish children leave their church they should not be in the position of making their way in the world without the education available in the one or two additional years the State requires. However, on this record, that argument is highly speculative. There is no specific evidence of the loss of Amish adherents by attrition, nor is there any showing that upon leaving the Amish community Amish children, with their practical agricultural training and habits of industry and self-reliance, would become burdens on society because of educational shortcomings. Indeed, this argument of the State appears to rest primarily on the State's mistaken assumption, already noted, that the Amish do not provide any education for their children beyond the eighth grade, but allow them to grow in "ignorance." To the contrary, not only do the Amish accept the necessity for formal schooling through the eighth grade level, but continue to provide what has been characterized by the undisputed testimony of expert educators as an "ideal" vocational education for their children in the adolescent years.

. . .

Insofar as the State's claim rests on the view that a brief additional period of formal education is imperative to enable the Amish to participate effectively and intelligently in our democratic process, it must fall. The Amish alternative to formal secondary school education has enabled them to function effectively in their day-to-day life under self-imposed limitations on relations with the world, and to survive and prosper in contemporary society as a separate, sharply identifiable and highly self-sufficient community for more than 200 years in this country. In itself this is strong evidence that they are capable of fulfilling the social and political responsibilities of citizenship without compelled attendance beyond the eighth grade at the price of jeopardizing their free exercise of religious belief. . . .

. . .

IV

. . .

Indeed it seems clear that if the State is empowered, as *parens patriae*, to "save" a child from himself or his Amish parents by requiring an additional two years of compulsory formal high school education, the State will in large measure influence, if not determine, the religious future of the child. . . .

. . . [A]ccommodating the religious objections of the Amish by forgoing one, or at most two, additional years of compulsory education will not impair the physical or mental health of the child, or result in an inability to be self-supporting or to discharge the duties and responsibilities of citizenship, or in any other way materially detract from the welfare of society.

V

. . . [W]e hold . . . that the First and Fourteenth amendments prevent the State from compelling respondents to cause their children to attend formal high school to age 16. . . .

Aided by a history of three centuries as an identifiable religious sect and a long history as a successful and self-sufficient segment of American society, the Amish in this case have convincingly demonstrated the sincerity of their religious beliefs, the interrelationship of belief with their mode of life, the vital role that belief and daily conduct play in the continued survival of Old Order Amish communities and their religious organization, and the hazards presented by the State's enforcement of a statute generally valid as to others. . . .

. . .

Affirmed.

Justice DOUGLAS, dissenting in part.

I

I agree with the Court that the religious scruples of the Amish are opposed to the education of their children beyond the grade schools, yet I disagree with the Court's conclusion that the matter is within the dispensation of parents alone. The Court's analysis assumes that the only interests at stake in the case are those of the Amish parents on the one hand, and those of the State on the other. The difficulty with this approach is that, despite the Court's claim, the parents are seeking to vindicate not only their own free exercise claims, but also those of their high-school-age children.

. . .

Religion is an individual experience. It is not necessary, nor even appropriate, for every Amish child to express his views on the subject in a prosecution of a single adult. Crucial, however, are the views of the child whose parent is the subject of the suit. Frieda Yoder has in fact testified that her own religious views are opposed to high-school education. I therefore join the judgment of the Court as to respondent Jonas Yoder. But Frieda Yoder's views may not be those of Vernon Yutzy or Barbara Miller. I must dissent, therefore, as to respondents Adin Yutzy and Wallace Miller as their motion to dismiss also raised the question of their children's religious liberty.

II

. . .

These children are "persons" within the meaning of the Bill of Rights. We have so held over and over again.

In *Tinker v. Des Moines School District* we dealt with 13-year-old, 15-year-old, and 16-year-old students who wore armbands to public schools and were disciplined for doing so. We gave them relief, saying that their First Amendment rights had been abridged.

In *West Virginia State Board of Education v. Barnette* we held that school-children, whose religious beliefs collided with a school rule requiring them to salute the flag, could not be required to do so. While the sanction included expulsion of the students and prosecution of the parents, the vice of the regime was its interference with the child's free exercise of religion. We said: "Here . . . we are dealing with a compulsion of students to declare a belief." . . .

On this important and vital matter of education, I think the children should be entitled to be heard. While the parents, absent dissent, normally speak for the entire family, the education of the child is a matter on which the child will often have decided views. He may want to be a pianist or an astronaut or an oceanographer. To do so he will have to break from the Amish tradition.[4]

It is the future of the student, not the future of the parents, that is imperiled by today's decision. If a parent keeps his child out of school beyond the grade school, then the child will be forever barred from entry into the new and amazing world of diversity that we have today. The child may decide that is the preferred course, or he may rebel. It is the student's judgment, not his parents', that is essential if we are to give full meaning to what we have said about the Bill of Rights and of the right of students to be masters of their own destiny. If he is harnessed to the Amish way of life by those in authority over him and if his education is truncated, his entire life may be stunted and deformed. The child, therefore, should be given an opportunity to be heard before the State gives the exemption which we honor today.

. . .

III

I think the emphasis of the Court on the "law and order" record of this Amish group of people is quite irrelevant. A religion is a religion irrespective of what the misdemeanor or felony records of its members might be. I am not at all sure how the Catholics, Episcopalians, the Baptists, Jehovah's Witnesses, the Unitarians, and my own Presbyterians would make out if subjected to such a test. . . .

JUSTICE WILLIAM O. DOUGLAS (1898–1980) was born poor and sickly in the town of Maine, Minnesota. Because he had polio, he was small and faced ridicule by other children. He turned to sports and outdoor activities to build up his body and self-esteem and thus began a lifelong passion for nature and the environment. He went to Whitman College in Walla Walla, Washington, and in the fall of 1922 hitchhiked his way across the country, sleeping and eating with hobos, in order to enter Columbia Law School, where he graduated second in his class. Douglas spent many years at the Securities and Exchange Commission and was a key component of the New Deal brain trust in Washington, D.C. President Franklin Delano Roosevelt appointed him to the Supreme Court in 1939. He served as a justice for thirty-six years, longer than any other justice.

HIGHLIGHTS

➤ Douglas was married four times.

➤ Douglas was the foremost naturalist, explorer, and hiker ever to serve on the Court, and frequently hiked the C&O Canal in Washington, D.C.

➤ A prolific writer, Justice Douglas was especially fond of writing about his adventuresome travels abroad. In 1974, he published the first volume of his autobiography, titled *Go East, Young Man: The Early Years*. Later, the second volume appeared, titled *The Court Years, 1939 to 1975: The Autobiography of William O. Douglas*.

FOR THE CLASS

HIGHER EDUCATION OR THE HEAVENLY CHURCH? On October 17, 1996, Reginald and Meredith Ackers were charged with failing to enroll their children in school. Moot state law required parents to enroll their children in a public school, an accredited private school, or a home-schooling program that administers annual academic progress exams until age seventeen or graduation from high school. Police officers delivered the citation to the home that the Ackers shared with twelve other couples, eighteen children, including their daughters Chloe and Ruth, and thirty-one single adults. The large and self-sufficient communal farm where the Ackers lived was known as Billings Hill. Daniel Billings, a fifty-two-year-old high school drop-out, millionaire investor, and self-described "messianic visionary," owned the house and preached the teachings of a religion he founded in 1985, called "the Heavenly Church."

The religion, based on Christianity, had some startling tenets. The religion was against the schooling of children by the secular state or any school that participated in mixing people of different religious faiths. It also vehemently opposed monogamy, the higher education of women, and equality between the sexes. Because of these rules, every Billingsist parent had chosen to "home-school" their children at the massive communal compound in which they all lived. While the religion was decidedly against the higher education of women, it was deemed necessary for young girls to attend school until the age of fifteen in order to learn "basic religious values and essential survival skills." Chloe was sixteen and Ruth was eight.

Mr. and Mrs. Ackers declined to enroll Chloe in any school since she had turned fifteen and had terminated her home-schooling lessons. (She had passed all of her state equivalency exams.) Chloe was preparing to marry another Billingsist when she turned seventeen, the lawful age for marriage in the state. Meanwhile, Ruth had successfully passed the state's Second and Third Grade Equivalent Academic Progress Exams for home-schooled children in English and Math, but had failed miserably in Science and Social Studies. The Ackers claimed that Ruth was a "brilliant young lady" and only failed the exams because the Science section tested "alleged 'knowledge' of evolution and astronomy," which the Heavenly Church considered "abominations and profane ideas." They also protested that the Social Studies section on different world cultures and governments "was an attempt to expose our daughter to devilish influences and One World Government that are completely antithetical to our religious faith and our sustained effort to create an insular and protective environment for our children."

A lower court found that the Ackers were violating state law and were ordered to enroll Chloe immediately in eleventh grade or to resume her home-schooling studies, leaving her in school at least until age seventeen or graduation. It also found that Ruth was not succeeding academically in home-schooling and ordered that she be sent immediately to public school in her area or an accredited private school. The court found that both girls "agreed with their parents and did not want to go to public school, but had been brainwashed and terrorized by the cult leader about drugs and fights at public schools."

The Ackers have appealed both orders to the Moot State Supreme Court. They say that Chloe is mature enough to make her own decision and wants to begin studying housework and motherhood and preparing for marriage. They also say that forcing her to go back to school would violate their religious freedom under *Wisconsin v. Yoder*. As to Ruth's situation, they say that forcing them to send Ruth to any public or private school would also violate their religious rights "because it would force us to subject our daughter to negative secular influences, drugs, persons from alien religions, and teachings that undermine our religious beliefs."

Select nine students to play the roles of the Moot State Supreme Court judges. Select two additional students to represent the Ackers and two more students to represent the state.

The students representing the Ackers should argue that the facts of the case alongside the holding in *Yoder* call for the reversal of the lower court decisions. Have one of the students argue that Chloe should be allowed to stay out of school and the other argue that Ruth should be allowed to continue with her home-schooling program. The attorneys for the state will oppose these arguments. One of the state's attorneys should argue in support of the lower court ruling concerning Chloe and the other should argue in support of the lower court ruling concerning Ruth. The oral arguments for each lawyer should run ten minutes.

The judges should ask questions of the lawyers throughout the oral arguments and then meet privately before coming back with their decision. (Remember, there can be both majority and minority opinions.) Each judge should be able to explain the reasoning behind his or her vote.

The Theory of Evolution and the Story of Creation: Ongoing Duel in the Classroom

What happens in high school classrooms when science makes discoveries about the natural world that contradict the religious beliefs of a large number of citizens? Should such scientific theories be taught in the classroom? Should they be censored? Should they be balanced with "equal time" for religiously based theories? Or is there no place at all for religious indoctrination in the classroom?

Nowhere has this problem been posed more dramatically than in the science classroom when it comes to teaching about human evolution and the doctrine that is sometimes called Darwinism. The classroom war between evolutionary science and religious creationism has gone on for more than seventy-five years.

One of the most famous trials in our nation's history was the so-called "Scopes Monkey Trial," which took place in the sweltering summer of 1925 in Tennessee. The case, which arose in the midst of rising religious fundamentalism, involved the criminal prosecution of John T. Scopes, a twenty-four-year-old science teacher and football coach, for teaching evolution in violation of a then-recently passed state law banning the theory of evolution from the classroom. Scopes had the support of the American Civil Liberties Union and was represented by the legendary Clarence Darrow, who wanted to show that the anti-evolution statute was an attempt to establish a religious law and substitute nonsense for knowledge. The lawyer for the state of Tennessee was the eloquent, populist political leader William Jennings Bryan. Bryan, a former secretary of state in the Woodrow Wilson administration, saw the trial as a showdown between evolution and Christianity.

The key moment in the trial arrived when Darrow called Bryan himself to the stand and examined him on whether or not he believed that everything recorded in the Bible was literally true. After interrogating him about biblical stories like the Tower of Babel and Jonah being swallowed by the whale, Darrow zeroed in on the origins of Earth:

Q: "Do you think the earth was made in six days?"
A: "Not six days of 24 hours. . . . My impression is they were periods. . . . "
Q: "Now, if you call those periods, they may have been a very long time?"
A: "They might have been."
Q: "The creation might have been going on for a very long time?"
A: "It might have continued for millions of years. . . . "

Thus, Darrow exploded Bryan's determination not to depart from the Biblical text and radically shifted public sentiment in favor of Scopes and evolution. Still, the jury returned with a guilty verdict and the judge ordered Scopes to pay a fine of $100, the lowest allowed under the law. In his parting words to the court, Scopes said: "Your Honor, I feel that I have been convicted of violating an unjust statute. I will continue in the future . . . to oppose this law in any way I can. Any other action would be in violation of my idea of academic freedom."

Scopes' conviction was later reversed in the Tennessee Supreme Court on technical grounds.

The Scopes trial did not put the controversy over teaching evolution to rest. In 1968, the issue finally reached the Supreme Court in the landmark case *Epperson v. Arkansas*. There, the Court struck down a similar "anti-evolution" law in Arkansas that made it illegal for public school teachers "to teach the theory or doctrine that mankind ascended or descended from a lower order of animals." The Court found that this law violated the Establishment Clause of the First Amendment because it "selects from the body of knowledge a particular segment which it proscribes for the sole reason that it is deemed to conflict with a particular religious doctrine." The Court said that it was "clear that fundamentalist sectarian conviction was . . . the law's reason for existence."

Epperson was a relatively easy case. But what about *Edward v. Aguillard*, a case that reached the Court almost twenty years later in 1987? In that decision, the Supreme Court struck down a Louisiana statute that prevented public school teachers from "teaching the theory of evolution in public schools unless accompanied by instruction in 'creation science'," the controversial scientific claims developed to support the belief in the biblical version of creation. Despite the fact that the stated purpose of this law was to enhance academic freedom, the Court considered this a "sham" since the law did "not grant teachers a flexibility that they did not already possess to supplement the present science curriculum with the presentation of theories, besides evolution, about the origin of life." Rather, the "primary purpose of the Creationism Act" was "to endorse a particular religious doctrine" and thus violated the Establishment Clause as well.

EXERCISE 4.9. Does the holding in *Epperson* make sense because the clear purpose of the law struck down was to neutralize and counteract the teaching of evolution with a wholly religious doctrine? Or has the Court unfairly taken sides in a legitimate scientific controversy by declaring one viewpoint religious and in effect banning it? Does the decision actually ban the teaching of creation science even when teachers undertake it voluntarily, or does it just forbid a mandatory "equal time" arrangement? Can courts decide on what scientific truth is?

FOR THE CLASS

PUT ON THE PLAY. The dramatic events that took place at the Scopes Monkey Trial inspired the great play *Inherit the Wind*, by Jerome Lawrence and Robert E. Lee. Check out the play from your school library and have the class act out the whole trial, including the amazing interchange between Darrow and Bryan.

SCHOOL BOARD EXERCISE. Pretend that your class is a school board trying to define a policy governing the teaching of evolution and creation in high school classes. Consider the following options:

1. Teach only the theory of evolution.
2. Teach only the theory of evolution, but include scientific criticisms of it. Explain that many Christians believe in Creation for religious reasons.
3. Teach both the theory of evolution and Creation-science as two equally plausible alternatives.
4. Allow each individual teacher to teach whatever he or she wants according to individual conscience and belief.
5. Allow each individual school to select its preferred curriculum.
6. Teach only Creation-science, explaining that while this practice is unconstitutional, the school will engage in it as a form of civil disobedience.
7. Teach only the theory of evolution, but allow individual teachers to state their personal beliefs about the origins of humanity.

After discussing the various options (including any others of your own), try to form a majority consensus around a solution and take a vote. Do you think your plan is constitutional?

In the spring of 1999, the Kansas State Board of Education voted 6–4 to reduce and minimize the teaching of evolution in public school classrooms as part of its new science standards. This move reignited national conflict over religiously inspired attacks on the theory of evolution. The governor of Kansas called the new policy an "embarrassment," and many parents worried that it would disadvantage their children in applying to college and finding jobs in science and technology. At the same time, many people in Kansas applauded the change, which followed closely upon the heels of an incident in a biology class at Lawrence Free State High School where a popular and effective teacher named Stan Roth was openly dismissive of a student, Anna Harvey, who asked him about creationism. "Mr. Roth? When are we going to learn about creationism?" Harvey asked when they finished their section on Darwin and the theory of evolution. According to Harvey, the teacher lost his cool and replied: "When are you going to stop believing that crap your parents teach you?" (Roth himself admitted to describing Creationist beliefs as "nonscientific crap.") The resulting firestorm from parents and students led to "an ignominious end . . . to a brilliant and iconoclastic teaching career that spanned four decades."[5] Despite the fact that he was widely regarded as one of the state's finest science teachers, Roth was involuntarily removed from the classroom and told that if he wanted to remain in the school system he could do so only as caretaker of the school district's science equipment.

EXERCISE 4.10. Was Roth's response to his student, Harvey, when she asked about creationism, appropriate or disproportionate? What should he have said? Was the school's response to the incident appropriate or disproportionate? Was the Board of Education's decision to demote and de-emphasize the teaching of evolution appropriate? Do you think it is constitutional for a state board of education to tell individual schools that they do not have to teach evolution if they do not want to? Is there a secular purpose behind such a law or an impermissible religious purpose?

Notes

1. ". . . Apart from the Court's admission that New Jersey's present action approaches the verge of her power, it would seem that a statute, ordinance or resolution which on its face singles out one sect only by name for enjoyment of the same advantages as public schools or their students, should be held discriminatory on its face by virtue of that fact alone, unless it were positively shown that no other sects sought or were available to receive the same advantages."

2. Found at *http://www.stjohndc.org/command/Command.htm* (accessed on 2/10/00).

3. Found at *http://www.saintirene.org/davidf/essays/tencomm.htm* (accessed on 2/10/00).

4. "A significant number of Amish children do leave the Old Order. Professor Hostetler notes that '[t]he loss of members is very limited in some Amish districts and considerable in others.' In one Pennsylvania church, he observed a defection rate of 30%. Rates up to 50% have been reported by others."

5. *Washington Post,* November 4, 1999, A1.

Read On

Muller, Robert, and Ronald Flowers. *Toward Benevolent Neutrality: Church, State, and the Supreme Court.* 3d ed. Waco, Texas: Markham Press Fund, 1987.

Smith, Rodney K. *Public Prayer and the Constitution.* Wilmington, Del.: Scholarly Resources, 1987.

5 THE FOURTH AMENDMENT: SEARCHES OF STUDENTS AND THEIR BELONGINGS

"The right of the people to be secure in their persons, houses, papers, and effects, against unreasonable searches and seizures, shall not be violated. . . ." THE FOURTH AMENDMENT

"Every breath you take, every move you make, I'll be watching you . . . " THE POLICE

All of us want to be free from government invasion of our personal space. But we also want to be in safe environments, free of violence and dangerous weapons. This tension between our competing desires for freedom and security sets up the problem to be explored in this chapter: when government authorities may invade our expectations of privacy for the sake of community security.

The Fourth Amendment does not protect against all government searches and seizures, only *unreasonable* searches and seizures. In theory, this means that government agents cannot conduct a search without a search warrant, but in practice the Supreme Court has greatly relaxed this requirement.

In the context of public education, the Supreme Court has granted school authorities very broad discretion to search both the persons and belongings of students in different kinds of situations. We know that many schools have become dangerous places, but is the Court going too far today in allowing schools to search students and their property without first obtaining search warrants? Are we allowing government to treat students like criminal suspects without

meaningful constitutional rights? Or, alternatively, does the well-recognized need for discipline and order in the schools require us to give school systems the same discretion that mothers and fathers have to search their children and their children's belongings? Does it make a difference what the schools plan to do with the fruits of their searches?

POINTS TO PONDER

How does the right to be free from unreasonable searches and seizures apply to public school students?

- Should school officials have the authority to search students' belongings?
- Can school authorities require student athletes to participate in random drug testing?
- Can school authorities subject students to strip searches?

The Reduced Rights of Students to Expect Privacy in Their Belongings

"Smoking in the Boys' Room," a once-famous rock-and-roll song, reminds America's youth that "smoking ain't allowed in school." In the following case, a high school freshman in New Jersey was caught doing just that. This infraction resulted in a series of escalating searches of the girl's belongings; ultimately, the high school's vice principal found marijuana in the offender's purse. This discovery, in turn, led to a court's finding that the girl—who was identified only as T.L.O.—was criminally delinquent. The Supreme Court took the case in order to determine whether or not the searches of T.L.O.'s purse were lawful. If not, the evidence could be excluded—this is the "exclusionary rule"—and the conviction reversed. Despite the fact that the school authorities had no search warrant and no probable cause to search, the Court upheld the delinquency finding. Why? What is the standard governing searches by school authorities?

NEW JERSEY
v.
T.L.O.

Supreme Court of the United States
Argued March 28, 1984.
Reargued Oct. 2, 1984.
Decided Jan. 15, 1985.

Justice WHITE delivered the opinion of the Court.

. . . [W]e here address . . . the questions of the proper standard for assessing the legality of searches conducted by public school officials and the application of that standard to the facts of this case.

I

On March 7, 1980, a teacher at Piscataway High School in Middlesex County, N.J., discovered two girls smoking in a lavatory. One of the two girls was . . . T.L.O., who at that time was a 14-year-old high school freshman. Because smoking in the lavatory was a violation of a school rule, the teacher took the two girls to the Principal's office, where they met with Assistant Vice Principal Theodore Choplick. In response to questioning by Mr. Choplick, T.L.O.'s companion admitted that she had violated the rule. T.L.O., however, denied that she had been smoking in the lavatory and claimed that she did not smoke at all.

Mr. Choplick asked T.L.O. to come into his private office and demanded to see her purse. Opening the purse, he found a pack of cigarettes, which he removed from the purse and held before T.L.O. as he accused her of having lied to him. As he reached into the purse for the cigarettes, Mr. Choplick also noticed a package of cigarette rolling papers. In his experience, possession of rolling papers by high school students was closely associated with the use of marihuana. Suspecting that a closer examination of the purse might yield further evidence of drug use, Mr. Choplick proceeded to search the purse thoroughly. The search revealed a small amount of marihuana, a pipe, a number of empty plastic bags, a substantial quantity of money in one-dollar bills, an index card that appeared to be a list of students who owed T.L.O. money, and two letters that implicated T.L.O. in marihuana dealing.

Mr. Choplick notified T.L.O.'s mother and the police, and turned the evidence of drug dealing over to the police. At the request of the police, T.L.O.'s mother took her daughter to police headquarters, where T.L.O. confessed that she had been selling marihuana at the high school. On the basis of the confession and the evidence seized by Mr. Choplick, the State brought delinquency charges against T.L.O. in the Juvenile and Domestic Relations Court of Middlesex County. Contending that Mr. Choplick's search of her purse violated the Fourth Amendment, T.L.O. moved to suppress the evidence found in her purse as well as her confession, which, she argued, was tainted by the allegedly unlawful search. The Ju-

venile Court denied the motion to suppress. Although the court concluded that the Fourth Amendment did apply to searches carried out by school officials, it held that

> a school official may properly conduct a search of a student's person if the official has a reasonable suspicion that a crime has been or is in the process of being committed, or reasonable cause to believe that the search is necessary to maintain school discipline or enforce school policies.

Applying this standard, the court concluded that the search conducted by Mr. Choplick was a reasonable one. The initial decision to open the purse was justified by Mr. Choplick's well-founded suspicion that T.L.O. had violated the rule forbidding smoking in the lavatory. Once the purse was open, evidence of marihuana violations was in plain view, and Mr. Choplick was entitled to conduct a thorough search to determine the nature and extent of T.L.O.'s drug-related activities. Having denied the motion to suppress, the court on March 23, 1981, found T.L.O. to be a delinquent and on January 8, 1982, sentenced her to a year's probation.

. . .

. . . [W]e are satisfied that the search did not violate the Fourth Amendment.

II

In determining whether the search at issue in this case violated the Fourth Amendment, we are faced initially with the question whether that Amendment's prohibition on unreasonable searches and seizures applies to searches conducted by public school officials. We hold that it does.

. . .

. . . In carrying out searches and other disciplinary functions pursuant to such policies, school officials act as representatives of the State, not merely as surrogates for the parents, and they cannot claim the parents' immunity from the strictures of the Fourth Amendment.

III

To hold that the Fourth Amendment applies to searches conducted by school authorities is only to begin the inquiry into the standards governing such searches. Although the underlying command of the Fourth Amendment is always that searches and seizures be reasonable, what is reasonable depends on the context within which a search takes place. The determination of the standard of reasonableness governing any specific class of searches requires "balancing the need to search against the invasion which the search entails." On one side of the balance are arrayed the individual's legitimate expectations of privacy and personal security; on the other, the government's need for effective methods to deal with breaches of public order.

We have recognized that even a limited search of the person is a substantial invasion of privacy. We have also recognized that searches of closed items of personal luggage are intrusions on protected privacy interests, for "the Fourth Amendment provides protection to the owner of every container that conceals its contents from plain view." A search of a child's person or of a closed purse or other bag carried on her person,[1] no less than a similar search carried out on an adult, is undoubtedly a severe violation of subjective expectations of privacy.

. . . To receive the protection of the Fourth Amendment, an expectation of privacy must be one that society is "prepared to recognize as legitimate." The State of New Jersey has argued that because of the pervasive supervision to which children in the schools are necessarily subject, a child has virtually no legitimate expectation of privacy in articles of personal property "unnecessarily" carried into a school. This argument has two factual premises: (1) the fundamental incompatibility of expectations of privacy with the maintenance of a sound educational environment; and (2) the minimal interest of the child in bringing any items of personal property into the school. Both premises are severely flawed.

Although this Court may take notice of the difficulty of maintaining discipline in the public schools today, the situation is not so dire that students in the schools may claim no legitimate expectations of privacy. We have recently recognized that the need to maintain order in a prison is such that prisoners retain no legitimate expectations of privacy in their cells, but it goes almost without saying that "[t]he prisoner and the schoolchild stand in wholly different circumstances, separated by the harsh facts of criminal conviction and incarceration." We are not yet ready to hold that the schools and the prisons need be equated for purposes of the Fourth Amendment.

Nor does the State's suggestion that children have no legitimate need to bring personal property into the schools seem well anchored in reality. Students at a minimum must bring to school not only the supplies needed for their studies, but also keys, money, and the necessaries of personal hygiene and grooming. In addition, students may carry on their persons or in purses or wallets such nondisruptive yet highly personal items as photographs, letters, and diaries. Finally, students may have perfectly legitimate reasons to carry with them articles of property needed in connection with extracurricular or recreational activities. In short, schoolchildren may find it necessary to carry with them a variety of legitimate, noncontraband items, and there is no reason to conclude that they have necessarily waived all rights to privacy in such items merely by bringing them onto school grounds.

Against the child's interest in privacy must be set the substantial interest of teachers and administrators in maintaining discipline in the classroom and on school grounds. Maintaining order in the classroom has never been easy, but in recent years, school disorder has often taken particularly ugly forms: drug use and violent crime in the schools have become major social problems. Even in schools that have been spared the most severe disciplinary problems, the preservation of order and a proper educational environment requires close supervision of schoolchildren, as well as the enforcement of rules against conduct that would be perfectly permissible if undertaken by an adult. "Events calling for discipline are frequent occurrences and sometimes require immediate, effective action.". . .

How, then, should we strike the balance between the schoolchild's legitimate expectations of privacy and the school's equally legitimate need to maintain an environment in

Most students consider the contents of their lockers private, but the Court in *T.L.O.* held that even students' private property can be searched at school based on "reasonable suspicions" that school rules or laws are being violated. Many schools have more sweeping policies that allow locker searches at any time. Are such policies constitutional?

which learning can take place? It is evident that the school setting requires some easing of the restrictions to which searches by public authorities are ordinarily subject. The warrant requirement, in particular, is unsuited to the school environment: requiring a teacher to obtain a warrant before searching a child suspected of an infraction of school rules (or of the criminal law) would unduly interfere with the maintenance of the swift and informal disciplinary procedures needed in the schools. Just as we have in other cases dispensed with the warrant requirement when "the burden of obtaining a warrant is likely to frustrate the governmental purpose behind the search," we hold today that school officials need not obtain a warrant before searching a student who is under their authority.

The school setting also requires some modification of the level of suspicion of illicit activity needed to justify a search. Ordinarily, a search—even one that may permissibly be carried out without a warrant—must be based upon "probable cause" to believe that a violation of the law has occurred. However, "probable cause" is not an irreducible requirement of a valid search. . . .

We join the majority of courts that have examined this issue in concluding that the accommodation of the privacy interests of schoolchildren with the substantial need of teachers and administrators for freedom to maintain order in the schools does not require strict adherence to the requirement that searches be based on probable cause to believe that the subject of the search has violated or is violating the law. Rather, the legality of a search of a student should depend simply on the reasonableness, under all the circumstances, of the search. Determining the reasonableness of any search involves a twofold inquiry: first, one must consider "whether the . . . action was justified at its inception," second, one must determine whether the search as actually conducted "was reasonably related in scope to the circumstances which justified the interference in the first place." Under ordinary circumstances, a search of a student by a teacher or other school official will be "justified at its inception" when there are reasonable grounds for suspecting that the search will turn up evidence that the student has violated or is violating either the law or the rules of the school. Such a search will be permissible in its scope when the measures adopted are reasonably related to the objectives of the search and not excessively intrusive in light of the age and sex of the student and the nature of the infraction.

. . .

IV

. . .

The incident that gave rise to this case actually involved two separate searches, with the first—the search for cigarettes—providing the suspicion that gave rise to the second— the search for marihuana. Although it is the fruits of the second search that are at issue here, the validity of the search for marihuana must depend on the reasonableness of the initial search for cigarettes, as there would have been no reason to suspect that T.L.O. possessed marihuana had the first search not taken place. Accordingly, it is to the search for cigarettes that we first turn our attention.

The New Jersey Supreme Court pointed to two grounds for its holding that the search for cigarettes was unreasonable. First, the court observed that possession of cigarettes was not in itself illegal or a violation of school rules. Because the contents of T.L.O.'s purse would therefore have "no direct bearing on the infraction" of which she was accused (smoking in a lavatory where smoking was prohibited), there was no reason to search her purse. Second, even assuming that a search of T.L.O.'s purse might under some circumstances be reasonable in light of the accusation made against T.L.O., the New Jersey court concluded that Mr. Choplick in this particular case had no reasonable grounds to suspect that T.L.O. had cigarettes in her purse. At best, according to the court, Mr. Choplick had "a good hunch."

Both these conclusions are implausible. T.L.O. had been accused of smoking, and had denied the accusation in the strongest possible terms when she stated that she did not smoke at all. Surely it cannot be said that under these circumstances, T.L.O.'s possession of cigarettes would be irrelevant to the charges against her or to her response to those charges. T.L.O.'s possession of cigarettes, once it was discovered, would both corroborate the report that she had been smoking and undermine the credibility of her defense to the charge of smoking. To be sure, the discovery of the cigarettes would not prove that T.L.O. had been smoking in the lavatory; nor would it, strictly speaking, necessarily be inconsistent with her claim that she did not smoke at all. But it is universally recognized that evidence, to be relevant to an inquiry, need not conclusively prove the ultimate fact in issue, but only have "any tendency to make the existence of any fact that is of consequence to the determination of the action more probable or less probable than it would be without the evidence." The relevance of T.L.O.'s possession of cigarettes to the question whether she had been smoking and to the credibility of her denial that she smoked supplied the necessary "nexus" between the item searched for and the infraction under investigation. Thus, if Mr. Choplick in fact had a reasonable suspicion that T.L.O. had cigarettes in her purse, the search was justified despite the fact that the cigarettes, if found, would constitute "mere evidence" of a violation.

Of course, the New Jersey Supreme Court also held that Mr. Choplick had no reasonable suspicion that the purse would contain cigarettes. This conclusion is puzzling. A teacher had reported that T.L.O. was smoking in the lavatory. Certainly this report gave Mr. Choplick reason to suspect that T.L.O. was carrying cigarettes with her; and if she did have cigarettes, her purse was the obvious place in which to find them. Mr. Choplick's suspicion that there were cigarettes in the purse . . . was the sort of "common-sense conclusio[n] about human behavior" upon which "practical people"—including government officials—are entitled to rely. . . . [I]t cannot be said that Mr. Choplick acted unreasonably when he examined T.L.O.'s purse to see if it contained cigarettes.[2]

Our conclusion that Mr. Choplick's decision to open T.L.O.'s purse was reasonable brings us to the question of the further search for marihuana once the pack of cigarettes was located. The suspicion upon which the search for marihuana was founded was provided when Mr. Choplick observed a package of rolling papers in the purse as he removed the pack of cigarettes. Although T.L.O. does not dispute the reasonableness of Mr. Choplick's belief that the rolling papers indicated the presence of marihuana, she does contend that the scope of the search Mr. Choplick conducted exceeded permissible bounds when he seized and read certain letters that implicated T.L.O. in drug dealing. This argument, too, is unpersuasive. The discovery of the rolling papers concededly gave rise to a reasonable suspicion that T.L.O. was carrying marihuana as well as cigarettes in her purse. This suspicion justified further exploration of T.L.O.'s purse, which turned up more evidence of drug-related activities: a pipe, a number of plastic bags of the type commonly used to store marihuana, a small quantity of marihuana, and a fairly substantial amount of money. Under these circumstances, it was not unreasonable to extend the search to a separate zippered compartment of the purse; and when a search of that compartment revealed an index card containing a list of "people who owe me money" as well as two letters, the inference that T.L.O. was involved in marihuana trafficking was substantial enough to justify Mr. Choplick in examining the letters to determine whether they contained any further evidence. In short, we cannot conclude that the search for marihuana was unreasonable in any respect.

. . .

Reversed.

Justice BRENNAN, with whom Justice MARSHALL joins, concurring in part and dissenting in part.

. . .

. . . Today's decision sanctions school officials to conduct full-scale searches on a "reasonableness" standard whose only definite content is that it *is not* the same test as the "probable cause" standard found in the text of the Fourth Amendment. In adopting this unclear, unprecedented, and unnecessary departure from generally applicable Fourth Amendment standards, the Court carves out a broad exception to standards that this Court has developed over years of considering Fourth Amendment problems. . . .

I

. . .

B

I emphatically disagree with the Court's decision to cast aside the constitutional probable-cause standard when assessing the constitutional validity of a schoolhouse search. . . .

. . .

II

. . .

. . . Just as a police officer could not obtain a warrant to search a home based solely on his claim that he had seen a package of cigarette papers in that home, Mr. Choplick was not entitled to search possibly the most private possessions of T.L.O. based on the mere presence of a package of cigarette papers. . . .

Justice STEVENS, with whom Justice MARSHALL joins, and with whom Justice BRENNAN joins as to Part I, concurring in part and dissenting in part.

. . .

III

. . .

In this case, Mr. Choplick overreacted to what appeared to be nothing more than a minor infraction—a rule prohibiting smoking in the bathroom of the freshmen's and sophomores' building. It is, of course, true that he actually found evidence of serious wrongdoing by T.L.O., but no one claims that the prior search may be justified by his unexpected discovery. As far as the smoking infraction is concerned, the search for cigarettes merely tended to corroborate a teacher's eyewitness account of T.L.O.'s violation of a minor regulation designed to channel student smoking behavior into designated locations. Because this conduct was neither unlawful nor significantly disruptive of school order or the educational process, the invasion of privacy associated with the forcible opening of T.L.O.'s purse was entirely unjustified at its inception.

. . . Although I agree that school administrators must have broad latitude to maintain order and discipline in our classrooms, that authority is not unlimited.

The schoolroom is the first opportunity most citizens have to experience the power of government. Through it passes every citizen and public official, from schoolteachers to policemen and prison guards. The values they learn there, they take with them in life. One of our most cherished ideals is the one contained in the Fourth Amendment: that the government may not intrude on the personal privacy of its citizens without a warrant or compelling circumstance. The Court's decision today is a curious moral for the Nation's youth. . . .

I respectfully dissent.

EXERCISE 5.1. The *T.L.O.* decision allows searches of students' property whenever school officials have "reasonable suspicion" that there is something criminal or impermissible under school rules taking place. This degree of suspicion—which is lower than the "probable cause" required of law enforcement officers searching adults—is acceptable to the Court because of the school setting. What happened to the *Tinker* decision, which stated that students do not shed their constitutional rights at school doors? What is special about schools that leads the Court to grant more leeway to officials who want to search for contraband?

Searching the Student Body: Drug Tests and Strip Searches

While *New Jersey v. T.L.O.* gave schools much latitude to search the belongings of students, it did not directly deal with the question of when school officials can search the students themselves. Consider the next case, which deals with a body fluid search in the context of the War on Drugs in a junior high school. In *Vernonia School District v. Acton* (1995), the Court confronts the question of whether or not a school can impose random drug tests on all students who participate in school athletics.

What are the legitimate privacy claims of students who want to avoid urinanalysis drug testing? Do such tests pose an affront to dignity? Do they open a chemical window onto other aspects of a student's life that he or she may want to keep private, such as use of medications or pregnancy? Or is a school just doing its job in attempting to deal with the problem of drug use, which can clearly interfere with the educational process? If a school is operating *in loco parentis*—in essence, standing in the place of the parents—does it not have a moral, even legal, obligation to intervene if it sees that its students are putting themselves in danger?

Tenth-grader James Acton, center, along with friends and family members, leaves the Supreme Court on March 28, 1995, after the Court considered his challenge to Vernonia's compulsory urinalysis drug testing of student athletes, a policy to which he was subjected in junior high school. Although plaintiffs in a case like this may attend the Court's oral argument to see their lawyers argue on their behalf, the Court's rules forbid lawyers to introduce their clients to the Court.

VERNONIA SCHOOL DISTRICT
v.
ACTON

Supreme Court of the United States
Argued March 28, 1995.
Decided June 26, 1995.

Justice SCALIA delivered the opinion of the Court.

The Student Athlete Drug Policy adopted by School District 47J in the town of Vernonia, Oregon, authorizes random urinalysis drug testing of students who participate in the District's school athletics programs. We granted certiorari to decide whether this violates the Fourth and Fourteenth Amendments to the United States Constitution.

I

A

Petitioner Vernonia School District 47J (District) operates one high school and three grade schools in the logging community of Vernonia, Oregon. As elsewhere in small-town America, school sports play a prominent role in the town's life, and student athletes are admired in their schools and in the community.

Drugs had not been a major problem in Vernonia schools. In the mid-to-late 1980's, however, teachers and administrators observed a sharp increase in drug use. Students began to speak out about their attraction to the drug culture, and to boast that there was nothing the school could do about it. Along with more drugs came more disciplinary problems. Between 1988 and 1989 the number of disciplinary referrals in Vernonia schools rose to more than twice the number reported in the early 1980's, and several students were suspended. Students became increasingly rude during class; outbursts of profane language became common.

Not only were student athletes included among the drug users but . . . athletes were the leaders of the drug culture. This caused the District's administrators particular concern, since drug use increases the risk of sports-related injury. Expert testimony at the trial confirmed the deleterious effects of drugs on motivation, memory, judgment, reaction, coordination, and performance. The high school football and wrestling coach witnessed a severe sternum injury suffered by a wrestler, and various omissions of safety procedures and misexecutions by football players, all attributable in his belief to the effects of drug use.

Initially, the District responded to the drug problem by offering special classes, speakers, and presentations designed to deter drug use. It even brought in a specially trained dog to detect drugs, but the drug problem persisted. . . . At that point, District officials began considering a drug-testing program. They held a parent "input night" to discuss the proposed Student Athlete Drug Policy (Policy), and the parents in attendance gave their unanimous approval. The school board approved the Policy for implementation in the fall of 1989. Its expressed purpose is to prevent student athletes from using drugs, to protect their health and safety, and to provide drug users with assistance programs.

B

The Policy applies to all students participating in interscholastic athletics. Students wishing to play sports must sign a form consenting to the testing and must obtain the written consent of their parents. Athletes are tested at the beginning of the season for their sport. In addition, once each week of the season the names of the athletes are placed in a "pool" from which a student, with the supervision of two adults, blindly draws the names of 10% of the athletes for random testing. Those selected are notified and tested that same day, if possible.

The student to be tested completes a specimen control form which bears an assigned number. Prescription medications that the student is taking must be identified by providing a copy of the prescription or a doctor's authorization. The student then enters an empty locker room accompanied by an adult monitor of the same sex. Each boy selected produces a sample at a urinal, remaining fully clothed with his back to the monitor, who stands approximately 12 to 15 feet behind the student. Monitors may (though do not always) watch the student while he produces the sample, and they listen for normal sounds of urination. Girls produce samples in an enclosed bathroom stall, so that they can be heard but not observed. After the sample is produced, it is given to the monitor, who checks it for temperature and tampering and then transfers it to a vial.

. . .

If a sample tests positive, a second test is administered as soon as possible to confirm the result. If the second test is negative, no further action is taken. If the second test is positive, the athlete's parents are notified, and the school principal convenes a meeting with the student and his parents, at which the student is given the option of (1) participating for six weeks in an assistance program that includes weekly urinalysis, or (2) suffering suspension from athletics for the remainder of the current season and the next athletic season. The student is then retested prior to the start of the next athletic season for which he or she is eligible. The Policy states that a second offense results in automatic imposition of option (2); a third offense in suspension for the remainder of the current season and the next two athletic seasons.

C

In the fall of 1991, . . . James Acton, then a seventh-grader, signed up to play football at one of the District's grade schools. He was denied participation, however, because he and his parents refused to sign the testing consent forms. The Actons filed suit.

II

The Fourth Amendment to the United States Constitution provides that the Federal Government shall not violate "[t]he right of the people to be secure in their persons, houses, papers, and effects, against unreasonable searches and seizures, ..." We have held that the Fourteenth Amendment extends this constitutional guarantee to searches and seizures by state officers, including public school officials. [We have] held that state-compelled collection and testing of urine, such as that required by the Student Athlete Drug Policy, constitutes a "search" subject to the demands of the Fourth Amendment.

As the text of the Fourth Amendment indicates, the ultimate measure of the constitutionality of a governmental search is "reasonableness." . . .

We have found . . . "special needs" to exist in the public-school context. There, the warrant requirement "would unduly interfere with the maintenance of the swift and informal disciplinary procedures [that are] needed," and "strict adherence to the requirement that searches be based upon probable cause" would undercut "the substantial need of teachers and administrators for freedom to maintain order in the schools." The school search we approved in *T.L.O.*, while not based on probable cause, *was* based on individualized *suspicion* of wrongdoing. As we explicitly acknowledged, however, " 'the Fourth Amendment imposes no irreducible requirement of such suspicion.' " We have upheld suspicionless searches and seizures to conduct drug testing of railroad personnel involved in train accidents, to conduct random drug testing of federal customs officers who carry arms or are involved in drug interdiction and to maintain automobile checkpoints looking for illegal immigrants and contraband and drunk drivers.

III

The first factor to be considered is the nature of the privacy interest upon which the search here at issue intrudes. The Fourth Amendment does not protect all subjective expectations of privacy, but only those that society recognizes as "legitimate.". . .Central, in our view, to the present case is the fact that the subjects of the Policy are (1) children, who (2) have been committed to the temporary custody of the State as schoolmaster.

Traditionally at common law, and still today, unemancipated minors lack some of the most fundamental rights of self-determination including even the right of liberty in its narrow sense, i.e., the right to come and go at will. They are subject, even as to their physical freedom, to the control of their parents or guardians. When parents place minor children in private schools for their education, the teachers and administrators of those schools stand in loco parentis over the children entrusted to them.

In *T.L.O.* we rejected the notion that public schools, like private schools, exercise only parental power over their students, which of course is not subject to constitutional constraints. . . . But while denying that the State's power over schoolchildren is formally no more than the delegated power of their parents, *T.L.O.* did not deny, but indeed emphasized, that the nature of that power is custodial and tutelary, permitting a degree of supervision and control that could not be exercised over free adults. . . . [W]hile children assuredly do not "shed their constitutional rights . . . at the schoolhouse gate," the nature of those rights is what is appropriate for children in school.

Fourth Amendment rights, no less than First and Fourteenth Amendment rights, are different in public schools than elsewhere; the "reasonableness" inquiry cannot disregard the schools' custodial and tutelary responsibility for children. For their own good and that of their classmates, public school children are routinely required to submit to various physical examinations, and to be vaccinated against various diseases. . . . Particularly with regard to medical examinations and procedures, therefore, "students within the school environment have a lesser expectation of privacy than members of the population generally."

Legitimate privacy expectations are even less with regard to student athletes. School sports are not for the bashful. They require "suiting up" before each practice or event, and showering and changing afterwards. Public school locker rooms, the usual sites for these activities, are not notable for the privacy they afford. The locker rooms in Vernonia are typical: no individual dressing rooms are provided; shower heads are lined up along a wall, unseparated by any sort of partition or curtain; not even all the toilet stalls have doors. As the United States Court of Appeals for the Seventh Circuit has noted, there is "an element of 'communal undress' inherent in athletic participation."

There is an additional respect in which school athletes have a reduced expectation of privacy. By choosing to "go out for the team," they voluntarily subject themselves to a degree of regulation even higher than that imposed on students generally. In Vernonia's public schools, they must submit to a preseason physical exam (James testified that his included the giving of a urine sample), they must acquire adequate insurance coverage or sign an insurance waiver, maintain a minimum grade point average, and comply with any "rules of conduct, dress, training hours and related matters as may be established for each sport by the head coach and athletic director with the principal's approval." Somewhat like adults who choose to participate in a "closely regulated industry," students who voluntarily participate in school athletics have reason to expect intrusions upon normal rights and privileges, including privacy.

IV

Having considered the scope of the legitimate expectation of privacy at issue here, we turn next to the character of the intrusion that is complained of. We recognized in *Skinner* that collecting the samples for urinalysis intrudes upon "an excretory function traditionally shielded by great privacy." We noted, however, that the degree of intrusion depends upon the manner in which production of the urine sample is monitored. Under the District's Policy, male students produce samples at a urinal along a wall. They remain fully clothed and are only observed from behind, if at all. Female students produce samples in an enclosed stall, with a female monitor standing outside listening only for sounds of tampering. These conditions are nearly identical to those typically encountered in public restrooms, which men, women, and especially school children use daily. Under such conditions, the privacy interests compromised by the process of obtaining the urine sample are in our view negligible.

The other privacy-invasive aspect of urinalysis is, of course, the information it discloses concerning the state of the subject's body, and the materials he has ingested. In this regard it is significant that the tests at issue here look only for drugs, and not for whether the student is, for example, epileptic, pregnant, or diabetic. Moreover, the drugs for which the samples are screened are standard, and do not vary according to the identity of the student. And finally, the results of the tests are disclosed only to a limited class of school personnel who have a need to know; and they are not turned over to law enforcement authorities or used for any internal disciplinary function.

. . .

The General Authorization Form that [the Actons] refused to sign, which refusal was the basis for James's exclusion from the sports program, said only . . . : "I . . . authorize the Vernonia School District to conduct a test on a urine specimen which I provide to test for drugs and/or alcohol use. I also authorize the release of information concerning the results of such a test to the Vernonia School District and to the parents and/or guardians of the student." While the practice of the District seems to have been to have a school official take medication information from the student at the time of the test, that practice is not set forth in, or required by, the Policy, which says simply: "Student athletes who . . . are or have been taking prescription medication must provide verification (either by a copy of the prescription or by doctor's authorization) prior to being tested." It may well be that, if and when James was selected for random testing at a time that he was taking medication, the School District would have permitted him to provide the requested information in a confidential manner—for example, in a sealed envelope delivered to the testing lab. Nothing in the Policy contradicts that, and when [the Actons] choose, in effect, to challenge the Policy on its face, we will not assume the worst. Accordingly, we reach the same conclusion as in *Skinner*: that the invasion of privacy was not significant.

V

Finally, we turn to consider the nature and immediacy of the governmental concern at issue here, and the efficacy of this means for meeting it. . . . [T]he District Court held that because the District's program also called for drug testing in the absence of individualized suspicion, the District "must demonstrate a 'compelling need' for the program." . . . It is a mistake, however, to think that the phrase "compelling state interest," in the Fourth Amendment context, describes a fixed, minimum quantum of governmental concern, so that one can dispose of a case by answering in isolation the question: Is there a compelling state interest here? Rather, the phrase describes an interest which appears *important enough* to justify the particular search at hand, in light of other factors which show the search to be relatively intrusive upon a genuine expectation of privacy. Whether that relatively high degree of government concern is necessary in this case or not, we think it is met.

That the nature of the concern is important—indeed, perhaps compelling—can hardly be doubted. Deterring drug use by our Nation's schoolchildren is at least as important as enhancing efficient enforcement of the Nation's laws against the importation of drugs. . . . School years are the time when the physical, psychological, and addictive effects of drugs are most severe. "Maturing nervous systems are more critically impaired by intoxicants than mature ones are; childhood losses in learning are lifelong and profound"; "children grow chemically dependent more quickly than adults, and their record of recovery is depressingly poor." And of course . . . the educational process is disrupted. In the present case, moreover, the necessity for the State to act is magnified by the fact that this evil is being visited not just upon individuals at large, but upon children for whom it has undertaken a special responsibility of care and direction. Finally, it must not be lost sight of that this program is directed more narrowly to drug use by school athletes, where the risk of immediate physical harm to the drug user or those with whom he is playing his sport is particularly high. Apart from psychological effects, which include impairment of judgment, slow reaction time, and a lessening of the perception of pain, the particular drugs screened by the District's Policy have been demonstrated to pose substantial physical risks to athletes.

As for the immediacy of the District's concerns: We are not inclined to question" . . . the District Court's conclusion that "a large segment of the student body, particularly those involved in interscholastic athletics, was in a state of rebellion," that "[d]isciplinary actions had reached 'epidemic proportions,'" and that "the rebellion was being fueled by alcohol and drug abuse as well as by the student's misperceptions about the drug culture." . . .

As to the efficacy of this means for addressing the problem: It seems to us self-evident that a drug problem largely fueled by the "role model" effect of athletes' drug use, and of particular danger to athletes, is effectively addressed by making sure that athletes do not use drugs. . . .

VI

Taking into account all the factors we have considered above—the decreased expectation of privacy, the relative unobtrusiveness of the search, and the severity of the need met by the search—we conclude Vernonia's Policy is reasonable and hence constitutional.

. . .

Justice GINSBURG, concurring.

The Court constantly observes that the School District's drug-testing policy applies only to students who voluntarily participate in interscholastic athletics. Correspondingly, the most severe sanction allowed under the District's policy is suspension from extracurricular athletic programs. I comprehend the Court's opinion as reserving the question whether the District, on no more than the showing made here, constitutionally could impose routine drug testing not only on those seeking to engage with others in team sports, but on all students required to attend school.

Justice O'CONNOR, with whom Justice STEVENS and Justice SOUTER join, dissenting.

The population of our Nation's public schools, grades 7 through 12, numbers around 18 million. By the reasoning of today's decision, the millions of these students who participate in interscholastic sports, an overwhelming majority of whom have given school officials no reason whatsoever to suspect they use drugs at school, are open to an intrusive bodily search.

. . .

. . . For most of our constitutional history, mass, suspicionless searches have been generally considered *per se* unreasonable within the meaning of the Fourth Amendment. . . . I dissent.

I

A

. . .

. . .[W]hat the Framers of the Fourth Amendment most strongly opposed, with limited exceptions wholly inapplicable here, were general searches—that is, searches by general warrant, by writ of assistance, by broad statute, or by any other similar authority.

. . .

Perhaps most telling of all, as reflected in the text of the Warrant Clause, the particular way the Framers chose to curb the abuses of general warrants—and by implication, all general searches—was not to impose a novel "evenhandedness" requirement; it was to retain the individualized suspicion requirement contained in the typical general warrant, but to make that requirement meaningful and enforceable, for instance, by raising the required level of individualized suspicion to objective probable cause. . . .

. . . Protection of privacy, not evenhandedness, was then and is now the touchstone of the Fourth Amendment.

. . . [C]ertainly monitored urination combined with urine testing is more intrusive than some personal searches we have said trigger Fourth Amendment protections in the past. Finally, the collection and testing of urine is, of course, a search of a person, one of only four categories of suspect searches the Constitution mentions by name.

Thus, it remains the law that the police cannot, say, subject to drug testing every person entering or leaving a certain drug-ridden neighborhood in order to find evidence of crime. And this is true even though it is hard to think of a more compelling government interest than the need to fight the scourge of drugs on our streets and in our neighborhoods. . . .

. . .

. . . The great irony of this case is that most (though not all) of the evidence the District introduced to justify its suspicionless drug-testing program consisted of first or second-hand stories of particular, identifiable students acting in ways that plainly gave rise to reasonable suspicion of in-school drug use and thus that would have justified a drug-related search under our *T.L.O.* decision. Small groups of students, for example, were observed by a teacher "passing joints back and forth" across the street at a restaurant before school and during school hours. Another group was caught skipping school and using drugs at one of the students' houses. Several students actually admitted their drug use to school officials (some of them being caught with marijuana pipes). One student presented himself to his teacher as "clearly obviously inebriated" and had to be sent home. Still another was observed dancing and singing at the top of his voice in the back of the classroom; when the teacher asked what was going on, he replied, "Well, I'm just high on life." To take a final example, on a certain road trip, the school wrestling coach smelled marijuana smoke in a hotel room occupied by four wrestlers, an observation that (after some questioning) would probably have given him reasonable suspicion to test one or all of them.

In light of all this evidence of drug use by particular students, there is a substantial basis for concluding that a vigorous regime of suspicion-based testing would have gone a long way toward solving Vernonia's school drug problem while preserving the Fourth Amendment rights of James Acton and others like him. . . . In these circumstances, the Fourth Amendment dictates that a mass, suspicionless search regime is categorically unreasonable.

I recognize that a suspicion-based scheme, even where reasonably effective in controlling in-school drug use, may not be as effective as a mass, suspicionless testing regime. In one sense, that is obviously true just as it is obviously true that suspicion-based law enforcement is not as effective as mass, suspicionless enforcement might be. "But there is nothing new in the realization" that Fourth Amendment protections come with a price. Indeed, the price we pay is higher in the criminal context, given that police do not closely observe the entire class of potential search targets (all citizens in the area) and must ordinarily adhere to the rigid requirements of a warrant and probable cause.

The principal counter argument to all this, central to the Court's opinion, is that the Fourth Amendment is more lenient with respect to school searches. That is no doubt correct, for, as the Court explains, schools have traditionally had special guardian-like responsibilities for children that necessitate a degree of constitutional leeway. . . .

The instant case, however, asks whether the Fourth Amendment is even more lenient than that, *i.e.*, whether it is *so* lenient that students may be deprived of the Fourth Amendment's only remaining, and most basic, categorical protection: its strong preference for an individualized suspicion requirement, with its accompanying antipathy toward personally intrusive, blanket searches of mostly innocent people. It is not at all clear that people in *prison* lack this categorical protection, and we have said "we are not yet ready to hold that the schools and the prisons need be equated for purposes of the Fourth Amendment."

For the contrary position, the Court relies on cases such as *T.L.O., Ingraham v. Wright*, and *Goss v. Lopez*. But I find the Court's reliance on these cases ironic. If anything, they affirm that schools have substantial constitutional leeway in carrying out their traditional mission of responding to *particularized* wrongdoing.

By contrast, intrusive, blanket searches of school children, most of whom are innocent, for evidence of serious wrongdoing are not part of any traditional school function of which I am aware. Indeed, many schools, like many parents, prefer to trust their children unless given reason to do otherwise. As James Acton's father said on the witness stand, "[suspicionless testing] sends a message to children that are trying to be responsible citizens . . . that they have to prove that they're innocent . . ., and I think that kind of sets a bad tone for citizenship."

. . .

II

. . .

. . . I find unreasonable the school's choice of student athletes as the class to subject to suspicionless testing. . . .

. . .[I]t seems to me that the far more reasonable choice would have been to focus on the class of students found to have violated published school rules against severe disruption in class and around campus—disruption that had a strong nexus to drug use, as the District established at trial. Such a choice would share two of the virtues of a suspicion-based regime: testing dramatically fewer students, tens as against hundreds, and giving students control, through their behavior, over the likelihood that they would be tested. Moreover, there would be a reduced concern for the accusatory nature of the search, because the Court's feared "badge of shame," would already exist, due to the antecedent accusation and finding of severe disruption.

III

It cannot be too often stated that the greatest threats to our constitutional freedoms come in times of crisis. But we must also stay mindful that not all government responses to such times are hysterical overreactions; some crises are quite real, and when they are, they serve precisely as the compelling state interest that we have said may justify a measured intrusion on constitutional rights. The only way for judges to mediate these conflicting impulses is to do what they should do anyway: stay close to the record in each case that appears before them, and make their judgments based on that alone. Having reviewed the record here, I cannot avoid the conclusion that the District's suspicionless policy of testing all student-athletes sweeps too broadly, and too imprecisely, to be reasonable under the Fourth Amendment.

EXERCISE 5.2. What if the Vernonia School District's policy of random drug-testing of student athletes does not work to reduce drug use in the student body and the principal decides next to randomly test (a) student council candidates; (b) students trying out for the cheerleading squad; (c) students who fail classes; (d) students on the honor roll; (e) sports coaches, student government advisers, and science teachers? Do you think that testing each of these categories of people is consistent with the Fourth Amendment? Consider the government's interest in the search and the level of privacy intrusion. What are the pros and cons of drug-testing each group?

EXERCISE 5.3. In determining whether or not a search is "reasonable" under *New Jersey v. T.L.O.*, the Court conducts a two-part analysis. First, the Court determines whether the search was "justified at its inception"—that is, whether there were reasonable grounds for suspecting the search would turn up evidence that the student was violating either the law or school rules. Second, the Court asks whether the search was reasonably related in scope to the purpose of the search and not overly intrusive in light of the student's age and sex and the nature of the infraction. In order to analyze this second issue, the Court must balance the importance of the government's interest against the level of violation of privacy rights.

Draw a line down the middle of a piece of paper and make two columns. At the top of the left-hand column, write "Level of Privacy Intrusion"; at the top of the right-hand column, write "Nature of Government Interest." To do a balancing test, you must compare the severity of the privacy intrusion against the weight of the government interest. (For example, in *Vernonia*, what is the nature of intrusion on privacy interests? What is the government's interest in the drug test?)

Read through the following list of procedures established at various public high schools facing the problems of drug and alcohol use among students. In the "Intrusion" column of your chart, list what you think the intrusion is for each procedure and rank how intrusive you think the procedure is on a scale of 1 to 10 (10 being the highest) and why. In the "Government Interest" column, write down what you think the government interest is in the drug-testing policy and how high that interest ranks on a scale of 1 to 10. If you think one example is not a "search" at all, write it on your chart and explain why.

(a) Students entering the building at Madison High must walk through a metal detector.
(b) Students at Hamilton High must walk through a metal detector and put their book bags through an x-ray machine before entering the building.
(c) Jefferson High reserves the right to "tap" all the pay phones in the hallways of the school and listen in on conversations. Students are informed of this at the beginning of each school year.
(d) Martin Luther King High has a counselor available to talk to students about their problems. Any teacher can "sign out" from the counselor's office student files that contain notes kept on each student's sessions.

(e) Big City High has video cameras in the hallways filming the rows of student lockers. If students act suspiciously around their lockers, the principal searches their lockers for drugs or weapons. Videotapes are routinely turned over to the police.

(f) Small City High conducts random locker searches of all boys' lockers and has removed all doors from the toilet stalls in the girls' bathroom.

(g) At Kaynine High, trained police dogs sniff outside student lockers, and school officials open and search lockers when the dogs bark and alert teachers to the presence of narcotics.

(h) Southeast High has trained police dogs at school doorways sniffing each student's backpack or bookbag as students enter the building.

(i) Detection High places young-looking undercover police officers into the senior class to befriend students and uncover information about drug dealing and about students obtaining abortions without the parental consent required under state law. They turn in several of their "friends."

(j) As a requirement for advancing to the next grade at J. Edgar Hoover High, all students must take a polygraph ("lie-detector") test and answer one question: "Did you cheat on any of your final exams this year?"

(k) At Thurgood Marshall High's homecoming dance, all of the chaperones carry an alcohol tester. Throughout the dance, the chaperones may approach any student and have him or her blow into the machine. If alcohol is detected, a red light goes on and the student's parents are called to take the student home.

(l) At John Marshall High's homecoming dance, students who test positive using the same device are expelled.

Sometimes school authorities trying to stop drugs go too far for the federal courts, which are generally sympathetic to the need for sweeping security measures. In the following case we see both tendencies at work: the Seventh Circuit Court of Appeals upholds a massive dog-sniffing drug search of the entire student body at an Indiana junior and senior high school but firmly draws the line at a strip search of a thirteen-year-old student. Does this decision let the police go too far, make them stop too soon, or get the balance about right?

——

DOE
v.
RENFROW

United States Court of Appeals Seventh Circuit
Argued April 3, 1980.
Decided July 18, 1980.

PER CURIAM.

[Petitioner Diane Doe is a 13-year-old student at Highland Junior High School in Highland, Ind., a community of approximately 30,000 residents. Highland has one junior high school and one senior high school, located in adjacent buildings. There are 2,780 students total enrolled in the two schools.]

On the morning of March 23, 1979, [Doe] went to her first-period class as usual. Shortly before 9:15, when the class was scheduled to adjourn, Doe's teacher ordered everyone to remain seated until further notice. An assistant principal, accompanied by a police-trained German shepherd, a dog handler, and a uniformed police officer, then entered the classroom as one of six teams conducting simultaneous raids at the Highland schools. For the next 2-1/2 hours, Doe and her classmates were required to sit quietly in their seats with their belongings in view and their hands upon their desks. They were forbidden to use the washroom unless accompanied by an escort. Uniformed police officers and school administrators were stationed in the halls. Guards were posted at the schoolhouse doors. While no student was allowed to leave the schoolhouse, representatives of the press and other news media, on invitation of the school authorities, were permitted to enter the classrooms to observe the proceedings.

The dogs were led up and down each aisle of the classroom, from desk to desk, and from student to student. Each student was probed, sniffed, and inspected by at least 1 of the 14 German shepherds detailed to the school. When the search team assigned to Doe's classroom reached Doe, the police dog pressed forward, sniffed at her body, and repeatedly pushed its nose and muzzle into her legs. The uniformed officer then ordered Doe to stand and empty her pockets, apparently because the dog "alerted" to the presence of drugs. However, no drugs were found. After Doe emptied her pockets, the dog again sniffed her body and again it apparently "alerted." Doe was then escorted to the nurse's office for a more thorough physical inspection.

Doe was met at the nurse's office by two adult women, one a uniformed police officer. After denying that she had ever used marihuana, Doe was ordered to strip. She did so, removing her clothing in the presence of the two women. The women then looked over Doe's body, inspected her clothing, and touched and examined the hair on her head. Again, no drugs were found. Doe was subsequently allowed to dress and was escorted back to her classroom.

Each of the 2,780 students present at Highland Junior and Senior High Schools that day was subjected to the mass detention and general exploratory search. Eleven students, including Doe, were subjected to body searches. Although the police dogs "alerted" 50 times, no junior high school students, and only 17 senior high school students, were found to be in possession of contraband. This contraband included marihuana, drug "paraphernalia," and three cans of beer.

. . .

It does not require a constitutional scholar to conclude that a nude search of a thirteen-year-old child is an invasion of constitutional rights of some magnitude. More than that: it is a violation of any known principle of human decency. Apart from any constitutional readings and rulings, simple common sense would indicate that the conduct of the school officials in permitting such a nude search was not only unlawful but outrageous under "settled indisputable principles of law."

[The court] accords immunity to school officials who act in good faith *and within the bounds of reason*. We suggest as strongly as possible that the conduct herein described ex-

A full-time police officer roams in school halls in Webster Groves High School in St. Louis, Missouri—evidence of a new security consciousness in high schools today.

ceeded the "bounds of reason" by two and a half country miles. It is not enough for us to declare that the little girl involved was indeed deprived of her constitutional and basic human rights. We must also permit her to seek damages from those who caused this humiliation and did indeed act as though students "shed at the schoolhouse door rights guaranteed by . . . any . . . constitutional provision." . . .

SWYGERT, Circuit Judge, dissenting. . . .

I am deeply troubled by this court's holding that the dragnet inspection of the entire student body of the Highland Senior and Junior High Schools by trained police dogs and their dog-handlers did not constitute a search under the Fourth Amendment. No doctrine of *in loco parentis* or diminished constitutional rights for children in a public school setting excuses this alarming invasion by police and school authorities of the constitutional rights of thousands of innocent children.

EXERCISE 5.4. Do you think there are any cases in which schools should be allowed to conduct strip searches of students? Many other courts have invalidated strip searches, such as the Northern District Court of New York in *Bellnier v. Lund* (1977), which held unlawful the (ultimately fruitless) strip search of an entire fifth-grade homeroom class down to its underwear in order to find three dollars.

However, courts in other cases have upheld strip searches. For example, in *Rone v. Daviess County Board of Education* (1983), the Kentucky Court of Appeals allowed the strip search of a student who had furnished pharmaceuticals and marijuana to classmates. He was forced to lower his pants and undershorts to his thighs. The court ruled the search justifiable because law officers were not present and he was not going to be criminally prosecuted. In *Williams v. Ellington* (1991), school authorities searched a female student by demanding that she take off her T-shirt and lower her blue jeans to the knees. The search produced no contraband, but the Sixth Circuit Court of Appeals held that the search was reasonable because there had been previous reports that she was using and distributing drugs and a prior search of her purse yielded a vial of the drug called "rush."

We know that, according to *New Jersey v. T.L.O.*, a strip search will only be found reasonable if it was justified at its inception and if it was done in a way consistent with the age and sex of the student and the general requirements of the situation. Do you think that it makes sense to evaluate strip searches on a case-by-case basis like this, or would it be better for the Supreme Court to lay down a categorical, "bright-line" rule that says "teachers and administrators may never strip search students"? What are the pros and cons on each side? If you were a member of the school board and you were asked to develop a policy on strip searches for your school district, what would it say? Discuss the issue with your classmates and see if you can draft a school system-wide policy on strip searches that a majority of the class will support.

Notes

1. "We do not address the question, not presented by this case, whether a schoolchild has a legitimate expectation of privacy in lockers, desks, or other school property provided for the storage of school supplies. Nor do we express any opinion on the standards (if any) governing searches of such areas by school officials or by other public authorities acting at the request of school officials."

2. "T.L.O. contends that even if it was reasonable for Mr. Choplick to open her purse to look for cigarettes, it was not reasonable for him to reach in and take the cigarettes out of her purse once he found them. Had he not removed the cigarettes from the purse, she asserts, he would not have observed the rolling papers that suggested the presence of marihuana, and the search for marihuana could not have taken place. T.L.O.'s argument is based on the fact that the cigarettes were not 'contraband,' as no school rule forbade her to have them. Thus, according to T.L.O., the cigarettes were not subject to seizure or confiscation by school authorities, and Mr. Choplick was not entitled to take them out of T.L.O.'s purse regardless of whether he was entitled to peer into the purse to see if they were there. Such hairsplitting argumentation has no place in an inquiry addressed to the issue of reasonableness. If Mr. Choplick could permissibly search T.L.O.'s purse for ciga-

rettes, it hardly seems reasonable to suggest that his natural reaction to finding them—picking them up—could be a constitutional violation. We find that neither in opening the purse nor in reaching into it to remove the cigarettes did Mr. Choplick violate the Fourth Amendment."

Read On

Arbetman, Lee, and Edward O'Brien. *Street Law.* St. Paul, Minn.: West Educational Publishing, 1999.

LaFave, Wayne R. *Search and Seizure.* 2d ed. St. Paul, Minn.: West Publishing, 1987.

DISCIPLINE AND PUNISHMENT: DUE PROCESS AND THE EIGHTH AMENDMENT

6

"[N]or shall any State deprive any person of life, liberty, or property, without due process of law. . . ."
THE FOURTEENTH AMENDMENT

"Excessive bail shall not be required, nor excessive fines imposed, nor cruel and unusual punishment inflicted." THE EIGHTH AMENDMENT

When a student gets into trouble for misbehaving at school and faces disciplinary measures, school authorities need not bring the student to court in order to suspend or even expel him or her. Disciplinary sanctions like these are deemed civil, not criminal, in nature. Therefore, the school system can set up its own preferred process to investigate, examine, and dispose of cases of student misconduct. But what kind of process *is* due to a student in trouble at school? Are there any kinds of discipline so severe that they violate the Eighth Amendment's ban on cruel and unusual punishment? We take up these questions here.

Should procedural Due Process rights and Eighth Amendment protections against cruel and unusual punishment be extended to public school students?

- What procedural rights to be heard do students have when facing suspension and other forms of discipline by school authorities?
- Should school teachers be allowed to use physical force to discipline students?

Due Process

When school officials want to suspend students from school for several days or weeks, should the students first get to have a fair hearing in which they have an opportunity to tell their side of the story?

The opportunity to be heard is the basic keystone of procedural due process. Generally, constitutional due process requires some sort of official proceeding and hearing before any part of the government may take action against any person. The hearings and trial required before a person can be convicted of a crime are examples of procedural due process.

The events in the following case, *Goss v. Lopez,* arose in Columbus, Ohio, in 1971 during a period of unrest in American high schools over school policies that many African-Americans and other racial minorities saw as discriminatory. In most of the incidents discussed in the case, school officials simply suspended students whom they thought were involved in various incidents without filing any formal charges against them, without giving them any opportunity to be heard or to challenge the administrator's conclusions, and without submitting the cases to any consideration by neutral third parties.

The Court struck down the discipline in these cases, which mostly involved ten-day suspensions of the students involved. The Court found that there must be a fair hearing before a student is suspended or otherwise disciplined. Notice that a hearing before a principal is nothing like a trial: there is no right to be represented by a lawyer, to cross-examine witnesses, or to produce evidence. But the idea of some due process—any due process—for high school students was revolutionary enough for many at the time, as evidenced by the vigorous dissent in this case in which the justices complained about the Court's intervention into the traditional realm of local education.

GOSS
v.
LOPEZ

Supreme Court of the United States
Argued Oct. 16, 1974.
Decided Jan. 22, 1975.

Justice WHITE delivered the opinion of the Court.

. . .

The nine named [students], each of whom alleged that he or she had been suspended from public high school in Columbus for up to 10 days without a hearing . . . filed an action under 42 U.S.C. § 1983 against the Columbus Board of Education and various administrators of the CPSS [Columbus, Ohio, Public School System]. The complaint sought a declaration that § 3313.66 [of an Ohio Law] was unconstitutional in that it permitted public school administrators to deprive plaintiffs of their rights to an education without a hearing of any kind, in violation of the procedural due process component of the Fourteenth Amendment. It also sought to enjoin the public school officials from issuing future suspensions . . . and to require them to remove references to the past suspensions from the records of the students in question.

. . . [T]he suspensions arose out of a period of widespread student unrest in the CPSS during February and March 1971. Six of the named plaintiffs, Rudolph Sutton, Tyrone Washington, Susan Cooper, Deborah Fox, Clarence Byars, and Bruce Harris, were students at the Marion-Franklin High School and were each suspended for 10 days on account of disruptive or disobedient conduct committed in the presence of the school administrator who ordered the suspension. One of these, Tyrone Washington, was among a group of students demonstrating in the school auditorium while a class was being conducted there. He was ordered by the school principal to leave, refused to do so, and was suspended. Rudolph Sutton, in the presence of the principal, physically attacked a police officer who was at-

9 IN COLUMBUS DENIED RIGHTS
High Court Rules
In Student Favor

tempting to remove Tyrone Washington from the auditorium. He was immediately suspended. The other four Marion-Franklin students were suspended for similar conduct. None was given a hearing to determine the operative facts underlying the suspension, but each, together with his or her parents, was offered the opportunity to attend a conference, subsequent to the effective date of the suspension, to discuss the student's future.

Two named plaintiffs, Dwight Lopez and Betty Crome, were students at the Central High School and McGuffey Junior High School, respectively. The former was suspended in connection with a disturbance in the lunchroom which involved some physical damage to school property. Lopez testified that at least 75 other students were suspended from his school on the same day. He also testified below that he was not a party to the destructive conduct but was instead an innocent bystander. Because no one from the school testified with regard to this incident, there is no evidence in the record indicating the official basis for concluding otherwise. Lopez never had a hearing.

Betty Crome was present at a demonstration at a high school other than the one she was attending. There she was arrested together with others, taken to the police station, and released without being formally charged. Before she went to school on the following day, she was notified that she had been suspended for a 10-day period. Because no one from the school testified with respect to this incident, the record does not disclose how the McGuffey Junior High School principal went about making the decision to suspend Crome, nor does it disclose on what information the decision was based. It is clear from the record that no hearing was ever held.

. . .

II

At the outset, [the school administrators] contend that because there is no constitutional right to an education at public expense, the Due Process Clause does not protect against expulsions from the public school system. This position misconceives the nature of the issue and is refuted by prior decisions. The Fourteenth Amendment forbids the State to deprive any person of life, liberty, or property without due process of law. . . .

. . .

Here, on the basis of state law, [the students] plainly had legitimate claims of entitlement to a public education. . . . It is true that § 3313.66 of the Code permits school principals to suspend students for up to 10 days; but suspensions may not be imposed without any grounds whatsoever. All of the schools had their own rules specifying the grounds for expulsion or suspension. Having chosen to extend the right to an education to people of appellees' class generally, Ohio may not withdraw that right on grounds of misconduct, absent fundamentally fair procedures to determine whether the misconduct has occurred.

. . . "The Fourteenth Amendment, as now applied to the States, protects the citizen against the State itself and all of its creatures—Boards of Education not excepted." . . . [T]he State is constrained to recognize a student's legitimate entitlement to a public education as a property interest which is protected by the Due Process Clause and which may not be taken away for misconduct without adherence to the minimum procedures required by that Clause.

The Due Process Clause also forbids arbitrary deprivations of liberty. "Where a person's good name, reputation, honor, or integrity is at stake because of what the government is doing to him," the minimal requirements of the Clause must be satisfied. School authorities here suspended appellees from school for periods of up to 10 days based on charges of misconduct. If sustained and recorded, those charges could seriously damage the students' standing with their fellow pupils and their teachers as well as interfere with later opportunities for higher education and employment. It is apparent that the claimed right of the State to determine unilaterally and without process whether that misconduct has occurred immediately collides with the requirements of the Constitution.

. . .

A short suspension is, of course, a far milder deprivation than expulsion. But, "education is perhaps the most important function of state and local governments," and the total exclusion from the educational process for more than a trivial period, and certainly if the suspension is for 10 days, is a serious event in the life of the suspended child. Neither the property interest in educational benefits temporarily denied nor the liberty interest in reputation, which is also implicated, is so insubstantial that suspensions may constitutionally be imposed by any procedure the school chooses, no matter how arbitrary.

III

"Once it is determined that due process applies, the question remains what process is due.". . .

. . . "The fundamental requisite of due process is the opportunity to be heard," a right that "has little reality or worth unless one is informed that the matter is ending and can choose for himself whether to . . . contest." At the very minimum, therefore, students facing suspension and the consequent interference with a protected property interest must be given *some* kind of notice and afforded *some* kind of hearing. "Parties whose rights are to be affected are entitled to be heard; and in order that they may enjoy that right they must first be notified."

. . . The student's interest is to avoid unfair or mistaken exclusion from the educational process, with all of its unfortunate consequences. The Due Process Clause will not shield him from suspensions properly imposed, but it disserves both his interest and the interest of the State if his suspension is in fact unwarranted. The concern would be mostly academic if the disciplinary process were a totally accurate, unerring process, never mistaken and never unfair. Unfortunately, that is not the case, and no one suggests that it is. Disciplinarians, although proceeding in utmost good faith, frequently act on the reports and advice of others; and the controlling facts and the nature of the conduct under challenge are often disputed. . . .

The difficulty is that our schools are vast and complex. Some modicum of discipline and order is essential if the educational function is to be performed. Events calling for discipline are frequent occurrences and sometimes require immediate, effective action. Suspension is considered not only to be a necessary tool to maintain order but a valuable educational device. The prospect of imposing elaborate hearing requirements in every suspension case is viewed with great concern, and many school authorities may well prefer the untrammeled power to act unilaterally, unhampered by rules about notice and hearing. But it would be a strange disciplinary system in an educational institution if no communication was sought by the disciplinarian with the student in an effort to inform him of his dereliction and to let him tell his side of the story in order to make sure that an injustice is not done. "[F]airness can rarely be obtained by secret, one-sided determination of facts decisive of rights. . . ." "Secrecy is not congenial to truth-seeking and self-righteousness gives too slender an assurance of rightness. No better instrument has been devised for arriving at truth than to give a person in jeopardy of serious loss notice of the case against him and opportunity to meet it."

. . . Students facing temporary suspension have interests qualifying for protection of the Due Process Clause, and due process requires, in connection with a suspension of 10 days or less, that the student be given oral or written notice of the charges against him and, if he denies them, an explanation of the evidence the authorities have and an opportunity to present his side of the story. . . .

. . . We hold only that, in being given an opportunity to explain his version of the facts at this discussion, the student first be told what he is accused of doing and what the basis of the accusation is. . . .

Justice POWELL, with whom The Chief Justice, Justice BLACKMUN, and Justice REHNQUIST join, dissenting.

. . .

II

. . .

C

One of the more disturbing aspects of today's decision is its indiscriminate reliance upon the judiciary, and the adversary process, as the means of resolving many of the most routine problems arising in the classroom. In mandating due process procedures the Court misapprehends the reality of the normal teacher-pupil relationship. There is an ongoing relationship, one in which the teacher must occupy many roles—educator, adviser, friend, and, at times, parent-substitute. It is rarely adversary in nature except with respect to the chronically disruptive or insubordinate pupil whom the teacher must be free to discipline without frustrating formalities.

. . . We have relied for generations upon the experience, good faith and dedication of those who staff our public schools, and the nonadversary means of airing grievances that always have been available to pupils and their parents. One would have thought before today's opinion that this informal method of resolving differences was more compatible with the interests of all concerned than resort to any constitutionalized procedure, however blandly it may be defined by the Court.

D

. . .

Nor does the Court's due process 'hearing' appear to provide significantly more protection than that already available. The Court holds only that the principal must listen to the student's "version of the events," either before suspension or thereafter—depending upon the circumstances. Such a truncated 'hearing' is likely to be considerably less meaningful than the opportunities for correcting mistakes already available to students and parents.

In its rush to mandate a constitutional rule, the Court appears to give no weight to the practical manner in which suspension problems normally would be worked out under Ohio law.[1] One must doubt, then, whether the constitutionalization of the student-teacher relationship, with all of its attendant doctrinal and practical difficulties, will assure in any meaningful sense greater protection than that already afforded under Ohio law.

III

No one can foresee the ultimate frontiers of the new 'thicket' the Court now enters. Today's ruling appears to sweep within the protected interest in education a multitude of discretionary decisions in the educational process. Teachers and other school authorities are required to make many decisions that may have serious consequences for the pupil. They must decide, for example, how to grade the student's work, whether a student passes or fails a course, whether he is to be promoted, whether he is required to take certain subjects, whether he may be excluded from interscholastic athletics or other extracurricular activities, whether he may be removed from one school and sent to another, whether he may be bused long distances when available schools are nearby, and whether he should be placed in a "general," "vocational," or "college-preparatory" track.

In these and many similar situations claims of impairment of one's educational entitlement identical in principle to those before the Court today can be asserted with equal or greater justification. Likewise, in many of these situations, the pupil can advance the same types of speculative and subjective injury given critical weight in this case. The District Court, relying upon generalized opinion evidence, concluded that a suspended student may suffer psychological injury in one or more of the ways set forth in the margin below.[2] The Court appears to adopt this rationale.

It hardly need be said that if a student, as a result of a day's suspension, suffers "a blow" to his "self esteem," "feels powerless," views "teachers with resentment," or feels "stigmatized by his teachers," identical psychological harms will flow from many other routine and necessary school decisions. The student who is given a failing grade, who is not promoted, who is excluded from certain extracurricular activities, who is assigned to a school reserved for children of less than average ability, or who is placed in the "vocational" rather than the "college preparatory" track, is unlikely to suffer any less psychological injury than if he were suspended for a day for a relatively minor infraction.[3]

If, as seems apparent, the Court will now require due process procedures whenever such routine school decisions are challenged, the impact upon public education will be serious indeed. The discretion and judgment of federal courts across the land often will be substituted for that of the 50 state legislatures, the 14,000 school boards, and the 2,000,000 teachers who heretofore have been responsible for the administration of the American public school system. If the Court perceives a rational and analytically sound distinction between the discretionary decision by school authorities to suspend a pupil for a brief period, and the types of discretionary school decisions described above, it would be prudent to articulate it in today's opinion. Otherwise, the federal courts should prepare themselves for a vast new role in society.

IV

Not so long ago, state deprivations of the most significant forms of state largesse were not thought to require due process protection on the ground that the deprivation resulted only in the loss of a state-provided "benefit." In recent years the Court, wisely in my view, has rejected the "wooden distinction between 'rights' and 'privileges,'" and looked instead to the significance of the state-created or state-enforced right and to the substantiality of the alleged deprivation. Today's opinion appears to abandon this reasonable approach by holding in effect that government infringement of any interest to which a person is entitled, no matter what the interest or how inconsequential the infringement, requires constitutional protection. As it is difficult to think of any less consequential infringement than suspension of a junior high school student for a single day, it is equally difficult to perceive any principled limit to the new reach of procedural due process.[4]

EXERCISE 6.1. In his dissenting opinion, Justice Powell suggests that a disciplinary suspension from school is no big deal. It "leaves no scars" and "affects no reputations." He even suggests that "it often may be viewed by the young as a badge of some distinction and a welcome holiday." Do you agree that suspension from school is so commonplace that it warrants no constitutional protections? Debate Justice Powell's position.

EXERCISE 6.2. What are the stages of the disciplinary process at your school? Are there published rules available from the school or the school board? Do you think that these rules comply with the (rather minimal) requirements of *Goss v. Lopez*? If you were asked to revise these rules, what would you change? Would you give students more rights or fewer rights? Would you allow the testimony of witnesses? Opening and closing statements? The opportunity to open the hearing to the public and the media? Should the principal decide on the final action or should a panel of teachers and/or administrators and students make that decision?

EXERCISE 6.3. Draft your own set of ideal rules for disciplinary proceedings in school. Should students be involved in the process as judges, prosecutors, or defenders? Compare your rules to those of your classmates.

Corporal Punishment

The Eighth Amendment protects citizens against infliction of cruel and unusual punishment. This right primarily comes into play when someone convicted of a crime claims that his or her punishment is exceptionally painful, disproportionate, or outrageous.

In the following case, students who were paddled on the buttocks multiple times by their teachers asserted that the corporal punishment they were subjected to was cruel and unusual punishment. Does the Court agree? Does the Court even allow the Eighth Amendment to apply to corporal punishment in the schools?

INGRAHAM
v.
WRIGHT

Supreme Court of the United States
Argued Nov. 2–3, 1976.
Decided April 19, 1977.

Justice POWELL delivered the opinion of the Court.

This case presents [a question] concerning the use of corporal punishment in public schools: . . . whether the paddling of students as a means of maintaining school discipline constitutes cruel and unusual punishment in violation of the Eighth Amendment.

I

. . .

. . . In the 1970–1971 school year many of the 237 schools in Dade County used corporal punishment as a means of maintaining discipline pursuant to Florida legislation [Fla. Stat. Ann. §232.27 (1961)] and a local School Board regulation [Dade County School Board policy 5144]. The statute then in effect authorized limited corporal punishment by negative inference, proscribing punishment which was "degrading or unduly severe" or which was inflicted without prior consultation with the principal or the teacher in charge of the school. The regulation . . . contained explicit directions and limitations.[5] The authorized punishment consisted of paddling the recalcitrant student on the buttocks with a flat wooden paddle measuring less than two feet long, three to four inches wide, and about one-half inch thick. The normal punishment was limited to one to five "licks" or blows with the paddle and resulted in no apparent physical injury to the student. School au-

Willie Wright, shown here in April 1977, administered paddling to the rear ends of students in a Florida public school. The Court ruled that such corporal punishment was not "cruel and unusual" within the meaning of the Eight Amendment.

Summery
Partly cloudy with highs in the 80s and lows in the 70s. Winds 15 to 20 m.p.h. (Details, Page 2A.)
TUESDAY'S TEMPERATURES

The Miami Herald

Final Edition
15 Cents
Newsstand price higher in air delivery cities
47th Year — No. 141

Wednesday, April 20, 1977 · · *Florida's Complete Newspaper*   86 Pages
A Latin American Edition Is Published Daily

Corporal Punishment Not 'Cruel and Unusual'

High Court OKs Paddling

thorities viewed corporal punishment as a less drastic means of discipline than suspension or expulsion. Contrary to the procedural requirements of the statute and regulation, teachers often paddled students on their own authority without first consulting the principal.

. . . The evidence, consisting mainly of the testimony of 16 students, suggests that the regime at Drew [High School] was exceptionally harsh. The testimony of Ingraham and Andrews, in support of their individual claims for damages, is illustrative. Because he was slow to respond to his teacher's instructions, Ingraham was subjected to more than 20 licks with a paddle while being held over a table in the principal's office. The paddling was so severe that he suffered a hematoma[6] requiring medical attention and keeping him out of school for several days. Andrews was paddled several times for minor infractions. On two occasions he was struck on his arms, once depriving him of the full use of his arm for a week.

. . .

II

. . . We . . . begin by examining the way in which our traditions and our laws have responded to the use of corporal punishment in public schools.

The use of corporal punishment in this country as a means of disciplining school children dates back to the colonial period. . . . Despite the general abandonment of corporal punishment as a means of punishing criminal offenders, the practice continues to play a role in the public education of school children in most parts of the country.

At common law a single principle has governed the use of corporal punishment since before the American Revolution: Teachers may impose reasonable but not excessive force to discipline a child. . . . The basic doctrine has not changed. The prevalent rule in this country today privileges such force as a teacher or administrator "reasonably believes to be necessary for [the child's] proper control, training, or education." To the extent that the force is excessive or unreasonable, the educator in virtually all States is subject to possible civil and criminal liability.

. . . All of the circumstances are to be taken into account in determining whether the punishment is reasonable in a particular case. Among the most important considerations are the seriousness of the offense, the attitude and past behavior of the child, the nature and severity of the punishment, the age and strength of the child, and the availability of less severe but equally effective means of discipline.

Of the 23 States that have addressed the problem through legislation, 21 have authorized the moderate use of corporal punishment in public schools. . . . Only two States, Massachusetts and New Jersey, have prohibited all corporal punishment in their public schools.

Against this background of historical and contemporary approval of reasonable corporal punishment, we turn to the constitutional questions before us.

III

The Eighth Amendment provides: "Excessive bail shall not be required, nor excessive fines imposed, nor cruel and unusual punishments inflicted." . . . An examination of the history of the Amendment and the decisions of this Court construing the proscription against cruel and unusual punishment confirms that it was designed to protect those convicted of crimes. We adhere to this longstanding limitation and hold that the Eighth Amendment does not apply to the paddling of children as a means of maintaining discipline in public schools.

. . .

B

. . . [I]t is not surprising to find that every decision of this Court considering whether a punishment is "cruel and unusual" within the meaning of the Eighth and Fourteenth Amendments has dealt with a criminal punishment.

. . .

C

Petitioners . . . urge nonetheless that the prohibition should be extended to ban the paddling of schoolchildren. Observing that the Framers of the Eighth Amendment could not have envisioned our present system of public and compulsory education, with its opportunities for noncriminal punishments, petitioners contend that extension of the prohibition against cruel punishments is necessary lest we afford greater protection to criminals than to schoolchildren. It would be anomalous, they say, if schoolchildren could be beaten without constitutional redress, while hardened criminals suffering the same beatings at the hands of their jailers might have a valid claim under the Eighth Amendment. Whatever force this logic may have in other settings, we find it an inadequate basis for wrenching the Eighth Amendment from its historical context and extending it to traditional disciplinary practices in the public schools.

The prisoner and the schoolchild stand in wholly different circumstances, separated by the harsh facts of criminal conviction and incarceration. The prisoner's conviction entitles the State to classify him as a "criminal," and his incarceration deprives him of the freedom "to be with family and friends and to form the other enduring attachments of normal life." Prison brutality, as the Court of Appeals observed in this case, is "part of the total punishment to which the individual is being subjected for his crime and, as such, is a proper subject for Eighth Amendment scrutiny." Even so, the protection afforded by the Eighth Amendment is limited. After incarceration, only the "unnecessary and wanton infliction of pain," constitutes cruel and unusual punishment forbidden by the Eighth Amendment.

The schoolchild has little need for the protection of the Eighth Amendment. Though attendance may not always be voluntary, the public school remains an open institution. Except perhaps when very young, the child is not physically restrained from leaving school during school hours; and at the end of the school day, the child is invariably free to return home. Even while at school, the child brings with him the support of family and friends and is rarely apart from teachers and other pupils who may witness and protest any instances of mistreatment.

The openness of the public school and its supervision by the community afford significant safeguards against the kinds of abuses from which the Eighth Amendment protects the prisoner. In virtually every community where corporal punishment is permitted in the schools, these safeguards are reinforced by the legal constraints of the common law. Public school teachers and administrators are privileged at common law to inflict only such corporal punishment as is reasonably necessary for the proper education and discipline of the child; any punishment going beyond the privilege may result in both civil and criminal liability.

We conclude that when public school teachers or administrators impose disciplinary corporal punishment, the Eighth Amendment is inapplicable.

Affirmed.

Justice WHITE, with whom Justice BRENNAN, Justice MARSHALL, and Justice STEVENS join, dissenting.

Today the Court holds that corporal punishment in public schools, no matter how severe, can never be the subject of the protections afforded by the Eighth Amendment.

The Eighth Amendment places a flat prohibition against the infliction of "cruel and unusual punishments." This reflects a societal judgment that there are some punishments that are so barbaric and inhumane that we will not permit them to be imposed on anyone, no matter how opprobrious the offense. If there are some punishments that are so barbaric that they may not be imposed for the commission of crimes, designated by our social system as the most thoroughly reprehensible acts an individual can commit, then . . . similar punishments may not be imposed on persons for less culpable acts, such as breaches of school discipline. Thus, if it is constitutionally impermissible to cut off someone's ear for the commission of murder, it must be unconstitutional to cut off a child's ear for being late to class. Although there were no ears cut off in this case, the record reveals beatings so severe that if they were inflicted on a hardened criminal for the commission of a serious crime, they might not pass constitutional muster.

Nevertheless, the majority holds that the Eighth Amendment "was designed to protect [only] those convicted of crimes," relying on a vague and inconclusive recitation of the history of the Amendment. . . . Certainly the fact that the Framers did not choose to insert the word "criminal" into the language of the Eighth Amendment is strong evidence that the Amendment was designed to prohibit all inhumane or barbaric punishments, no matter what the nature of the offense for which the punishment is imposed.

No one can deny that spanking of schoolchildren is "punishment" under any reasonable reading of the word, for the similarities between spanking in public schools and other forms of punishment are too obvious to ignore. Like other forms of punishment, spanking of schoolchildren involves an institutionalized response to the violation of some official rule or regulation proscribing certain conduct and is imposed for the purpose of rehabilitating the offender, deterring the offender and others like him from committing the violation in the future, and inflicting some measure of social retribution for the harm that has been done.

. . .

. . .

The essence of the majority's argument is that schoolchildren do not need Eighth Amendment protection because corporal punishment is less subject to abuse in the public schools than it is in the prison system. However, it cannot be reasonably suggested that just because cruel and unusual punishments may occur less frequently under public scrutiny, they will not occur at all. The mere fact that a public flogging or a public execution would be available for all to see would not render the punishment constitutional if it were otherwise impermissible. Similarly, the majority would not suggest that a prisoner

JUSTICE LEWIS F. POWELL, JR. (1907–1998) was born in a suburb of Norfolk, Virginia. He went to Washington & Lee College for both undergraduate and law school study and also took a year at Harvard Law School. After service in World War II as an Air Force intelligence officer, he launched a career in corporate law in Virginia and became increasingly active in local affairs in Richmond. As chairman of the Richmond School Board between 1952 and 1961, he defended racial segregation in the schools during a time when much of the South had declared a policy of "massive resistance" to *Brown v. Board of Education*. President Richard Nixon appointed Powell to the Supreme Court in 1971. He retired in 1987.

HIGHLIGHTS

➤ Powell served in North Africa during World War II and was decorated with the Legion of Merit, the Bronze Star, and the French Croix de Guerre. He was instrumental in cracking the Nazis' secret ULTRA code.

➤ As a lawyer, Powell was a member of the board of directors of eleven large corporations over a period of time, including Philip Morris.

who is placed in a minimum-security prison and permitted to go home to his family on the weekends should be any less entitled to Eighth Amendment protections than his counterpart in a maximum-security prison. In short, if a punishment is so barbaric and inhumane that it goes beyond the tolerance of a civilized society, its openness to public scrutiny should have nothing to do with its constitutional validity.

Nor is it an adequate answer that schoolchildren may have other state and constitutional remedies available to them. Even assuming that the remedies available to public school students are adequate under Florida law, the availability of state remedies has never been determinative of the coverage or of the protections afforded by the Eighth Amendment. The reason is obvious. The fact that a person may have a state-law cause of action against a public official who tortures him with a thumbscrew for the commission of an antisocial act has nothing to do with the fact that such official conduct is cruel and unusual punishment prohibited by the Eighth Amendment.

D

By holding that the Eighth Amendment protects only criminals, the majority adopts the view that one is entitled to the protections afforded by the Eighth Amendment only if he is punished for acts that are sufficiently opprobrious for society to make them "criminal."

The issue presented in this phase of the case is limited to whether corporal punishment in public schools can *ever* be prohibited by the Eighth Amendment. I am therefore not suggesting that spanking in the public schools is in every instance prohibited by the Eighth Amendment. My own view is that it is not. I only take issue with the extreme view of the majority that corporal punishment in public schools, no matter how barbaric, inhumane, or severe, is never limited by the Eighth Amendment. Where corporal punishment becomes so severe as to be unacceptable in a civilized society, I can see no reason that it should become any more acceptable just because it is inflicted on children in the public schools.

EXERCISE 6.4. The Supreme Court has often said that the Eighth Amendment prohibits two kinds of government practices: those that were cruel and unusual when the Constitution was written, and those that offend the "evolving standards" of decency of the society. Do you think that the standards of American society have changed sufficiently in the last two decades such that corporal punishment today might violate the Eighth Amendment? Why or why not? Are we becoming a more or less violent society?

EXERCISE 6.5. Even though a specific action may not be unconstitutional, we often say that its commission makes for *bad policy*. Does corporal punishment make for bad policy or good policy? Assume that the school board for your community asks you to draft a policy for elementary, junior high, and high school teachers on the use of physical punishment in the classroom. Draft a policy on when, if ever, physical force or corporal punishment may be used against students in the classroom. Present it to your classmates as if they were members of the school board and give them the opportunity to ask questions about your policy.

Corporal Punishment in the Aftermath of *Ingraham v. Wright*

Ingraham v. Wright was a huge disappointment to the opponents of corporal punishment in the schools, but they redoubled their efforts to ban the practice over the next two decades. At the time of the decision in 1977, only two states banned corporal punishment, but by 1998 twenty-five states banned corporal punishment outright and even in those states that had not gotten rid of it, many counties and cities had adopted their own policies against the practice.

Furthermore, while *Ingraham* established that corporal punishment in schools does not violate the Eighth Amendment, a number of federal circuit courts have found that *excessive* physical force against students *does* violate their due process rights. In the 1980 case of *Hall v. Tawney,* the Fourth Circuit Court of Appeals allowed money damages to a seventh-grade student who had been beaten so severely with a thick rubber paddle that she had to receive emergency medical treatment and was hospitalized for ten days.

Similarly, the Tenth Circuit allowed for money damages in a civil rights lawsuit based on extreme corporal punishment in the 1987 case of *Garcia v. Miera.* The plaintiff in *Garcia,* a nine-year-old student, was held upside down by her ankles while the school principal beat her on the front of her legs with a paddle that was "split right down the middle, so it was two pieces, and when it hit it clapped and grabbed." After the paddling, the student's classroom teacher noticed blood coming through her clothes. The student's injuries left a permanent scar. Responding to complaints from the student's parents, the principal agreed not to spank the child again without first contacting her parents. But the student was again seriously injured a month later.

The Third Circuit, in the 1988 case of *Metzger v. Osbeck,* also allowed students to sue schools for injuries suffered in severe attacks by teachers. In *Metzger,* a teacher punished a student for using abusive language by choking the student while lifting him from the ground. The student lost consciousness and fell face down on a concrete floor suffering lip lacerations, a broken nose, broken teeth, and other injuries.

The courts have generally allowed students to recover money damages against schools where there is a severe injury and the force applied was wholly disproportionate to the underlying problem or misbehavior.

EXERCISE 6.6. What do you think leads to scandalous types of violent incidents like these? What can be done to prevent violence in schools?

EXERCISE 6.7. Research how much violence there is in the schools in your community—both among students and teachers or other employees—and then what sorts of things are being done to stop it. What strategies and policies can you suggest, based on your research and interviews, to reduce violence and "increase the peace" in your community?

Notes

1. "The Court itself recognizes that the requirements it imposes are, 'if anything, less than a fair-minded school principal would impose upon himself in order to avoid unfair suspensions.'"

2. "The psychological injuries so perceived were as follows:

'1. The suspension is a blow to the student's self-esteem.
'2. The student feels powerless and helpless.
'3. The student views school authorities and teachers with resentment, suspicion and fear.
'4. The student learns withdrawal as a mode of problem solving.
'5. The student has little perception of the reasons for the suspension. He does not know what offending acts he committed.
'6. The student is stigmatized by his teachers and school administrators as a deviant. They expect the student to be a troublemaker in the future.'"

3. "There is, no doubt, a school of modern psychological or psychiatric persuasion that maintains that *any* discipline of the young is detrimental. Whatever one may think of the wisdom of this unproved theory, it hardly affords dependable support for a *constitu-*

tional decision. Moreover, even the theory's proponents would concede that the magnitude of injury depends primarily upon the individual child or teenager. A classroom reprimand by the teacher may be more traumatic to the shy, timid introvert than expulsion would be to the aggressive, rebellious extrovert. In my view we tend to lose our sense of perspective and proportion in a case of this kind. For average, normal children—the vast majority—suspension for a few days is simply not a detriment; it is a commonplace occurrence, with some 10% of all students being suspended; it leaves no scars; affects no reputations; indeed, it often may be viewed by the young as a badge of some distinction and a welcome holiday."

4. "Some half dozen years ago, the Court extended First Amendment rights under limited circumstances to public school pupils. Mr. Justice Black, dissenting, viewed the decision as ushering in 'an entirely new era in which the power to control pupils by the elected "officials of state supported public schools" . . . is in ultimate effect transferred to the Supreme Court.' *Tinker.* There were some who thought Mr. Justice Black was unduly concerned. But his prophecy is now being fulfilled. In the few years since *Tinker* there have been literally hundreds of cases by schoolchildren alleging violation of their constitutional rights. This flood of litigation, between pupils and school authorities, was triggered by a narrowly written First Amendment opinion which I could well have joined on its facts. One can only speculate as to the extent to which public education will be disrupted by giving every school-child the power to contest *in court* any decision made by his teacher which arguably infringes the state-conferred right to education."

5. "In the 1970–1971 school year, Policy 5144 authorized corporal punishment where the failure of other means of seeking cooperation from the student made its use necessary. The regulation specified that the principal should determine the necessity for corporal punishment, that the student should understand the seriousness of the offense and the reason for the punishment, and that the punishment should be administered in the presence of another adult in circumstances not calculated to hold the student up to shame or ridicule. The regulation cautioned against using corporal punishment against a student under psychological or medical treatment, and warned that the person administering the punishment 'must realize his own personal liabilities' in any case of physical injury.

While this litigation was pending in the District Court, the Dade County School Board amended Policy 5144 to standardize the size of the paddles used in accordance with the description in the text, to proscribe striking a child with a paddle elsewhere than on the buttocks, to limit the permissible number of 'licks' (five for elementary and intermediate grades and seven for junior and senior grades), and to require a contemporaneous explanation of the need for the punishment to the student and a subsequent notification to the parents."

6. [Hematoma is defined as] "[a] localized mass of extravasated blood that is relatively or completely confined within an organ or tissue . . . ; the blood is usually clotted (or partly clotted), and, depending on how long it has been there, may manifest various degrees of organization and decolorization."

Read On

Devine, John. *Maximum Security: The Culture of Violence in Inner-City Schools.* Chicago: University of Chicago Press, 1996.

Hoffan, Allan M. *Schools, Violence and Society.* Westport, Conn.: Praeger, 1996.

Hyman, Irwin A. *Corporal Punishment in American Education: Readings in History, Practice, and Alternatives*. Philadelphia: Temple University Press, 1979.

Lantieri, Linda, and Janet Patti. *Waging Peace in Our Schools*. Boston: Beacon Press, 1998.

For Further Information

Parents and Teachers Against Violence in Education (PTAVE) at *www.nospank.org*.

Keep Schools Safe Project at *www.keepschoolssafe.org*.

EQUAL PROTECTION AND THE CONSTITUTIONAL STRUGGLE FOR INTEGRATED SCHOOLS

7

"[N]or shall any State deprive any person of life, liberty, or property, without due process of law; nor deny to any person within its jurisdiction the equal protection of the laws."
THE FOURTEENTH AMENDMENT

All laws involve line-drawing. For example, we allow people age sixteen and over to drive cars but make it illegal for those fifteen and under to drive. The courts accept this classification even though some fifteen-and-a-half-year-olds might make excellent drivers and some seventeen-year-olds poor drivers. The line drawn at age sixteen is thought to be a reasonable one, and the courts do not regard classifications based on age as inherently suspicious or discriminatory. Similarly, the vast majority of counties and municipalities allow people to register to vote in local elections only if they live within the borders of the relevant jurisdiction. The Supreme Court views residency as a reasonable qualification for voting and does not approach residency requirements as demanding any special government justification beyond a "rational basis."

But the Supreme Court's deference to government classifications based on age or residency falls away when it comes to other kinds of line-drawing, most notably differing legal treatment based on race or gender. The Fourteenth Amendment was added to the Constitution in 1868 as part of the Reconstruction effort to purge the Constitution of white supremacy and racism, and so the Court has made it clear that Equal Protection forbids the use of racial categorization to separate, demean, stigmatize, or disadvantage people in our country. Although the framers of the Fourteenth Amendment did not actually have it in mind to protect women against discrimination, in the last quarter of the twentieth century the Supreme Court has taken the broad principle of Equal Protection and used it to invalidate laws that treat women differently from men (barring some very good reason).

The Court has not applied "strict scrutiny" (which applies to racial classifications) or "heightened scrutiny" (which applies to gender classifications) to laws that draw lines according to wealth and money. When you study the last case presented here, *San Antonio Independent School District v. Rodriguez,* consider whether or not you think wealth-based classifications should be treated as inherently suspect.

POINTS TO PONDER

How do the Equal Protection guarantees of the Fourteenth Amendment apply to students in public schools?

- Are our schools today racially integrated? Do students have a right to attend integrated schools or just schools that are not formally segregated?
- Should public education be a fundamental right that is protected by the Constitution?
- Should states be able to fund single-sex schools?
- Should states have to spend proportionately equal resources in local school districts?

The Persistent Legacy of Slavery and Racism

Slavery was America's original sin. It was given the full force of law for centuries, until the Civil War and the Thirteenth Amendment abolished that form of institutionalized cruelty and exploitation. Today, even though most Americans take pride in the diversity of our people, we are still dealing on a daily basis with the complicated legacies of racism and discrimination.

Children in African-American and minority communities have often been the victims of racial exclusion and violence. Yet, the country has placed a large burden of hope on such children to liberate America from the injustices of the past. *Brown v. Board of Education,* perhaps the most famous of the Supreme Court's twentieth-century rulings, is the landmark 1954 case that deals with the rights of black schoolchildren not to be forced by their states into segregated schools. It led to a period of intense struggle—and violence—in which children, especially in the African-American community, were put on the front lines of the effort to create an integrated America.

Brown has become the very symbol of the nation's commitment to an interracial, integrated, and "color-blind" society. It marked a turning point for the Supreme Court, which has most often in our history been a force for racial conservatism. In 1857, in the infamous *Dred Scott* case, the Court upheld the expansion of slavery and found that African-Americans were not "persons" eligible to sue in federal court within the meaning of the Constitution. In 1896, the Court, in *Plessy v. Ferguson,* ruled in support of the Jim Crow doctrine of "separate but equal" by upholding racial segregation in public places and services. It would be more than fifty years before *Brown* would strike at the heart of the *Plessy* decision and herald a radically new direction for the country.

— —

PLESSY
v.
FERGUSON

Supreme Court of the United States
Argued April 13, 1896.
Decided May 18, 1896.

[The plaintiff, Homer Plessy, challenged a Louisiana statute requiring that railway passenger cars have "equal but separate accommodations for the white and colored races." Stating he was "seven-eighths Caucasian and one-eighth African blood" and that "the mixture of colored blood was not discernible in him . . . and that he was entitled to every right [of] the white race," Plessy was arrested and convicted for refusing to leave a seat on a car reserved for whites only.]

Justice BROWN . . . delivered the opinion of the court.

. . .

That [the statute] does not conflict with the thirteenth amendment, which abolished slavery and involuntary servitude, except as a punishment for crime, is too clear for argument. Slavery implies involuntary servitude,—a state of bondage; the ownership of mankind as a chattel, or, at least, the control of the labor and services of one man for the benefit of another, and the absence of a legal right to the disposal of his own person, property, and services. . . . [T]his amendment was regarded by the statesmen of that day as insufficient to protect the colored race from certain laws imposing upon the colored race onerous disabilities and burdens, and curtailing their rights in the pursuit of life, liberty, and property to such an extent that their freedom was of little value; and that the fourteenth amendment was devised to meet this exigency.

The author of this opinion, **JUSTICE HENRY BILLINGS BROWN** (1836–1913), was born into an affluent New England family and received his education at prep school, Yale University, and Harvard Law School. After a career as a marshal, United States Attorney, lawyer, and judge, Brown was appointed by President Benjamin Harrison to the Supreme Court in 1890. He served until 1906.

HIGHLIGHTS

➢   Justice Brown employed a substitute to avoid the draft during the Civil War.

➢   Late in his life, Justice Brown acknowledged that he had been naive to think that the Louisiana statute in *Plessy v. Ferguson* was not meant principally to keep African-Americans out of white train cars.

. . .

The object of the amendment was undoubtedly to enforce the absolute equality of the two races before the law, but, in the nature of things, it could not have been intended to abolish distinctions based upon color, or to enforce social, as distinguished from political, equality, or a commingling of the two races upon terms unsatisfactory to either. Laws permitting, and even requiring, their separation, in places where they are liable to be brought into contact, do not necessarily imply the inferiority of either race to the other, and have been generally, if not universally, recognized as within the competency of the state legislatures in the exercise of their police power. The most common instance of this is connected with the establishment of separate schools for white and colored children, which have been held to be a valid exercise of the legislative power even by courts of states where the political rights of the colored race have been longest and most earnestly enforced.

. . .

Laws forbidding the intermarriage of the two races may be said in a technical sense to interfere with the freedom of contract, and yet have been universally recognized as within the police power of the state. . . .

[The Court lists various State and Federal cases in which segregation on public transportation has been held to be constitutional.]

. . .

. . . [It is suggested] that the same argument that will justify the state legislature in requiring railways to provide separate accommodations for the two races will also authorize them to require separate cars to be provided for people whose hair is of a certain color, or who are aliens, or who belong to certain nationalities, or to enact laws requiring colored people to walk upon one side of the street, and white people upon the other, or requiring white men's houses to be painted white, and colored men's black, or their vehicles or business signs to be of different colors, upon the theory that one side of the street is as good as the other, or that a house or vehicle of one color is as good as one of another color. The reply to all this is that every exercise of the police power must be reasonable, and extend only to such laws as are enacted in good faith for the promotion of the public good, and not for the annoyance or oppression of a particular class.

. . . In determining the question of reasonableness, [the government] is at liberty to act with reference to the established usages, customs, and traditions of the people, and with a view to the promotion of their comfort, and the preservation of the public peace and good order. Gauged by this standard, we cannot say that a law which authorizes or even requires the separation of the two races in public conveyances is unreasonable, or more obnoxious to the fourteenth amendment than the acts of congress requiring separate schools for colored children in the District of Columbia, the constitutionality of which does not seem to have been questioned, or the corresponding acts of state legislatures.

We consider the underlying fallacy of the plaintiff's argument to consist in the assumption that the enforced separation of the two races stamps the colored race with a badge of inferiority. If this be so, it is not by reason of anything found in the act, but solely because the colored race chooses to put that construction upon it. . . . The argument also assumes that social prejudices may be overcome by legislation, and that equal rights cannot be secured to the negro except by an enforced commingling of the two races. We cannot accept this proposition. If the two races are to meet upon terms of social equality, it must be the result of natural affinities, a mutual appreciation of each other's merits, and a voluntary consent of individuals. . . . Legislation is powerless to eradicate racial instincts, or to abolish distinctions based upon physical differences, and the attempt to do so can only result in accentuating the difficulties of the present situation. If the civil and political rights of both races be equal, one cannot be inferior to the other civilly or politically. If one race be inferior to the other socially, the constitution of the United States cannot put them upon the same plane.

. . .

Affirmed.

Justice HARLAN, dissenting.

. . .

. . . [I] deny that any legislative body or judicial tribunal may have regard to the race of citizens when the civil rights of those citizens are involved. . . .

It was said in argument that the statute of Louisiana does not discriminate against either race, but prescribes a rule applicable alike to white and colored citizens. But this argument does not meet the difficulty. Every one knows that [the statute] had its origin in the purpose, not so much to exclude white persons from railroad cars occupied by blacks, as to exclude colored people from coaches occupied by or assigned to white persons. . . . The fundamental objection, therefore, to the statute, is that it interferes with the personal freedom of citizens.

. . .

Under the Jim Crow system of "separate but equal" racial segregation upheld in *Plessy v. Ferguson,* African-American children were segregated from whites and forced to go to underfunded schools with underpaid teachers and poor resources.

The white race deems itself to be the dominant race in this country. And so it is, in prestige, in achievements, in education, in wealth, and in power. So, I doubt not, it will continue to be for all time, if it remains true to its great heritage, and holds fast to the principles of constitutional liberty. But in view of the constitution, in the eye of the law, there is in this country no superior, dominant, ruling class of citizens. There is no caste here. Our constitution is color-blind, and neither knows nor tolerates classes among citizens. In respect of civil rights, all citizens are equal before the law. The humblest is the peer of the most powerful. The law regards man as man, and takes no account of his surroundings or of his color when his civil rights as guaranteed by the supreme law of the land are involved.

In my opinion, the judgment this day rendered will, in time, prove to be quite as pernicious as the decision made by this tribunal in the *Dred Scott Case,* [which held that] the descendants of Africans who were imported into this country, and sold as slaves, were not included nor intended to be included under the word "citizens" in the Constitution; . . . that, at time of the adoption of the Constitution, they were "considered as a subordinate and inferior class of beings, who had been subjugated by the dominant race, and, whether emancipated or not, yet remained subject to their authority, and had no rights or privileges but such as those who held the power and the government might choose to grant them." The recent amendments of the constitution, it was supposed, had eradicated these principles from our institutions. . . . What can more certainly arouse race hate, what more certainly create and perpetuate a feeling of distrust between these races, than state enactments, which, in fact, proceed on the ground that colored citizens are so inferior and degraded that they cannot be allowed to sit in public coaches occupied by white citizens?

. . .

. . . The thin disguise of "equal" accommodations for passengers in railroad coaches will not mislead any one, nor atone for the wrong this day done. . . .

EXERCISE 7.1. Why do you think Homer Plessy argued that he was wrongly classified as "colored" rather than "white" before he even tried to challenge the government's power to segregate by race? Do you think this was a more palatable argument to a racially conservative Supreme Court?

EXERCISE 7.2. The Court in *Plessy* rejected the "slippery slope" argument that allowing states to racially segregate the train cars would also allow them to segregate people according to eye color or hair color or to require people from different groups to paint their houses different colors. "The reply to all this is that every exercise of the police power must be reasonable, and extend only to such laws as are enacted in good faith for the promotion of the public good, and not for the annoyance or oppression of a particular class." Why did the Court think racial segregation was "reasonable"? Why did it not see segregation as annoying and oppressing a "particular class"? Does it make sense to base constitutional rights on the "established usages, customs, and traditions of the people"?

EXERCISE 7.3. What did the Court see as the "underlying fallacy" of the argument against segregation? If there is a stigma attached to segregation, where does it come from? When people of different races live in different neighborhoods or

JUSTICE JOHN MARSHALL HARLAN (1833–1911) was born in Boyle County, Kentucky. He studied nearby at Centre College and acquired his legal education from professors at Transylvania University. President Rutherford B. Hayes appointed him to the Supreme Court in 1877, where he remained until his death.

HIGHLIGHTS

➤ Harlan was named for then–Chief Justice John Marshall.

➤ Harlan opposed the secessionists during the Civil War, although he firmly believed in a slave owner's right to slaves as property.

➤ He also opposed the Emancipation Proclamation and Thirteenth Amendment, abolishing slavery.

➤ Harlan formed and fought with the 10th Kentucky Volunteers during the Civil War.

➤ He was raised to defend slavery but came to abhor racists.

hang out in different social milieus, what message does it send to young people? What message is sent when young people only eat and hang out with people of their own racial group?

In *Plessy,* the Court upheld the segregationist doctrine of "separate but equal" in public accommodations. More than fifty years later, the Court, in *Brown,* found that "in the field of public education the doctrine of 'separate but equal' has no place." The Court in 1954 ruled that "[s]eparate educational facilities are inherently unequal." Between 1896, when the Court found that the Equal Protection Clause *allows* racially segregated public facilities, and 1954, when it found that the Equal Protection Clause *disallows* racially segregated public facilities, the language of the Constitution did not change. So what did change? Why did the Supreme Court (with an entirely new membership) make a U-turn in its reading of the Constitution? What does the reversal teach us about the nature of Supreme Court interpretation? Does it consist of science, logic, morality, or politics, or some combination thereof?

——

BROWN

v.

BOARD OF EDUCATION OF TOPEKA

Supreme Court of the United States
Argued Dec. 9, 1952.
Reargued Dec. 7, 8, 9, 1953.
Decided May 17, 1954.

Chief Justice WARREN delivered the opinion of the Court.

These cases come to us from the States of Kansas, South Carolina, Virginia, and Delaware.

In each of the cases, minors of the Negro race, through their legal representatives, seek the aid of the courts in obtaining admission to the public schools of their community on a nonsegregated basis. In each instance, they have been denied admission to schools attended by white children under laws requiring or permitting segregation according to race. This segregation was alleged to deprive the plaintiffs of the equal protection of the laws under the Fourteenth Amendment. [Segregation has been legally justified by] the so-called "separate but equal" doctrine announced by this Court in *Plessy v. Ferguson.* Under that doctrine, equality of treatment is accorded when the races are provided substantially equal facilities, even though these facilities be separate.

The plaintiffs contend that segregated public schools are not "equal" and cannot be made "equal," and that hence they are deprived of the equal protection of the laws.

Reargument was largely devoted to the circumstances surrounding the adoption of the Fourteenth Amendment in 1868. . . . The most avid proponents of the post-War Amendments undoubtedly intended them to remove all legal distinctions among "all persons born or naturalized in the United States." Their opponents, just as certainly, were antagonistic to both the letter and the spirit of the Amendments and wished them to have the most limited effect. What others in Congress and the state legislatures had in mind cannot be determined with any degree of certainty.

. . .

In the first cases in this Court construing the Fourteenth Amendment, decided shortly after its adoption, the Court interpreted it as proscribing all state-imposed discriminations against the Negro race. The doctrine of "separate but equal" did not make its appearance in this court until 1896 in the case of *Plessy v. Ferguson,* involving not education but transportation. American courts have since labored with the doctrine for over half a century.

In the instant cases . . . there are findings . . . that the Negro and white schools involved have been equalized, or are being equalized, with respect to buildings, curricula, qualifications and salaries of teachers, and other "tangible" factors. Our decision, therefore, cannot turn on merely a comparison of these tangible factors in the Negro and white schools involved in each of the cases. We must look instead to the effect of segregation itself on public education.

In approaching this problem, we cannot turn the clock back to 1868 when the Amendment was adopted, or even to 1896 when *Plessy v. Ferguson* was written. We must consider public education in the light of its full development and its present place in American life throughout the Nation. Only in this way can it be determined if segregation in public schools deprives these plaintiffs of the equal protection of the laws.

Today, education is perhaps the most important function of state and local governments. Compulsory school attendance laws and the great expenditures for education both demonstrate our recognition of the importance of education to our democratic society. It is required in the performance of our most basic public responsibilities, even service in the armed forces. It is the very foundation of good citizenship. Today it is a principal instrument in awakening the child to cultural values, in preparing him for later professional training, and in helping him to adjust normally to his environment. In these days, it is doubtful that any child may reasonably be expected to succeed in life if he is denied the opportunity of an education. Such an opportunity, where the state has undertaken to provide it, is a right which must be made available to all on equal terms.

We come then to the question presented: Does segregation of children in public schools solely on the basis of race, even though the physical facilities and other "tangible" factors may be equal, deprive the children of the minority group of equal educational opportunities? We believe that it does.

In *Sweatt v. Painter,* in finding that a segregated law school for Negroes could not provide them equal educational opportunities, this Court relied in large part on "those qualities which are incapable of objective measurement but which make for greatness in a law school." In *McLaurin v. Oklahoma State Regents,* the Court, in requiring that a Negro admitted to a white graduate school be treated like all other students, again resorted to intangible considerations: ". . . his ability to study, to engage in discussions and exchange views with other students, and, in general, to learn his profession." Such considerations apply with added force to children in grade and high schools. To separate them from others of similar age and qualifications solely because of their race generates a feeling of inferiority as to their status in the community that may affect their hearts and minds in a way unlikely ever to be undone. The effect of this separation on their educational opportunities was well stated by a finding in the Kansas case by a court which nevertheless felt compelled to rule against the Negro plaintiffs:

> "Segregation of white and colored children in public schools has a detrimental effect upon the colored children. The impact is greater when it has the sanction of the law; for the policy of separating the races is usually interpreted as denoting the inferiority of the negro group. A sense of inferiority affects the motivation of a child to learn. Segregation with the sanction of law, therefore, has a tendency to [retard] the educational and mental development of Negro children and to deprive them of some of the benefits they would receive in a racial[ly] integrated school system."

Whatever may have been the extent of psychological knowledge at the time of *Plessy v. Ferguson*, this finding is amply supported by modern authority.[1] Any language in *Plessy v. Ferguson* contrary to this finding is rejected.

We conclude that in the field of public education the doctrine of "separate but equal" has no place. Separate educational facilities are inherently unequal. Therefore, we hold that the plaintiffs and others similarly situated for whom the actions have been brought are, by reason of the segregation complained of, deprived of the equal protection of the laws guaranteed by the Fourteenth Amendment.

. . . We have now announced that . . . segregation is a denial of the equal protection of the laws.

It is so ordered.

Spottswood Bolling, shown here rejoicing with his mother, Sarah, was one of five Washington, D.C. youngsters who served as plaintiffs in *Bolling v. Sharpe*, which struck down the congressionally authorized segregation of public schools in the District of Columbia.

EXERCISE 7.4. The *Brown* Court found segregation unconstitutional because it had such a negative effect on black children: "To separate them from others of similar age and qualifications solely because of their race generates a feeling of inferiority as to their status in the community that may affect their hearts and minds in a way unlikely ever to be undone." What do you think of this as the rationale for the Court's holding? Contrast it with the following hypothetical rationales that the Court might have used:

A. "To segregate white and black children solely because of their race generates a feeling of false inferiority in the black children and a feeling of false superiority in the white children that may affect their hearts and minds in a way unlikely ever to be undone."
B. "Segregation is a creation of white supremacy, which was invalidated by the Thirteenth Amendment's ban on slavery and the Fourteenth Amendment's guarantee of Equal Protection."
C. "The Constitution is color-blind, and so government may never take race into account for any purpose whatsoever."
D. "The premise of American democracy is freedom for all persons, but there is no freedom where the state segregates people on the basis of race."

What do you think is the best way to articulate what is wrong with racial segregation? How well did the Supreme Court do in its analysis? Choose the rationale you think best meets this purpose, either from the choices listed above or on your own, and defend your choice in a one-page essay.

EXERCISE 7.5. The Court in *Brown* seems to assume that all students are either black or white. Where do you suppose children who are neither "black" nor "white" fit into the picture? Do you think that the presence of millions of Hispanic, Asian-American, and Native American children in the United States improves the prospects for good race relations? What about students who cannot be readily categorized or who refuse to be defined or classified by race?

JUSTICE EARL WARREN (1891–1974) was born to a working-class family in Los Angeles and labored on the railroads as a boy. He worked his way through college and law school at the University of California. He had served as a district attorney, state attorney general, and three-term governor when, in 1953, President Dwight Eisenhower appointed him to the Supreme Court. He retired in 1969.

HIGHLIGHTS

➤ Warren was the first governor of California to be elected three times. In one primary election, he won both the Republican and Democratic nomination.

➤ Justice Warren was chair of the commission that investigated the assassination of President John F. Kennedy, a commission that continues to be controversial even today.

➤ As attorney general of California and a candidate for governor, Warren favored the internment and relocation of persons of Japanese ancestry on the West Coast during World War II. Yet, he became a key force on the Court against racial discrimination and segregation. Justice Warren later called his decision to back the internment of Japanese-Americans the major regret of his life.

Many people think that by allowing busing and limited affirmative action in education, the Court has followed through on the promise of *Brown*. Others, noting the Court's growing hostility to affirmative action and opposition to inter–school district remedies, think that the Court has taken up its former, passive role in the face of racism. Still others think that the Court should have no special commitment to racial integration and justice but should simply make sure that government is always "color-blind" in its policies. What do you think? Are we an integrated society today? Do we have integrated schools?

Two Steps Forward, One Step Back: "Massive Resistance" and Reaction to *Brown*

While the *Brown* decision was met with jubilation in the African-American community and among its civil rights allies in other racial groups, the decision set off a furious reaction among whites in the states of the Deep South. Almost every elected official from governors to school board members denounced the *Brown* decision and the Court in harsh terms. Herman Talmadge, the governor of Georgia, proclaimed in 1954 that "[b]lood will flow in the rivers." In Virginia, politicians and the white Establishment declared a policy of "Massive Resistance" to federally sanctioned desegregation. Ku Klux Klan membership swelled across the South, and racist violence spread. Many cars in the South featured bumper stickers that read: "Impeach Earl Warren."

One of the states where white politicians swore they would never integrate was Arkansas. There, Gov. Orval Faubus, on September 2, 1957, declared that "blood will run in the streets" if black children tried to attend Central High School. He ordered Arkansas national guardsmen to surround Central High to stop any attempt at integrating the student body. Elizabeth Eckford, an African-American high school student at the time, relates what it was like to be a black student trying to integrate Central High in the face of official hostility and mob violence:

> [The Arkansas national guardsmen] glared at me with a mean look and I was very frightened and didn't know what to do. I turned around and the crowd came toward me.
>
> They moved closer and closer. Somebody started yelling "Lynch her! Lynch her!"
>
> I tried to see a friendly face somewhere in the mob—someone who maybe would help. I looked into the face of an old woman and it seemed a kind face, but when I looked at her again, she spat on me.
>
> They came closer, shouting "No nigger bitch is going to get in our school. Get out of here![2]

Elizabeth did not make it into the school that day although she escaped with her life. Black students did not successfully integrate Central High School until the Supreme Court made it clear that the state had no power to stand in the way and President Dwight Eisenhower federalized the National Guard and ordered the troops to guarantee the safe passage of the students against the screaming mobs.

The following Supreme Court case made it clear that the defiance of government officials in Arkansas was unconstitutional and no state could exempt itself from the commands of Equal Protection and the Supremacy Clause, which makes the Constitution and federal laws supreme to state laws and power.

———

COOPER
v.
AARON

Supreme Court of the United States
Argued Sept. 11, 1958.
Decided Sept. 12, 1958.
Opinion announced Sept. 29, 1958.

[The school board of Little Rock, Arkansas, filed a petition to postpone desegregation plans of public schools due to "extreme public hostility." The district court granted the relief sought and the court of appeals reversed.]

Opinion of the Court by Chief Justice WARREN, Justice BLACK, Justice FRANKFURTER, Justice DOUGLAS, Justice HARLAN, Justice BRENNAN, and Justice WHITTAKER.

. . . We are urged to uphold a suspension of the Little Rock School Board's plan to do away with segregated public schools in Little Rock until state laws and efforts to upset and nullify our holding in *Brown v. Board of Education* have been further challenged and tested in the courts. We reject these contentions.

. . .

The constitutional rights of [the children] are not to be sacrificed or yielded to the violence and disorder which have followed upon the actions of the Governor and Legislature. As this Court said some 41 years ago in an unanimous opinion in a case involving another aspect of racial segregation: "It is urged that this proposed segregation will promote the public peace[,] . . . this aim cannot be accomplished by laws or ordinances which deny rights created or protected by the Federal Constitution." Thus law and order are not here to be preserved by depriving the Negro children of their constitutional rights.

. . . The command of the Fourteenth Amendment is that no "State" shall deny to any person within its jurisdiction the equal protection of the laws. . . . "Whoever, by virtue of

Nine African-American students leave the army station wagon that drove them to Central High School the morning of September 26, 1957. Two jeeps and paratroopers of the 101st airborne division form a tight cordon around them as they enter the school.

public position under a State government, . . . denies or takes away the equal protection of the laws, violates the constitutional inhibition; and as he acts in the name and for the State, and is clothed with the State's power, his act is that of the State. This must be so, or the constitutional prohibition has no meaning."

. . .

It is, of course, quite true that the responsibility for public education is primarily the concern of the States, but it is equally true that such responsibilities, like all other state activity, must be exercised consistently with federal constitutional requirements as they apply to state action. The Constitution created a government dedicated to equal justice under law. The Fourteenth Amendment embodied and emphasized that ideal. State support of segregated schools through any arrangement . . . cannot be squared with the Amendment's command that no State shall deny to any person within its jurisdiction the equal protection of the laws. The right of a student not to be segregated on racial grounds in schools so maintained is indeed so fundamental and pervasive that it is embraced in the concept of due process of law. The basic decision in *Brown* was unanimously reached by this Court . . . , and that decision is now unanimously reaffirmed. The principles announced in that decision and the obedience of the States to them, according to the command of the Constitution, are indispensable for the protection of the freedoms guaranteed by our fundamental charter for all of us. Our constitutional ideal of equal justice under law is thus made a living truth.

[*Reversed.*]

Just as white politicians in Arkansas used any legal or illegal means they could scare up to block the schoolhouse doors, white politicians in Virginia experimented with even more creative ways to stop desegregation. The school board in Prince Edward County, Virginia, simply closed down the public schools and reopened them as state-supported private schools. In *Griffin v. County School Board of Prince Edward County,* the Supreme Court also rejected that tactic. What was its reasoning?

—— ——

GRIFFIN
v.
COUNTY SCHOOL BOARD OF PRINCE EDWARD COUNTY

Supreme Court of the United States
Argued March 30, 1964.
Decided May 25, 1964.

[In 1959, following the order of the Supreme Court to desegregate public schools, Prince Edward County, Virginia, closed its public schools. In their place, private, for-white-students-only schools were supported by state and local authorities.]

Justice BLACK

. . .

. . . Having as early as 1956 resolved that they would not operate public schools "wherein white and colored children are taught together," the Supervisors of Prince Edward County refused to levy any school taxes for the 1959–1960 school year. . . . As a result, the country's public schools did not reopen in the fall of 1959 and have remained closed ever since, although the public schools of every other county in Virginia have continued to operate. . . . An offer to set up private schools for colored children in the county was rejected, the Negroes of Prince Edward preferring to continue the legal battle for desegregated public schools, and colored children were without formal education from 1959 to 1963, when federal, state, and county authorities cooperated to have classes conducted for Negroes and whites in school buildings owned by the county.

For reasons to be stated, we agree with the District Court that, under the circumstances here, closing the Prince Edward County school while public schools in all the other counties of Virginia were being maintained denied the petitioners and the class of Negro students they represent the equal protection of the laws guaranteed by the Fourteenth Amendment.

. . .

II

. . .

Virginia law, as here applied, unquestionably treats the school children of Prince Edward differently from the way it treats the school children of all other Virginia counties. Prince Edward children must go to a private school or none at all; all other Virginia children can go to public schools. Closing Prince Edward's schools bears more heavily on Negro children in Prince Edward County since white children there have accredited private schools which they can attend, while colored children until very recently have had no available private schools, and even the school they now attend is a temporary expedient. Apart from this expedient, the result is that Prince Edward County school children, if they go to school in their own county, must go to racially segregated schools which, although designated as private, are beneficiaries of county and state support.

A State, of course, has a wide discretion in deciding whether laws shall operate statewide or shall operate only in certain counties. . . . But the record in the present case could not be clearer that Prince Edward's public schools were closed and private schools operated in their place with state and county assistance, for one reason, and one reason only: to ensure, through measures taken by the county and the State, that white and colored children in Prince Edward County would not, under any circumstances, go to the same school. Whatever nonracial grounds might support a State's allowing a county to abandon public schools, the object must be a constitutional one, and grounds of race and opposition to desegregation do not qualify as constitutional.

. . . Accordingly, we agree with the District Court that closing the Prince Edward schools and meanwhile contributing to the support of the private segregated white schools that took their place denied petitioners the equal protection of the laws.

In cases like *Cooper* and *Griffin,* the Court was able to knock down the most overt brands of resistance to desegregating public schools. It also disallowed schemes that maintained separate black and white schools but gave individual students the freedom to "switch" from one to another. In *Swann v. Charlotte-Mecklenburg Board of Education* (1971), the Court also gave district courts enforcing *Brown* the green light to order the busing of students from one neighborhood to another—a controversial practice that led to brutal racist violence in many places, including Boston.

However hard courts tried to make integration work, in many places official attempts to evade *Brown*'s mandate were ingenious and successful. Yet even where desegregation did take hold, the underlying social dynamics often would not cooperate. In a sociological sense, the heart of the problem was "white flight," as countless white families decided to move rather than face the possibility of integration. With whites relocating across city and county lines in order to escape the implications of *Brown,* the question became whether courts could follow them by ordering desegregation and busing across school district lines.

In the next case, *Milliken v. Bradley* (1974), the Supreme Court found that federal courts may not normally order desegregation plans that cut across the lines of different school districts. A lower court had tried to order a desegregation plan that included not only Detroit but fifty-three neighboring suburbs. The Supreme Court rejected this approach, finding that municipal boundary lines were not automatically part of the problem of racial segregation and must be respected by the judiciary. Many people believe that this decision undermined *Brown* and encouraged white flight to the suburbs, halting the forward progress that had been made since 1954. What do you think of this decision? What do the dissenters say?

—•—

MILLIKEN
v.
BRADLEY

Supreme Court of the United States
Argued Feb. 27, 1974.
Decided July 25, 1974.

Chief Justice BURGER delivered the opinion of the Court.

We granted certiorari . . . to determine whether a federal court may impose a multidistrict, area-wide remedy to single-district *de jure* segregation problem absent any finding that the other included school districts have failed to operate unitary school systems within their districts, [and] absent any claim or finding that the boundary lines of any affected school district were established with the purpose of fostering racial segregation in public schools. . . .

. . .

II

Ever since *Brown v. Board of Education,* judicial consideration of school desegregation cases has begun with the standard:

"[I]n the field of public education the doctrine of 'separate by equal' has no place. Separate educational facilities are inherently unequal."

The target of the *Brown* holding was clear and forthright: the elimination of state-mandated or deliberately maintained dual school systems. . . . This duality and racial segregation were held to violate the Constitution. . . . In further refining the remedial process . . . the task is to correct, by a balancing of the individual and collective interests, "the condition that offends the Constitution." A federal remedial power may be exercised "only on the basis of a constitutional violation" and, "[a]s with any equity case, the nature of the violation determines the scope of the remedy."

. . . The District Court abruptly rejected the proposed Detroit-only plans. . . . Consequently, the court reasoned, it was imperative to "look beyond the limits of the Detroit school district for a solution . . . " since "school district lines are simply matters of political convenience and may not be used to deny constitutional rights."

. . .

. . . [I]t is obvious from the scope of the interdistrict remedy itself that absent a complete restructuring of the laws of Michigan relating to school districts the District Court will become first, a *de facto* "legislative authority.". . .

Of course, no state law is above the Constitution. School district lines and the present laws with respect to local control are not sacrosanct, and if they conflict with the Fourteenth Amendment federal courts have a duty to prescribe appropriate remedies. . . . But our prior holdings have been confined to violations and remedies within a single school district. We therefore turn to address, for the first time, the validity of a remedy mandating cross-district or interdistrict consolidation to remedy a condition of segregation found to exist in only one district.

The controlling principle consistently expounded in our holdings is that the scope of the remedy is determined by the nature and extent of the constitutional violation. Before the boundaries of separate and autonomous school districts may be set aside by consolidating the separate units for remedial purposes or by imposing a cross-district remedy, it must first be shown that there has been constitutional violation within one district that produces a significant segregative effect in another district. Specifically, it must be shown that racially discriminatory acts of the state or local school districts, or of single school district, have been a substantial cause of interdistrict segregation. Thus an interdistrict remedy might be in order where the racially discriminatory acts of one or more school districts caused racial segregation in an adjacent district, or where district lines have been deliberately drawn on the basis of race. In such circumstances an interdistrict remedy would be appropriate to eliminate the interdistrict segregation directly caused by the constitutional violation. Conversely, without an interdistrict violation and interdistrict effect, there is no constitutional wrong calling for an interdistrict remedy. . . .

With no showing of significant violation by the 53 outlying school districts and no evidence of any interdistrict violation or effect, the court went beyond the original theory of the case . . . and mandated a metropolitan remedy. To approve the remedy ordered by the court would impose on the outlying districts, not shown to have committed any constitutional violation, a wholly impermissible remedy based on a standard not hinted at in *Brown I* and *II* or any holding of this Court.

. . .

IV

. . .

. . . We conclude that the relief ordered by the District Court and affirmed by the Court of Appeals was based upon an erroneous standard and was unsupported by record evidence that acts of the outlying districts effected the discrimination found to exist in the schools of Detroit. Accordingly the judgment of the Court of Appeals is reversed and the case is remanded for further proceedings consistent with this opinion. . . .

Reversed and remanded.

Justice DOUGLAS, dissenting.

The Court of Appeals has acted responsibly in these cases and we should affirm its judgment.

. . . Here the Michigan educational system is unitary, maintained and supported by the legislature and under the general supervision of the State Board of Education. . . . State action is indeed challenged as violating the Equal Protection Clause. Whatever the reach of that claim may be, it certainly is aimed at discrimination based on race.

. . .

When we rule against the metropolitan area remedy we take a step that will likely put the problems of the blacks and our society back to the period that antedated the "separate but equal" regime.

Today's decision, given *Rodriguez* [*San Antonio School District v. Rodriguez*, holding that each school district must pay its own way], means that there is no violation of the Equal Protection Clause though the schools are segregated by race and though the black schools are not only "separate" but "inferior."

Justice WHITE, with whom Justice DOUGLAS, Justice BRENNAN, and Justice MARSHALL join, dissenting.

[The Court does not] question the obligation of the federal courts to devise a feasible and effective remedy. But it promptly cripples the ability of the judiciary to perform this task, which is of fundamental importance to our constitutional system, by fashioning a strict rule that remedies, in school cases, must stop at the school district line unless certain other conditions are met.

Regretfully, and for several reasons, I can join neither the Court's judgment nor its opinion. The core of my disagreement is that deliberate acts of segregation and their consequences will go unremedied, not because a remedy would be infeasible or unreasonable in terms of the usual criteria governing school desegregation cases, but because an effective remedy would cause what the Court considers to be undue administrative inconvenience to the State. The result is that the State of Michigan, the entity at which the Fourteenth Amendment is directed, has successfully insulated itself from its duty to provide effective desegregation remedies. . . .

I am . . . mystified as to how the Court can ignore the legal reality that the constitutional violations, even if occurring locally, were committed by governmental entities for which the state is responsible and that it is the State that must respond to the command of the Fourteenth Amendment. An interdistrict remedy for the infringements that occurred in this case is well within the confines and powers of the State, which is the governmental entity ultimately responsible for desegregating its schools.

I am therefore constrained to record my disagreement and dissent.

Justice MARSHALL, with whom Justice DOUGLAS, Justice BRENNAN, and Justice WHITE join, dissenting.

. . .

. . . [T]he Court today takes a giant step backwards. Notwithstanding a record showing widespread and pervasive racial segregation in the educational system provided by the State of Michigan for children in Detroit, this Court holds that the District Court was powerless to require the State to remedy its constitutional violation in any meaningful fashion. Ironically purporting to base its result on the principle that the scope of the remedy in a desegregation case should be determined by the nature and the extent of the constitutional violation, the Court's answer is to provide no remedy at all for the violation proved in this case, thereby guaranteeing that Negro children in Detroit will receive the same separate and inherently unequal education in the future as they have been unconstitutionally afforded in the past.

. . .

The rights at issue in this case are too fundamental to be abridged on grounds as superficial as those relied on by the majority today. . . . Our Nation, I fear, will be ill served by the Court's refusal to remedy separate and unequal education, for unless our children begin to learn together, there is little hope that our people will ever learn to live together.

. . .

III

. . .

Desegregation is not and was never expected to be an easy task. Racial attitudes ingrained in our Nation's childhood and adolescence are not quickly thrown aside in its middle years. But just as the inconvenience of some cannot be allowed to stand in the way of the rights of others, so public opposition, no matter how strident, cannot be permitted to divert this Court from the enforcement of the constitutional principles at issue in this case. Today's holding, I fear, is more a reflection of a perceived public mood that we have gone far enough in enforcing the Constitution's guarantee of equal justice than it is the product of neutral principles of law. In the short run, it may seem to be an easier course to allow our great metropolitan areas to be divided up each into two cities—one white, the other black—but it is a course, I predict, our people will ultimately regret. I dissent.

EXERCISE 7.6. Do you think that the suburban and urban schools in your area have racially distinctive populations? If so, do you think that the political boundary lines present an obstacle to meaningful integration of students?

As the Supreme Court grew more conservative in the last three decades of the twentieth century, it seemed to lose much of the fervor and energy it once had for promoting an end to segregated schools. In the following case, *Missouri v. Jenkins*, the Court overturned efforts by a district court to encourage integration in Kansas City, Missouri, by ordering the creation of an urban magnet school with well-paid teachers that would be able to attract students from the mostly white suburban and private schools. The majority in this decision finds that such relief goes too far. Why?

— — —

MISSOURI
v.
JENKINS

Supreme Court of the United States
Argued Jan. 11, 1995.
Decided June 12, 1995.

[Throughout eighteen years of litigation the federal court had finally decided that the Kansas City Missouri School District (KCMSD) effectively operated a segregated school system. Accordingly, the district court ordered the KCMSD to apply desegregation plans that included statewide measures. In addition, in 1986 the court ordered the implementation of a magnet school program to draw non-minority students into the inner-city district schools. This case challenged the ability of the district court to order the city to levy taxes in order to fund the desegregation programs.]

Chief Justice REHNQUIST delivered the opinion of the Court.

. . .

. . . In June 1985 the District Court issued its first remedial order and established as its goal the "elimination of all vestiges of state-imposed segregation."

. . .

The District Court . . . set out to desegregate the KCMSD but believed that "[t]o accomplish desegregation within the boundary lines of a school district whose enrollment remains 68.3% black is a difficult task." . . . [T]he District Court determined that "achievement of AAA status, improvement of the quality of education being offered at the KCMSD schools, magnet schools, as well as other components of this desegregation plan, can serve to maintain and hopefully attract non-minority student enrollment."

In November 1986 the District Court approved a comprehensive magnet school and capital improvements plan and held the State and the KCMSD jointly and severally liable for its funding.

. . .

. . . We granted certiorari to consider the following: (1) whether the District Court exceeded its constitutional authority when it granted salary increases to virtually all . . . employees of the KCMSD, and (2) whether the District Court properly relied upon the fact that student achievement test scores had failed to rise to some unspecified level when it declined to find that the State had achieved partial unitary status as to the quality education programs.

III

. . .

Almost 25 years ago, in *Swann v. Charlotte-Mecklenburg Bd. of Ed.,* we dealt with the authority of a district court to fashion remedies for a school district that had been segregated in law in violation of the Equal Protection Clause of the Fourteenth Amendment. Although recognizing the discretion that must necessarily adhere in a district court in fashioning a remedy, we also recognized the limits on such remedial power:

> "Elimination of racial discrimination in public schools is a large task and one that should not be retarded by efforts to achieve broader purposes lying beyond the jurisdiction of the school authorities. One vehicle can carry only a limited amount of baggage. It would not serve the important objective of *Brown* to seek to use school desegregation cases for purposes beyond their scope, although desegregation of schools ultimately will have impact on other forms of discrimination."

. . .

. . . [I]n *Milliken v. Bradley*, we articulated a three-part framework derived from our prior cases to guide district courts in the exercise of their remedial authority.

"In the first place, like other equitable remedies, the nature of the desegregation remedy is to be determined by the nature and scope of the constitutional violation. The remedy must therefore be related to 'the *condition* alleged to offend the Constitution. . . .' Second, the decree must indeed be *remedial* in nature, that is, it must be designed as nearly as possible 'to restore the victims of discriminatory conduct to the position they would have occupied in the absence of such conduct.' Third, the federal courts in devising a remedy must take into account the interests of state and local authorities in managing their own affairs, consistent with the Constitution."

. . .

. . . [W]e have rejected "the suggestion . . . that schools which have a majority of Negro students are not 'desegregated,' whatever the makeup of the school district's population and however neutrally the district lines have been drawn and administered."

Instead of seeking to remove the racial identity of the various schools within the KCMSD, the District Court has set out on a program to create a school district that was equal to or superior to the surrounding [school districts].

The purpose of desegregative attractiveness has been not only to remedy the systemwide reduction in student achievement, but also to attract nonminority students. . . . The District Court's remedial orders have converted every senior high school, every middle school, and one-half of the elementary schools in the KCMSD into "magnet" schools. . . .

. . . [T]his interdistrict goal is beyond the scope of the intradistrict violation identified by the District Court. In effect, the District Court has devised a remedy to accomplish indirectly what it admittedly lacks the remedial authority to mandate directly: the interdistrict transfer of students.

. . .

The District Court's pursuit of the goal of "desegregative attractiveness". . . is so far removed from the task of eliminating the racial identifiability of the schools within the KCMSD that we believe it is beyond the admittedly broad discretion of the District Court. In this posture, we conclude that the District Court's order of salary increases, which was "grounded in remedying the vestiges of segregation by improving the desegregative attractiveness of the KCMSD," is simply too far removed from an acceptable implementation of a permissible means to remedy previous legally mandated segregation.

Justice THOMAS, concurring.

It never ceases to amaze me that the courts are so willing to assume that anything that is predominantly black must be inferior. Instead of focusing on remedying the harm done to those black schoolchildren injured by segregation, the District Court here sought to convert the KCMSD into a "magnet district" that would reverse the "white flight" caused by desegregation. In this respect, I join the Court's decision concerning the two remedial issues presented for review. . . .

Two threads in our jurisprudence have produced this unfortunate situation, in which a District Court has taken it upon itself to experiment with the education of the KCMSD's black youth. First, the court has read our cases to support the theory that black students suffer an unspecified psychological harm from segregation that retards their mental and educational development. This approach not only relies upon questionable social science research rather than constitutional principle, but it also rests on an assumption of black inferiority. Second, we have permitted the federal courts to exercise virtually unlimited equitable powers to remedy this alleged constitutional violation. The exercise of this authority has trampled upon principles of federalism and the separation of powers and has freed courts to pursue other agendas unrelated to the narrow purpose of precisely remedying a constitutional harm.

Justice SOUTER, with whom Justice STEVENS, Justice GINSBURG, and Justice BREYER join, dissenting.

. . .

. . . [O]n the 20th anniversary of *Brown* in 1974, 39 of the 77 schools in the KCMSD had student bodies that were more that 90 percent black, and 80 percent of all black schoolchildren in the KCMSD attended those schools. . . . Because the State and the KCMSD intentionally created this segregated system of education, and subsequently failed to correct it, the District Court concluded that the State and the district had "defaulted in their obligation to uphold the Constitution."

. . . [I]n *Milliken v. Bradley* (*Milliken II*), we held that a district court is authorized to remedy all conditions flowing directly from the constitutional violations committed by state or local officials, including the educational deficits that result from a segregated school system. . . .

III

. . .

. . . [T]he Court violates existing case law even on its own apparent view of the facts, that the segregation violation within the KCMSD produced no proven effects, segregative or otherwise, outside it. Assuming this to be true, the Court's decision that the rule against interdistrict remedies for intradistrict violations applies to this case, solely because the remedy here is meant to produce effects outside the district in which the violation occurred, is flatly contrary to established precedent.

. . .

On its face, the District Court's magnet school concept falls entirely within the scope of equitable authority [of federal courts]. . . . The District Court's remedial measures go only to the operation and quality of schools within the KCMSD, and the burden of those measures accordingly falls only on the two proven constitutional wrongdoers in this case, the KCMSD and the State. And insofar the District Court has ordered those violators to undertake measures to increase the KCMSD's attractiveness to students from other districts and thereby to reverse the flight attributable to their prior segregative acts, its orders do not represent an abuse of discretion, but instead appear "wholly commensurate with the 'nature and extent of the constitutional violation.'"

Justice GINSBURG, dissenting.

. . .

The Court stresses that the present remedial programs have been in place for seven years. But compared to more than two centuries of firmly entrenched official discrimination, the experience with the desegregation remedies ordered by the District Court has been evanescent.

EXERCISE 7.7. "Resegregation in American Schools" is the title of a report issued in June 1999 by the Civil Rights Project at Harvard University's Graduate School of Education and Harvard Law School. The thesis of this end-of-the-century report is that progress toward integration came to a halt in the 1980s and that we have begun to return to the old baseline of mostly segregated schools.

The report finds that (1) "the American South is resegregating, after two and a half decades in which civil rights law broke the tradition of apartheid in the region's schools"; (2) "the data shows continuously increasing segregation for Latino students, who are rapidly becoming our largest minority group and have been more segregated than African Americans for several years"; (3) there are "large and increasing numbers of African American and Latino students enrolled in suburban schools," but at the same time "serious segregation within these communities"; and (4) "all racial groups except whites experience considerable diversity in their schools but whites are remaining in overwhelmingly white schools even in regions with very large non-white enrollments."

Do these conclusions accord or conflict with your own experience and observations? What can be done about these trends forty-five years after *Brown*? Should anything be done?

EXERCISE 7.8. Segregation remains an issue both *between* schools in the same school system and *within* individual schools themselves. It is not only a legal issue but a moral one as well. During the historic March on Washington on August 28, 1963, Rev. Martin Luther King, Jr., made his famous "I have a dream" speech, in which he said:

"I have a dream that one day on the red hills of Georgia the sons of former slaves and the sons of former slave owners will be able to sit down together at a table of brotherhood. I have a dream that one day even the state of Mississippi, a desert state, sweltering with the heat of injustice and oppression, will be transformed into an oasis of freedom and justice. I have a dream that my four children will one day live in a nation where they will not be judged by the color of their skin but by the content of their character. I have a dream today. I have a dream that one day the state of Alabama, whose governor's lips are presently dripping with the words of interposition and nullification, will be transformed into a situation where little black boys and black girls will be able to join hands with little white boys and white girls and walk together as sisters and brothers. I have a dream today!"

Write a one- to two-page letter to Chief Justice Warren in 1954 and Reverend King in 1963 telling them what your own city or county (or private) school system is like today—whether or not it is segregated or integrated or some mixture thereof. Include a description of the situation at your own school and indicate how well you think the teachers and students there are living up to the ideals of integration championed by Chief Justice Warren and Dr. King. Give your school system a grade, somewhere between F and A+, on its efforts to break down racial and ethnic barriers. Hang the letters on your school's community bulletin board to share with your fellow students. What do people think of your observations?

FOR THE CLASS

THE FREDERICK DOUGLASS SCHOOL. In response to growing signs that African-American teen-aged boys are at disproportionate risk of academic failure, delinquency, depression, drug and alcohol abuse, and illiteracy, several cities have begun to experiment with special schools set up just for African-American boys. The theory is that this at-risk population needs African-American male role models, closer supervision and discipline, and a curriculum specially geared to meet special needs. Private schools set up on this theory have had impressive academic success with their students.

Critics argue that not all young African-American males are at risk and so do not necessarily qualify to attend such schools, while many girls and kids from other backgrounds are at risk and could benefit from the same investment of resources. Further, critics maintain that setting up race- and sex-segregated schools violates the whole spirit and meaning of *Brown*, which insists that children learn best when they are not artificially segregated. Supporters of such schools note that schools are *de facto* segregated anyway, and that this formalized and positive group experience is the only possible solution to deal with a serious crisis within the most disadvantaged portion of the population.

Assume that a group of citizens in your city or town wants to charter a public school called the Frederick Douglass School that would admit only African-American boys. Have two teams of students research and debate this issue as a matter of both policy and constitutional law. Would a city-funded, all-black, male school be a good idea where you live? Would it violate Equal Protection as described in *Brown*? Why or why not? Would such a school stigmatize its students, or would it stigmatize those students who are excluded? Are the answers the same when it comes to race and gender? Make sure that you distinguish between *policy* arguments ("it's a bad idea") and *constitutional* arguments ("it would violate Equal Protection").

After the debate, each member of the class should write a one- or two-page essay stating whether or not such a school is a good idea and whether or not it would be constitutional. (It is perfectly fine to say that it is a bad idea but constitutional or a good idea yet unconstitutional.)

Rich Schools, Poor Schools: The Court's Treatment of "Separate but Equal" When It Comes to Money for Education

Schools can be segregated along *economic* lines as well as racial lines. In fact, economic lines sometimes closely parallel racial lines. How should the Supreme Court deal with legal challenges to public school systems in which certain schools have a lot more money and resources than others?

The following 1973 Supreme Court case held that wealth-based differences in public schools are *not* unconstitutional and that education is *not* a fundamental right. This holding is in tension with *Brown* and helps to explain why we still see tremendous disparities in public schools in different areas when it comes to teacher/student ratios, textbooks, science and art supplies, athletic equipment and fields, cleanliness, and so on.

The most common method of funding public schools involves, in at least substantial measure, tapping into money raised through local property taxes. This method favors residents of wealthier areas, where property taxes on real estate produce much more public revenue than is produced in poorer areas, where the property values are lower. This means that students who go to school in areas with higher property values will enjoy a higher rate of spending on their education than will those who go to school in areas with lower property values. Does this violate the Equal Protection guarantee? The Supreme Court says no. Why? What do you think?

SAN ANTONIO INDEPENDENT SCHOOL DISTRICT
v.
RODRIGUEZ

Supreme Court of the United States
Argued Oct. 12, 1972.
Decided March 21, 1973.

Justice POWELL delivered the opinion of the Court.

This suit attacking the Texas system of financing public education was initiated by Mexican-American parents whose children attend the elementary and secondary schools in the Edgewood Independent School District, an urban school district in San Antonio, Texas. They brought a class action on behalf of schoolchildren throughout the State who are members of minority groups or who are poor and reside in school districts having a low property tax base.

. . .

Until recent times, Texas was a predominantly rural State and its population and property wealth were spread relatively evenly across the State. Sizable differences in the value of assessable property between local school districts became increasingly evident as the State became more industrialized and as rural-to-urban population shifts became more

Demetrio Rodriguez and other Mexican-American parents challenged the property tax–based system of financing schools in Texas as a form of wealth discrimination that violated the fundamental right to education. The Court rejected their Equal Protection claim in 1973, holding that wealth-based classifications do not warrant any special scrutiny and that education is no fundamental right under the Equal Protection Clause.

pronounced. The location of commercial and industrial property began to play a significant role in determining the amount of tax resources available to each school district. These growing disparities in population and taxable property between districts were responsible in part for increasingly notable differences in levels of local expenditure for education.

. . .

The school district in which appellees reside, the Edgewood Independent School District, has been compared throughout this litigation with the Alamo Heights Independent School District. This comparison between the least and most affluent districts in the San Antonio area serves to illustrate the manner in which the dual system of finance operates and to indicate the extent to which substantial disparities exist despite the State's impressive progress in recent years. Edgewood is one of seven public school districts in the metropolitan area. Approximately 22,000 students are enrolled in its 25 elementary and secondary schools. The district is situated in the core-city sector of San Antonio in a residential neighborhood that has little commercial or industrial property. The residents are predominantly of Mexican-American descent: approximately 90% of the student population is Mexican-American and over 6% is Negro. The average assessed property value per pupil is $5,960—the lowest in the metropolitan area—and the median family income ($4,686) is also the lowest. At an equalized tax rate of $1.05 per $100 of assessed property—the highest in the metropolitan area—the district contributed $26 to the education of each child for the 1967–1968 school year above its Local Fund Assignment for the Minimum Foundation Program. The Foundation Program contributed $222 per pupil for a state-local total of $248. Federal funds added another $108 for a total of $356 per pupil.

Alamo Heights is the most affluent school district in San Antonio. Its six schools, housing approximately 5,000 students, are situated in a residential community quite unlike the Edgewood District. The school population is predominantly "Anglo," having only 18% Mexican-Americans and less than 1% Negroes. The assessed property value per pupil exceeds $49,000, and the median family income is $8,001. In 1967–1968 the local tax rate of $.85 per $100 of valuation yielded $333 per pupil over and above its contribution to the Foundation Program. Coupled with the $225 provided from that Program, the district was able to supply $558 per student. Supplemented by a $36 per-pupil grant from federal sources, Alamo Heights spent $594 per pupil.

. . .

. . . We must decide . . . whether the Texas system of financing public education operates to the disadvantage of some suspect class or impinges upon a fundamental right explicitly or implicitly protected by the Constitution, thereby requiring strict judicial scrutiny. If so, the judgment of the District Court should be affirmed.

. . . It is not the province of this Court to create substantive constitutional rights in the name of guaranteeing equal protection of the laws. Thus, the key to discovering whether education is "fundamental" is not to be found in comparisons of the relative societal significance of education as opposed to subsistence or housing. Nor is it to be found by weighing whether education is as important as the right to travel. Rather, the answer lies in assessing whether there is a right to education explicitly or implicitly guaranteed by the Constitution.

Education, of course, is not among the rights afforded explicit protection under our Federal Constitution. Nor do we find any basis for saying it is implicitly so protected. As we have said, the undisputed importance of education will not alone cause this Court to depart from the usual standard for reviewing a State's social and economic legislation. It is appellees' contention, however, that education is distinguishable from other services and benefits provided by the State because it bears a peculiarly close relationship to other rights and liberties accorded protection under the Constitution. Specifically, they insist that education is itself a fundamental personal right because it is essential to the effective exercise of First Amendment freedoms and to intelligent utilization of the right to vote. In asserting a nexus between speech and education, appellees urge that the right to speak is meaningless unless the speaker is capable of articulating his thoughts intelligently and persuasively. The "marketplace of ideas" is an empty forum for those lacking basic communicative tools. Likewise, they argue that the corollary right to receive information becomes little more than a hollow privilege when the recipient has not been taught to read, assimilate, and utilize available knowledge.

. . .

Even if it were conceded that some identifiable quantum of education is a constitutionally protected prerequisite to the meaningful exercise of either right, we have no indication that the present levels of educational expenditures in Texas provide an education that falls short. Whatever merit appellees' argument might have if a State's financing system occasioned an absolute denial of educational opportunities to any of its children, that argument provides no basis for finding an interference with fundamental rights where only relative differences in spending levels are involved and where—as is true in the present case—no charge fairly could be made that the system fails to provide each child with an opportunity to acquire the basic minimal skills necessary for the enjoyment of the rights of speech and of full participation in the political process.

Furthermore, the logical limitations on appellees' nexus theory are difficult to perceive. How, for instance, is education to be distinguished from the significant personal interests in the basics of decent food and shelter? Empirical examination might well buttress an assumption that the ill-fed, ill-clothed, and ill-housed are among the most ineffective participants in the political process, and that they derive the least enjoyment from the benefits of the First Amendment.

We have carefully considered each of the arguments supportive of the District Court's finding that education is a fundamental right or liberty and have found those arguments unpersuasive.

. . .

It should be clear, for the reasons stated above and in accord with the prior decisions of this Court, that this is not a case in which the challenged state action must be subjected to the searching judicial scrutiny reserved for laws that create suspect classifications or impinge upon constitutionally protected rights.

. . .

In sum, to the extent that the Texas system of school financing results in unequal expenditures between children who happen to reside in different districts, we cannot say that such disparities are the product of a system that is so irrational as to be invidiously discriminatory. Texas has acknowledged its shortcomings and has persistently endeavored—not without some success—to ameliorate the differences in levels of expenditures without sacrificing the benefits of local participation.

Reversed.

Justice BRENNAN, dissenting.

. . . I . . . record my disagreement with the Court's rather distressing assertion that a right may be deemed "fundamental" for the purposes of equal protection analysis only if it is "explicitly or implicitly guaranteed by the Constitution."

Here, there can be no doubt that education is inextricably linked to the right to participate in the electoral process and to the rights of free speech and association guaranteed by the First Amendment. This being so, any classification affecting education must be subjected to strict judicial scrutiny, and since even the State concedes that the statutory scheme now before us cannot pass constitutional muster under this stricter standard of review, I can only conclude that the Texas school-financing scheme is constitutionally invalid.

Justice MARSHALL, with whom Justice DOUGLAS concurs, dissenting.

The Court today decides, in effect, that a State may constitutionally vary the quality of education which it offers its children in accordance with the amount of taxable wealth located in the school districts within which they reside. The majority's decision represents an abrupt departure from the mainstream of recent state and federal court decisions concerning the unconstitutionality of state educational financing schemes dependent upon taxable local wealth. More unfortunately, though, the majority's holding can only be seen as a retreat from our historic commitment to equality of educational opportunity and as unsupportable acquiescence in a system which deprives children in their earliest years of the chance to reach their full potential as citizens. The Court does this despite the absence of any substantial justification for a scheme which arbitrarily channels educational resources in accordance with the fortuity of the amount of taxable wealth within each district.

In my judgment, the right of every American to an equal start in life, so far as the provision of a state service as important as education is concerned, is far too vital to permit state discrimination on grounds as tenuous as those presented by this record. Nor can I accept the notion that it is sufficient to remit these appellees to the vagaries of the political process which, contrary to the majority's suggestion, has proved singularly unsuited to the task of providing a remedy for this discrimination. I, for one, am unsatisfied with the hope of an ultimate "political" solution sometime in the indefinite future while, in the meantime, countless children unjustifiably receive inferior educations that "may affect their hearts and minds in a way unlikely ever to be undone." *Brown.* I must therefore respectfully dissent.

JUSTICE WILLIAM J. BRENNAN (1906–1997) was born in Newark, New Jersey, where his father was a popular local official in charge of public safety. Brennan attended Barringer High School and the Wharton School at the University of Pennsylvania. He went on to Harvard Law School. After a distinguished career as a labor lawyer, Brennan rose through the ranks of the New Jersey courts, landing on the New Jersey Supreme Court. President Dwight Eisenhower appointed him a justice of the U.S. Supreme Court in 1956, where he served until 1990.

HIGHLIGHTS

➤ Justice Brennan was a student of Justice Felix Frankfurter at Harvard Law School and later came to be both his colleague and frequent adversary on the Court.

➤ Unaware that President Eisenhower, a Republican, was considering nominating him to the Supreme Court, Brennan complained about having to go to Washington, D.C., when Herbert Brownell called him from the Attorney General's Office.

➤ Justice Brennan had a tremendous influence in promoting a progressive civil rights and civil liberties jurisprudence on the Court and was known as a great leader in forging consensus among his fellow justices.

EXERCISE 7.9. Sometimes people say that communities that truly want to support education will tax themselves at a higher rate while those that are less supportive will tax themselves at a lower rate. But in *Rodriguez,* the communities that imposed a higher tax rate actually ended up earning less tax revenue than the communities that imposed a lower tax rate. As a matter of arithmetic, why was that? Do you think that this fact undercuts the majority's argument?

EXERCISE 7.10. Is the Supreme Court's decision in *Rodriguez* consistent with the *Brown* decision? Why or why not? What is the spirit of this case relative to *Brown*? Which holding do you think is sturdier?

EXERCISE 7.11. Many state supreme courts, including the one in Texas, have done what the U.S. Supreme Court was unwilling to do: they have found that under their *state* constitutions students have a right to equal rates of spending in each school district. Do you agree with this approach? What would you think about a rule in your state that there has to be an equal number of dollars spent per pupil in each school district and school? Is that fair? What happens if a local parents' group wants to donate extra money or supplies? Is it okay for certain local public schools to acquire more resources by seeking private funding and/or holding fundraisers?

When adult experts debate the subject of school financing, a major issue is whether or not more money in a school system or school leads to improved educational outcomes. To what extent do financial resources actually buy a better education? Is money relevant or irrelevant to the success of your teachers and your education? Is it necessary to excellence but not sufficient? Is it sufficient but not necessary? Write a short essay (two pages) on how you think money, or the lack of it, either helps or hinders your experience in school.

EXERCISE 7.12. More than 90 percent of children go to public school, but many also go to private schools that are funded by their families and by alumni contributions. While some of these schools are relatively poor, many others are very rich and are able to give their students extraordinary resources and teacher attention. The Supreme Court in 1925 struck down an Oregon law that required all students to attend public schools rather than private ones. In *Pierce v. Society of Sisters*, the Court ruled that foreclosing alternatives to public school "unreasonably interferes with the liberty of parents and guardians to direct the upbringing and education of children under their control." Do you think that this decision was right, or should all students be required to go to public schools? What effect do private schools have on public schools? Should people have the right to send their children to any school they want, public or private, or do we lose something when families begin to sort themselves out according to wealth, religion, and race?

FOR THE CLASS

SCHOOL VOUCHERS: PRO OR CON? The 1990s saw the growth of a movement in favor of "school vouchers," the policy of granting parents tax-financed vouchers that they can redeem to pay tuition for their children at any school, public or private. The idea, launched in 1955 in an essay penned by free-market economist Milton Friedman, has been adopted in Milwaukee, Wisconsin, and Cleveland, Ohio, as well as by the state of Florida. Champions of vouchers say that every child, no matter how poor, should have the opportunity to attend the elite private schools typically reserved for the children of the wealthy and that the voucher program will stir a beneficial competition among schools for parents' voucher dollars. Opponents say that vouchers will simply strip the public schools of their best students, further undermine public support for public schools, and benefit only a tiny percentage of less affluent families since the vast majority will still not have enough money to go to the elite private schools. The rhetoric of proponents is "free choice for all" while the rhetoric of opponents is "don't destroy the public schools."

Pair up with one of your classmates and do some research on all sides of the school voucher debate, then present a report to the class on your views. Are there ways that we could have vouchers without undermining public schools? Are there ways we could provide more choice and competition within the public schools?

"Suspect" Classes and Sex-Based Segregation

Since *Brown* was decided in 1954, the Supreme Court has developed different tests for the various Equal Protection claims brought under the Fourteenth Amendment. If a law distinguishes people based on race, the Court reviews the case using "strict scrutiny," because the Court views race as an inherently suspect, or discriminatory, classification. In order to pass a strict scrutiny test, the government must show that its racial classification advances a compelling public interest in an effective and necessary way.

If a law treats people differently according to their gender, the government must show that the law's classification advances an "important" public interest in a way that is substantially related to its purpose. This is "heightened" or "intermediate scrutiny." If a law differentiates citizens based on physical handicap, wealth, sexual orientation, or many other categories, the Court reviews the case using only "rational basis scrutiny." The test employed essentially asks, "Is there any rational reason for the government to make this law that is not an arbitrary burden on a particular group of people, in violation of the Fourteenth Amendment's Equal Protection Clause?"

The nuances of Supreme Court Equal Protection analysis are rather complicated and abstract. But it is important that you be able to conceptualize the underlying notion that classifications based on race are the most difficult for the government to justify, while classifications based on sex, while suspicious, are a little easier to justify. Classifications based on other categories, while still requiring justification, have the most leeway of all. If Equal Protection analysis were drawn on a continuum, it would look something like this:

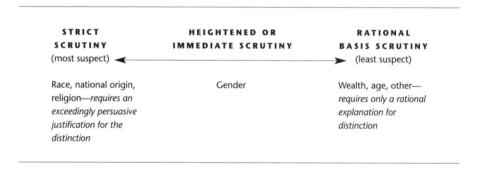

STRICT SCRUTINY (most suspect)	HEIGHTENED OR IMMEDIATE SCRUTINY	RATIONAL BASIS SCRUTINY (least suspect)
Race, national origin, religion—*requires an exceedingly persuasive justification for the distinction*	Gender	Wealth, age, other— *requires only a rational explanation for distinction*

The Supreme Court has said that higher scrutiny is triggered when government draws lines that adversely affect a "discrete and insular minority." This is a group defined by some "immutable" (unchangeable) trait, a history of being the object of bias and discrimination, and political powerlessness in society.

Why are race classifications so much more suspect than gender classifications? Is it because the history of race oppression in the United States is more severe or detrimental than the history of sex discrimination? Is it because women, the undoubted targets of discrimination, are not a minority? Or is it because there are real differences between the sexes but not the races?

In *United States v. Virginia,* the Supreme Court heard arguments for and against the power of a state-funded military college to exclude women. Virginia Military Institute (VMI) was the sole single-sex school among Virginia's public in-

Virginia Military Institute cadets stand at attention. Front and center is one of the first women admitted to VMI in the wake of the Court's landmark decision in *United States v. Virginia.*

stitutions of higher learning. VMI's distinctive mission is to produce "citizen-soldiers," individuals prepared for leadership in civilian life and in military service.

Using a harsh, marine-like, "adversative" method of training not available elsewhere in Virginia, VMI endeavors to instill physical and mental discipline in its cadets and impart to them a strong moral code. This model of education features physical rigor, mental stress, absolute equality of treatment, absence of privacy, minute regulation of behavior, and indoctrination in "desirable values." The adversative method "dissects the young student," and makes him aware of his "limits and capabilities," so that he knows "how far he can go with his anger, . . . how much he can take under stress, . . . exactly what he can do when he is physically exhausted." Because of this intense regimen, the alumni place high value on their VMI training, and VMI has the largest per-student endowment of all public undergraduate institutions in the nation.

The United States sued Virginia and VMI, alleging that VMI's males-only admission policy violated the Fourteenth Amendment's Equal Protection Clause. VMI initially received a favorable ruling from the district court. On review, the Fourth Circuit reversed and ordered Virginia to remedy the constitutional violation. In response, Virginia proposed a parallel program for women: Virginia Women's Institute for Leadership (VWIL), located at Mary Baldwin college, a private liberal arts school for women. The district court found that Virginia's proposal satisfied the Constitution's Equal Protection requirement, and the Fourth Circuit affirmed. The appeals court deferentially reviewed Virginia's plan and determined that provision of single-gender educational options was a legitimate objective. Maintenance of single-sex programs, the court concluded, was essential to that objective. The court recognized, however, that its analysis risked bypassing Equal Protection scrutiny, so it fashioned an additional test, asking whether VMI and VWIL students would receive "substantially comparable" benefits. Although the court of appeals acknowledged that the VWIL degree lacked the historical benefit and prestige of a VMI degree, the court nevertheless found the educational opportunities at the two schools sufficiently comparable.

The Supreme Court rejected this attempt to create a parallel all-women's institution and instead insisted that Virginia admit both men and women to VMI. Six justices made up the majority decision to find against Virginia in the VMI case: Justices Ginsburg, Stevens, O'Connor, Kennedy, Souter, and Breyer. Chief Justice Rehnquist filed an opinion concurring in the judgment. Justice Scalia dissented. (Justice Thomas abstained from both the consideration and the decision of the case because his son was a student at VMI at the time.)

Before discussing the fine points of both the majority and dissenting opinions, this analysis must identify the type of review, or scrutiny, the Court applies in this situation. As noted above, the Court uses intermediate scrutiny to evaluate the constitutionality of gender-based laws. Therefore, in *United States v. Virginia*, the Court, faced with a state school's gender-based discrimination policy, asked whether: (1) Virginia's interest in an all-male college is "important" to producing exemplary "citizen-soldiers," and (2) whether the all-male policy is "substantially related" to achievement of Virginia's goal of producing such soldiers.

Writing for the majority, Justice Ginsburg found that Virginia's arguments for a separate, all-female military college were unable to pass the test of intermediate scrutiny. Justice Ginsburg rejected Virginia's argument for a separate women's military college based on three principles. First, the Court affirmed its degree of scrutiny when confronted with gender-based classifications. In evaluating the case, Justice Ginsburg held that, although gender-based classifications are not categorically prohibited, categorization by sex may not be used to create or perpetuate the legal, social, or economic inferiority of women.

Second, Virginia failed to provide the Court with enough evidence that the exclusion of women was *substantially related* to the important state interest of VMI's adversative training method. In other words, the State had failed to offer enough proof that only an all-male setting would allow VMI's rigorous physical and mental conditioning program to operate. Why couldn't VMI continue to impose a tough set of academic and athletic protocols with women present? However, the Court was willing to allow the all-male policy to continue if the State could show that women were offered an alternative to VMI that would produce female graduates with opportunities substantially equal to those afforded male graduates of VMI.

Virginia, however, was unable to clear this final hurdle. The Supreme Court rejected Virginia's proposed all-female school because the disparity in geographic location and physical and mental training, and the inferior reputation of the institution itself, would not produce a result comparable to attending VMI. Therefore, the Court's enunciation of its conclusion that "separate" produced a result far from "equal" left VMI holding the bag with an unconstitutional all-male policy.

Justice Scalia dissented from this analysis because, in his view, the school had met its burdens under intermediate scrutiny. He attacked the majority's view of women, pointing out that women constitute a majority of the electorate and have the power of the ballot to change educational policies they find disagreeable. Applying a weaker standard of scrutiny for Virginia's program, Justice Scalia concluded that VMI's program promoted the precise goal Virginia aspired to— the creation of leaders through a strict moral code—and that this goal clearly passed constitutional muster.

In his spirited dissent, Justice Scalia included excerpts from the VMI cadet's training booklet. Read the following piece, entitled "The Code of a Gentleman," and decide for yourself whether it supports Justice Scalia's argument that the majority's decision unnecessarily trashed a noble masculine tradition in Virginia.

"A Gentleman . . .

Does not discuss his family affairs in public or with acquaintances.

Does not speak more than casually about his girl friend.

Does not go to a lady's house if he is affected by alcohol. He is temperate in the use of alcohol.

Does not lose his temper; nor exhibit anger, fear, hate, embarrassment, ardor or hilarity in public.

Does not hail a lady from a club window.

A gentleman never discusses the merits or demerits of a lady.

Does not mention names exactly as he avoids the mention of what things cost.

Does not borrow money from a friend, except in dire need. Money borrowed is a debt of honor, and must be repaid as promptly as possible. Debts incurred by a deceased parent, brother, sister or grown child are assumed by honorable men as a debt of honor.

Does not display his wealth, money or possessions.

Does not put his manners on and off, whether in the club or in a ballroom. He treats people with courtesy, no matter what their social position may be.

Does not slap strangers on the back nor so much as lay a finger on a lady.

Does not 'lick the boots of those above' nor 'kick the face of those below him on the social ladder.'

Does not take advantage of another's helplessness or ignorance and assumes that no gentleman will take advantage of him.

A Gentleman respects the reserves of others, but demands that others respect those which are his.

A Gentleman can become what he wills to be . . ."

Justice Scalia concluded his dissent with the following statement:

"I do not know whether the men of VMI lived by this Code; perhaps not. But it is powerfully impressive that a public institution of higher education still in existence sought to have them do so. I do not think any of us, women included, will be better off for its destruction."

EXERCISE 7.13. What do you think of the plain-spoken words with which Justice Scalia concludes his dissent? Note that inclusion of this "Code of a Gentleman" is unusual for a judicial opinion. Does it make you more likely, less likely, or about as likely to agree with Justice Scalia's perspective on VMI's admission of women? Why?

EXERCISE 7.14. What is your opinion on the validity of sex-segregated schools? Can all-female schools ever help women in a constitutionally permissible way? Is there ever justification for all-male schools?

EXERCISE 7.15. What would you think of one-sex-only classes within your school? An all-girls math class to prevent girls from being drowned-out by overly aggressive boys? All-girls and all-boys sex-education classes to prevent embarrassment on both sides?

FOR THE CLASS

SEX AND SECOND-CLASS CITIZENS. Pretend that you and your classmates are members of the state legislature or city council where you live. A group of parents appears before you to testify about the ways in which girls are often treated like second-class citizens in public high schools in your jurisdiction. It reports that boys are always elected to the student council and as class president and are also almost always chosen to be editor of the school newspaper. They enjoy numerous other prestigious positions in school as well. The group wants you to support the establishment of a statewide Eleanor Roosevelt Leadership Academy for Young Women, a special high school for girls only that would allow girls to occupy all the positions of leadership and influence that few now do in the co-ed high schools.

Discuss among yourselves the issue these parents have brought to the table. How do you deal with it? What creative solutions can you come up with? Do you vote to support creation of the Eleanor Roosevelt Leadership Academy, or can you think of some other legislation that will address the problem? Is there a problem?

Notes

1. K. B. Clark, *Effect of Prejudice and Discrimination on Personality Development* (Mid-century White House Conference on Children and Youth, 1950); Witmer and Kotinsky, *Personality in the Making* (1952), c. VI; Deutscher and Chein, *The Psychological Effects of Enforced Segregation: A Survey of Social Science Opinion*, 26 J. Psychol. 259 (1948); Chein, *What Are the Psychological Effects of Segregation Under Conditions of Equal Facilities?*, 3 Int. J. Opinion and Attitude Res. 229 (1949); Brameld, *Educational Costs, in Discrimination and National Welfare* (MacIver, ed., 1949), 44–48; Frazier, *The Negro in the United States* (1949), 674–681. And see generally Myrdal, *An American Dilemma* (1944).

2. Clayborne Carson et al., *Eyes on the Prize: Civil Rights Reader* (New York: Penguin Books, 1991), as quoted in Daisy Bates, *The Long Shadow of Little Rock* (New York: David McKay, 1962).

Read On

Bell, Derrick A., Jr. *Race, Racism and American Law.* Boston: Little, Brown, 1980.

Bickel, Alexander M. *The Least Dangerous Branch: The Supreme Court at the Bar of Politics.* Indianapolis: Bobbs-Merrill, 1962.

Carson, Clayborne, et al. *Eyes on the Prize: Civil Rights Reader.* New York: Penguin Books, 1991.

Kluger, Richard. *Simple Justice: The History of* Brown v. Board of Education *and Black America's Struggle for Equality.* New York: Knopf, 1975.

Kozol, Jonathan. *Savage Inequalities: Children in America's Schools.* New York: Crown Publishing, 1991.

Lagemann, Ellen C., and Lamar P. Miller, eds. Brown v. Board of Education: *The Challenge for Today's Schools.* New York: Teachers College Press, 1996.

Nelson, William E. *The Fourteenth Amendment: From Political Principle to Judicial Doctrine.* Cambridge, Mass.: Harvard University Press, 1988.

Whitman, Mark. *The Irony of Desegregation Law 1955–1995.* Princeton, N.J.: M. Wiener, 1998.

Wilkinson, J. Harvie. *From* Brown *to* Bakke: *The Supreme Court and School Integration, 1954–1978.* New York: Oxford University Press, 1979.

8 HARASSMENT IN THE HALLS: SEXUAL HARASSMENT ON CAMPUS

"No person in the United States shall, on the basis of sex, be excluded from participation in, be denied the benefits of, or be subjected to discrimination under any education program or activity receiving federal financial assistance." TITLE IX (20 U.S.C. § 1681)

"There were two or three boys touching me . . . and I'd tell them to stop but they wouldn't. This went on for . . . months. Finally I was in one of my classes when all of them came back and backed me into a corner and started touching me all over. . . . After the class I told the principal, and he and the boys had a little talk. And after the talk was up, the boys came out laughing because they got no punishment." QUOTED IN NAN STEIN AND LISA SJOSTRAM, *FLIRTING OR HURTING? A TEACHER'S GUIDE TO STUDENT-TO-STUDENT SEXUAL HARASSMENT IN SCHOOLS*

For most adults, high school evokes images of cramming for calculus tests, going to yearbook meetings, cheering on the home team, enjoying school musicals, and pinning on corsages at senior proms. But there has always been a dark side to high school as well: the teasing, put-downs, ridicule, and hazing that students sometimes visit on one another, and the abuse of power over students practiced by a few teachers and administrators. Sometimes these behaviors—bad enough on their own—turn even more serious, to the point that they become illegal. This is the case with *sexual harassment,* which is defined as unwanted and unwelcome sexual advances and conduct that interfere with a student's education.

Sexual harassment is a serious and pervasive problem in American schools. In 1993, the American Association of University Women released a study done by Louis Harris and Associates called *Hostile Hallways,* which surveyed more than 1,600 public high school students (grades 8 through 11) from all across America. The findings were astonishing: 85 percent of the girls and 76 percent of the boys reported experiencing some kind of sexual harassment, including unwanted sexual touching, grabbing, comments, and gestures. All told, four out of five students had, to one degree or another, personally encountered the problem of sexual harassment. The experience can undermine a student's academic performance and ruin her or his sense of physical, emotional, and mental well-being. While student-on-student harassment is most common, some students face sexual harassment from teachers, coaches, advisers, staff, and even principals.

Although the sexual harassment of students is not in any sense unconstitutional, it is definitely illegal under Title IX of the Education Amendments of 1972, a federal statute passed by Congress. Under Title IX, sexual harassment in any school receiving federal funds, whether public or private, is considered a form of illegal sex discrimination. Thus, any student, male or female, subjected to sexual harassment in any official school program or activity—whether in class or on the sports field, on campus or off campus—can bring suit against her or his school system under Title IX. The cases in this chapter define when a school system is, in fact, liable for such harassment.

Under Title IX, sexual harassment can assume two different forms: so-called quid pro quo sexual harassment and hostile environment sexual harassment. Quid pro quo harassment occurs when a school employee, such as a teacher or staff member, tries to convince a student to submit to unwanted sexual advances as a condition for participating in a school program or extracurricular activity, as a means of getting ahead in some way (such as getting a better grade or a starting position on a team), or as a necessary way to avoid negative consequences (like getting a bad grade or having rumors spread about). The harasser is essentially telling his or her victim that he or she will profit from sexual conduct in some way or lose out by refusing the unwanted advances: "If you have sexual relations with me, you will get the starring role in the school play," or, "Girls who have resisted my charms in the past have mysteriously ended up flunking out of history." These are examples of quid pro quo sexual harassment, and they are illegal.

Hostile environment sexual harassment occurs when unwelcome hostile conduct of a sexual nature is so severe, persistent, or pervasive that it interferes with a student's ability to benefit from school or creates an intimidating, threatening, or abusive academic environment. Such an environment might be created by teachers, administrators, other students, or some combination thereof. Examples of conduct that create a hostile environment include leers, sexual banter and ridicule, use of pornography to embarrass and humiliate, unwanted touching, squeezing and fondling, sexual graffiti, persistent negative rumors, sexual "ratings" of students, sexual gestures and mooning, exhibitionist displays, and so on.

There is, of course, some ambiguity about when unwelcome juvenile sexual conduct actually crosses the line and creates a hostile learning environment. Obviously, a couple of bad jokes or a single unwelcome invitation to the movies are not Title IX violations. But the law considers severe and pervasive sexual harassment a serious problem and is willing to gamble that courts will be able to distinguish between an innocent (if undesired) love poem left at someone's desk and a pattern of sexually hostile and demeaning behavior. If you are ever confronted with unwelcome conduct of a sexual nature, the best thing to do is to tell the other people involved that you are offended and ask them to stop. If they persist, it is time to get teachers and other authority figures involved.

POINTS TO PONDER

How can schools and courts tell the difference between innocent teasing or joking and illegal sexual harassment?

- What are the two different kinds of sexual harassment according to federal law?
- If a teacher sexually pressures and harasses one of his or her students, should the school system be held legally and financially responsible even if the teacher's superiors were unaware of the situation?
- Should school authorities be held responsible for student-on-student sexual harassment if they know about it and do nothing to stop it? What if they are unaware of what is going on?

When Teachers Harass Students

If a student brings a Title IX action alleging that she is being sexually harassed by a teacher and proves that this is in fact true, is the school automatically liable at that point for money damages? Or must the student first show that a proper authority at the school actually knew about the inappropriate behavior but failed to stop it? In *Gebser v. Lago Vista Independent School District* (1998), the Court found that a school district is liable for damages under Title IX for a teacher's sexual harassment of a student only if higher-up officials in the school know about it and choose to do nothing. Does this standard leave students too vulnerable to predatory adults? See what you think by reading both the majority and dissenting opinions.

GEBSER
v.
LAGO VISTA INDEPENDENT SCHOOL DISTRICT

Supreme Court of the United States
Argued March 25, 1998.
Decided June 22, 1998.

Justice O'CONNOR delivered the opinion of the Court.

The question in this case is when a school district may be held liable in damages in an implied right of action under Title IX of the Education Amendments (Title IX) for the sexual harassment of a student by one of the district's teachers. We conclude that damages may not be recovered in those circumstances unless an official of the school district who at a minimum has authority to institute corrective measures on the district's behalf has actual notice of, and is deliberately indifferent to, the teacher's misconduct.

I

In the spring of 1991, when petitioner Alida Star Gebser was an eighth-grade student at a middle school in respondent Lago Vista Independent School District (Lago Vista), she joined a high school book discussion group led by Frank Waldrop, a teacher at Lago Vista's high school. Lago Vista received federal funds at all pertinent times. During the book discussion sessions, Waldrop often made sexually suggestive comments to the students. Gebser entered high school in the fall and was assigned to classes taught by Waldrop in both semesters. Waldrop continued to make inappropriate remarks to the students, and he began to direct more of his suggestive comments toward Gebser, including during the substantial amount of time that the two were alone in his classroom. He initiated sexual contact with Gebser in the spring, when, while visiting her home ostensibly to give her a book, he kissed and fondled her. The two had sexual intercourse on a number of occasions during the remainder of the school year. Their relationship continued through the summer and into the following school year, and they often had intercourse during class time, although never on school property.

Gebser did not report the relationship to school officials, testifying that while she realized Waldrop's conduct was improper, she was uncertain how to react and she wanted to continue having him as a teacher. In October 1992, the parents of two other students complained to the high school principal about Waldrop's comments in class. The principal arranged a meeting, at which, according to the principal, Waldrop indicated that he did not believe he had made offensive remarks but apologized to the parents and said it would not happen again. The principal also advised Waldrop to be careful about his classroom comments and told the school guidance counselor about the meeting, but he did not report the parents' complaint to Lago Vista's superintendent, who was the district's Title IX coordinator. A couple of months later, in January 1993, a police officer discovered Waldrop and Gebser engaging in sexual intercourse and arrested Waldrop. Lago Vista terminated his employment, and subsequently, the Texas Education Agency revoked his teaching license. During this time, the district had not promulgated or distributed an official grievance procedure for lodging sexual harassment complaints; nor had it issued a formal anti-harassment policy.

. . .

III

. . .

. . . When a teacher's sexual harassment is imputed to a school district or when a school district is deemed to have "constructively" known of the teacher's harassment, by assumption the district had no actual knowledge of the teacher's conduct. Nor, of course, did the district have an opportunity to take action to end the harassment or to limit further harassment.

. . .

IV

. . .[W]e hold that a damages remedy will not lie under Title IX unless an official who at a minimum has authority to address the alleged discrimination and to institute corrective measures on the recipient's behalf has actual knowledge of discrimination in the recipient's programs and fails adequately to respond.

We think, moreover, that the response must amount to deliberate indifference to discrimination. The administrative enforcement scheme presupposes that an official who is advised of a Title IX violation refuses to take action to bring the recipient into compliance. The premise, in other words, is an official decision by the recipient not to remedy the violation. That framework finds a rough parallel in the standard of deliberate indifference. Under a lower standard, there would be a risk that the recipient would be liable in damages not for its own official decision but instead for its employees' independent actions. . . .

. . .

V

. . . [W]e will not hold a school district liable in damages under Title IX for a teacher's sexual harassment of a student absent actual notice and deliberate indifference. . . .

Justice STEVENS, with whom Justice SOUTER, Justice GINSBURG, and Justice BREYER join, dissenting.

. . .

. . . This case presents a paradigmatic example of a tort that was made possible, that was effected, and that was repeated over a prolonged period because of the powerful influence that Waldrop had over Gebser by reason of the authority that his employer, the school district, had delegated to him. As a secondary school teacher, Waldrop exercised even greater authority and control over his students than employers and supervisors exercise over their employees. His gross misuse of that authority allowed him to abuse his young student's trust.

. . . The Court's holding is also questionable as a factual matter. Waldrop himself surely had ample authority to maintain order in the classes that he conducted. Indeed, that is a routine part of every teacher's responsibilities. If petitioner had been the victim of sexually harassing conduct by other students during those classes, surely the teacher would have had ample authority to take corrective measures. The fact that he did not prevent his own harassment of petitioner is the consequence of his lack of will, not his lack of authority.

· · ·

. . . As long as school boards can insulate themselves from knowledge about this sort of conduct, they can claim immunity from damages liability. . . . Indeed, the rule that the Court adopts would preclude a damages remedy even if every teacher at the school knew about the harassment but did not have "authority to institute corrective measures on the district's behalf."

· · ·

IV

· · ·

A theme that seems to underlie the Court's opinion is a concern that holding a school district liable in damages might deprive it of the benefit of the federal subsidy—that the damages remedy is somehow more onerous than a possible termination of the federal grant. . . . It is not clear to me why the well-settled rules of law that impose responsibility on the principal for the misconduct of its agents should not apply in this case. As a matter of policy, the Court ranks protection of the school district's purse above the protection of immature high school students that those rules would provide. . . .

EXERCISE 8.1. What do you think of the dissenting justices' argument that the teacher, Frank Waldrop, *is* an authority figure within the school and therefore the school should be automatically or strictly liable for his conduct? The majority believes that it is not fair to hold the school financially accountable since school officials were not aware of the affair. Do you agree with the majority opinion (there must be actual knowledge and "deliberate indifference" before the school system becomes liable) or the dissenting opinion (the school must always be liable for the teacher's actions, even if there was no actual notice that a teacher was harassing a student or having an affair)? Compare your views with those of your classmates.

When Students Harass Students

If school systems are liable for sexual harassment of students by their own employees when school authorities are aware of offending behavior, what about when sexual harassment occurs at the hands of fellow students? One line of thought contends that schools are absolutely responsible and liable for anything that happens inside their walls; an opposing line of thought maintains that schools should never be responsible for actions taken by students (as opposed to employees). In fact, the Supreme Court has rejected both of these positions, ruling instead that under Title IX school systems will *sometimes* be liable for student-on-student sexual harassment. Under what conditions, then, does the Court find schools responsible? Write out the rule handed down in the following case when you see the Court define it. This is the holding of the case.

—•—

DAVIS
v.
MONROE COUNTY BOARD OF EDUCATION

Supreme Court of the United States
Argued Jan. 12, 1999.
Decided May 24, 1999.

Justice O'CONNOR delivered the opinion of the Court.

Petitioner brought suit against the Monroe County Board of Education and other defendants, alleging that her fifth-grade daughter had been the victim of sexual harassment by another student in her class. Among petitioner's claims was a claim for monetary and injunctive relief under Title IX of the Education Amendments of 1972. The District Court dismissed petitioner's Title IX claim on the ground that "student-on-student," or peer, harassment provides no ground for a private cause of action under the statute. The Court of Appeals for the Eleventh Circuit, sitting en banc, affirmed. We consider here whether a private damages action may lie against the school board in cases of student-on-student harassment. We conclude that it may, but only where the funding recipient acts with deliberate indifference to known acts of harassment in its programs or activities. Moreover, we conclude that such an action will lie only for harassment that is so severe, pervasive, and objectively offensive that it effectively bars the victim's access to an educational opportunity or benefit.

I

. . .

A

. . . According to petitioner's complaint, the harassment began in December 1992, when the classmate, G. F., attempted to touch LaShonda's breasts and genital area and made vulgar statements such as " 'I want to get in bed with you' " and " 'I want to feel your boobs.' " Similar conduct allegedly occurred on or about January 4 and January 20, 1993. LaShonda reported each of these incidents to her mother and to her classroom teacher, Diane Fort. Petitioner, in turn, also contacted Fort, who allegedly assured petitioner that the school principal, Bill Querry, had been informed of the incidents. Petitioner contends that, notwithstanding these reports, no disciplinary action was taken against G. F.

G. F.'s conduct allegedly continued for many months. In early February, G. F. purportedly placed a door stop in his pants and proceeded to act in a sexually suggestive manner toward LaShonda during physical education class. LaShonda reported G. F.'s behavior to her physical education teacher, Whit Maples. Approximately one week later, G. F. again allegedly engaged in harassing behavior, this time while under the supervision of another classroom teacher, Joyce Pippen. Again, LaShonda allegedly reported the incident to the teacher, and again petitioner contacted the teacher to follow up.

Petitioner alleges that G. F. once more directed sexually harassing conduct toward

LaShonda Davis (right) was only ten years old when she suffered through five months of crude sexual taunts and advances in the 1992–1993 school year.

LaShonda in physical education class in early March, and that LaShonda reported the incident to both Maples and Pippen. In mid-April 1993, G. F. allegedly rubbed his body against LaShonda in the school hallway in what LaShonda considered a sexually suggestive manner, and LaShonda again reported the matter to Fort.

The string of incidents finally ended in mid-May, when G. F. was charged with, and pleaded guilty to, sexual battery for his misconduct. The complaint alleges that LaShonda had suffered during the months of harassment, however; specifically, her previously high grades allegedly dropped as she became unable to concentrate on her studies, and, in April 1993, her father discovered that she had written a suicide note. The complaint further alleges that, at one point, LaShonda told petitioner that she " 'didn't know how much longer she could keep [G. F.] off her.' "

Nor was LaShonda G. F.'s only victim; it is alleged that other girls in the class fell prey to G. F.'s conduct. At one point, in fact, a group composed of LaShonda and other female students tried to speak with Principal Querry about G. F.'s behavior. According to the complaint, however, a teacher denied the students' request with the statement, " 'If [Querry] wants you, he'll call you.' "

Petitioner alleges that no disciplinary action was taken in response to G. F.'s behavior toward LaShonda. In addition to her conversations with Fort and Pippen, petitioner alleges that she spoke with Principal Querry in mid-May 1993. When petitioner inquired as to what action the school intended to take against G. F., Querry simply stated, " 'I guess I'll have to threaten him a little bit harder.' " Yet, petitioner alleges, at no point during the many months of his reported misconduct was G. F. disciplined for harassment. Indeed, Querry allegedly asked petitioner why LaShonda " 'was the only one complaining.' "

Nor, according to the complaint, was any effort made to separate G. F. and LaShonda. On the contrary, notwithstanding LaShonda's frequent complaints, only after more than three months of reported harassment was she even permitted to change her classroom seat so that she was no longer seated next to G. F. Moreover, petitioner alleges that, at the time of the events in question, the Monroe County Board of Education (Board) had not instructed its personnel on how to respond to peer sexual harassment and had not established a policy on the issue.

. . .

II

. . . [A]t issue here is the question whether a recipient of federal education funding may be liable for damages under Title IX under any circumstances for discrimination in the form of student-on-student sexual harassment.

A

. . .

We disagree with respondents' assertion, however, that petitioner seeks to hold the Board liable for G. F.'s actions instead of its own. Here, petitioner attempts to hold the Board liable for its own decision to remain idle in the face of known student-on-student harassment in its schools. In *Gebser,* we concluded that a recipient of federal education funds may be liable in damages under Title IX where it is deliberately indifferent to known acts of sexual harassment by a teacher. In that case, a teacher had entered into a sexual relationship with an eighth grade student, and the student sought damages under Title IX for the teacher's misconduct. . . .

Accordingly, we rejected the use of agency principles to impute liability to the district for the misconduct of its teachers. Likewise, we declined the invitation to impose liability under what amounted to a negligence standard—holding the district liable for its failure to react to teacher-student harassment of which it knew or *should have known.* Rather, we concluded that the district could be liable for damages only where the district itself intentionally acted in clear violation of Title IX by remaining deliberately indifferent to acts of teacher-student harassment of which it had actual knowledge. . . . [W]e concluded in *Gebser* that recipients could be liable in damages only where their own deliberate indifference effectively "cause[d]" the discrimination. . . .

. . .

We consider here whether the misconduct identified in *Gebser*—deliberate indifference to known acts of harassment—amounts to an intentional violation of Title IX, capable of supporting a private damages action, when the harasser is a student rather than a teacher. We conclude that, in certain limited circumstances, it does. . . .

. . .

. . . The statute's plain language confines the scope of prohibited conduct based on the recipient's degree of control over the harasser and the environment in which the harassment occurs. If a funding recipient does not engage in harassment directly, it may not be liable for damages unless its deliberate indifference "subject[s]" its students to harassment. That is, the deliberate indifference must, at a minimum, "cause [students] to undergo" harassment or "make them liable or vulnerable" to it. . . .

. . .

Where, as here, the misconduct occurs during school hours and on school grounds— the bulk of G. F.'s misconduct, in fact, took place in the classroom—the misconduct is taking place "under" an "operation" of the funding recipient. . . . In these circumstances, the recipient retains substantial control over the context in which the harassment occurs. More importantly, however, in this setting the Board exercises significant control over the harasser. We have observed, for example, "that the nature of [the State's] power [over public schoolchildren] is custodial and tutelary, permitting a degree of supervision and control that could not be exercised over free adults." . . .

. . .

While it remains to be seen whether petitioner can show that the Board's response to reports of G. F.'s misconduct was clearly unreasonable in light of the known circumstances, petitioner may be able to show that the Board "subject[ed]" LaShonda to discrimination by failing to respond in any way over a period of five months to complaints of G. F.'s in-school misconduct from LaShonda and other female students.

B

. . . Having previously determined that "sexual harassment" is "discrimination" in the school context under Title IX, we are constrained to conclude that student-on-student sexual harassment, if sufficiently severe, can likewise rise to the level of discrimination actionable under the statute. . . .

The most obvious example of student-on-student sexual harassment capable of triggering a damages claim would thus involve the overt, physical deprivation of access to school resources. Consider, for example, a case in which male students physically threaten their female peers every day, successfully preventing the female students from using a particular school resource—an athletic field or a computer lab, for instance. District administrators are well aware of the daily ritual, yet they deliberately ignore requests for aid from the female students wishing to use the resource. The district's knowing refusal to take any action in response to such behavior would fly in the face of Title IX's core principles, and such deliberate indifference may appropriately be subject to claims for monetary damages. It is not necessary, however, to show physical exclusion to demonstrate that students have been deprived by the actions of another student or students of an educational opportunity on the basis of sex. Rather, a plaintiff must establish sexual harassment of students that is so severe, pervasive, and objectively offensive, and that so undermines and detracts from the victims' educational experience, that the victim-students are effectively denied equal access to an institution's resources and opportunities.

Whether gender-oriented conduct rises to the level of actionable "harassment" thus "depends on a constellation of surrounding circumstances, expectations, and relationships," including, but not limited to, the ages of the harasser and the victim and the number of individuals involved, moreover, must bear in mind that schools are unlike the adult workplace and that children may regularly interact in a manner that would be unacceptable among adults. Indeed, at least early on, students are still learning how to interact appropriately with their peers. It is thus understandable that, in the school setting, students often engage in insults, banter, teasing, shoving, pushing, and gender-specific conduct that is upsetting to the students subjected to it. Damages are not available for simple acts of teasing and name-calling among school children, however, even where these comments target differences in gender. Rather, in the context of student-on-student harassment, damages are available only where the behavior is so severe, pervasive, and objectively offensive that it denies its victims the equal access to education that Title IX is designed to protect.

The dissent fails to appreciate these very real limitations on a funding recipient's liability under Title IX. It is not enough to show, as the dissent would read this opinion to provide, that a student has been "teased," or "called offensive names[.]" Comparisons to an "overweight child who skips gym class because the other children tease her about her size," the student "who refuses to wear glasses to avoid the taunts of 'four-eyes,'" and "the child who refuses to go to school because the school bully calls him a 'scardy-cat' at recess," are inapposite and misleading. Nor do we contemplate, much less hold, that a mere "decline in grades is enough to survive" a motion to dismiss. The drop-off in LaShonda's grades provides necessary evidence of a potential link between her education and G. F.'s misconduct, but petitioner's ability to state a cognizable claim here depends equally on the alleged persistence and severity of G. F.'s actions, not to mention the Board's alleged knowledge and deliberate indifference. We trust that the dissent's characterization of our opinion will not mislead courts to impose more sweeping liability than we read Title IX to require.

Moreover, the provision that the discrimination occur "under any education program or activity" suggests that the behavior be serious enough to have the systemic effect of denying the victim equal access to an educational program or activity. Although, in theory, a single instance of sufficiently severe one-on-one peer harassment could be said to have such an effect, we think it unlikely that Congress would have thought such behavior sufficient to rise to this level in light of the inevitability of student misconduct and the amount of litigation that would be invited by entertaining claims of official indifference to a single instance of one-on-one peer harassment. By limiting private damages actions to cases having a systemic effect on educational programs or activities, we reconcile the general principle that Title IX prohibits official indifference to known peer sexual harassment with the practical realities of responding to student behavior, realities that Congress could not have meant to be ignored. . . .

The fact that it was a teacher who engaged in harassment in *Franklin* and *Gebser* is relevant. The relationship between the harasser and the victim necessarily affects the extent to which the misconduct can be said to breach Title IX's guarantee of equal access to educational benefits and to have a systemic effect on a program or activity. Peer harassment, in particular, is less likely to satisfy these requirements than is teacher-student harassment.

C

Applying this standard to the facts at issue here, we conclude that the Eleventh Circuit erred in dismissing petitioner's complaint. Petitioner alleges that her daughter was the victim of repeated acts of sexual harassment by G. F. over a 5-month period, and there are allegations in support of the conclusion that G. F.'s misconduct was severe, pervasive, and objectively offensive. The harassment was not only verbal; it included numerous acts of objectively offensive touching, and, indeed, G. F. ultimately pleaded guilty to criminal sexual misconduct. Moreover, the complaint alleges that there were multiple victims who were sufficiently disturbed by G. F.'s misconduct to seek an audience with the school principal. Further, petitioner contends that the harassment had a concrete, negative effect on her daughter's ability to receive an education. The complaint also suggests that petitioner may be able to show both actual knowledge and deliberate indifference on the part of the Board, which made no effort whatsoever either to investigate or to put an end to the harassment.

Justice KENNEDY, with whom The Chief Justice, Justice SCALIA, and Justice THOMAS join, dissenting.

. . .

I am aware of no basis in law or fact . . . for attributing the acts of a student to a school and, indeed, the majority does not argue that the school acts through its students. . . . Discrimination by one student against another therefore cannot be "under" the school's program or activity as required by Title IX. . . .

B

. . .

The practical obstacles schools encounter in ensuring that thousands of immature students conform their conduct to acceptable norms may be even more significant than the legal obstacles. School districts cannot exercise the same measure of control over thousands of students that they do over a few hundred adult employees. The limited resources of our schools must be conserved for basic educational services. Some schools lack the resources even to deal with serious problems of violence and are already overwhelmed with disciplinary problems of all kinds.

Perhaps even more startling than its broad assumptions about school control over primary and secondary school students is the majority's failure to grapple in any meaningful way with the distinction between elementary and secondary schools, on the one hand, and universities on the other. The majority bolsters its argument that schools can control their students' actions by quoting our decision in *Vernonia School District v. Acton* for the proposition that " 'the nature of [the State's] power [over public school children] is custodial and tutelary, permitting a degree of supervision and control that could not be exercised over free adults.' " Yet the majority's holding would appear to apply with equal force to universities, which do not exercise custodial and tutelary power over their adult students.

A university's power to discipline its students for speech that may constitute sexual harassment is also circumscribed by the First Amendment. A number of federal courts have already confronted difficult problems raised by university speech codes designed to deal with peer sexual and racial harassment. . . .

The difficulties associated with speech codes simply underscore the limited nature of a university's control over student behavior that may be viewed as sexual harassment. . . .

. . .

II

. . .

The law recognizes that children—particularly young children—are not fully accountable for their actions because they lack the capacity to exercise mature judgment. It should surprise no one, then, that the schools that are the primary locus of most children's social development are rife with inappropriate behavior by children who are just learning to interact with their peers. [Those] on the front lines of our schools describe the situation best:

> "Unlike adults in the workplace, juveniles have limited life experiences or familial influences upon which to establish an understanding of appropriate behavior. The real world of school discipline is a rough-and-tumble place where students

practice newly learned vulgarities, erupt with anger, tease and embarrass each other, share offensive notes, flirt, push and shove in the halls, grab and offend."

No one contests that much of this "dizzying array of immature or uncontrollable behaviors by students" is inappropriate, even "objectively offensive" at times . . . and that parents and schools have a moral and ethical responsibility to help students learn to interact with their peers in an appropriate manner. It is doubtless the case, moreover, that much of this inappropriate behavior is directed toward members of the opposite sex, as children in the throes of adolescence struggle to express their emerging sexual identities.

It is a far different question, however, whether it is either proper or useful to label this immature, childish behavior gender discrimination. Nothing in Title IX suggests that Congress even contemplated this question, much less answered it in the affirmative in unambiguous terms.

. . .

The difficulties schools will encounter in identifying peer sexual harassment are already evident in teachers' manuals designed to give guidance on the subject. For example, one teachers' manual on peer sexual harassment suggests that sexual harassment in kindergarten through third grade includes a boy being "put down" on the playground "because he wants to play house with the girls" or a girl being "put down because she shoots baskets better than the boys." Yet another manual suggests that one student saying to another, "You look nice," could be sexual harassment, depending on the "tone of voice," how the student looks at the other, and "who else is around." Blowing a kiss is also suspect. This confusion will likely be compounded once the sexual-harassment label is invested with the force of federal law, backed up by private damages suits.

The only guidance the majority gives schools in distinguishing between the "simple acts of teasing and name-calling among school children," said not to be a basis for suit even when they "target differences in gender," and actionable peer sexual harassment is, in reality, no guidance at all. The majority proclaims that "in the context of student-on-student harassment, damages are available only in the situation where the behavior is so serious, pervasive, and objectively offensive that it denies its victims the equal access to education that Title IX is designed to protect." The majority does not even purport to explain, however, what constitutes an actionable denial of "equal access to education." Is equal access denied when a girl who tires of being chased by the boys at recess refuses to go outside? When she cannot concentrate during class because she is worried about the recess activities? When she pretends to be sick one day so she can stay home from school? It appears the majority is content to let juries decide.

. . .

The only real clue the majority gives schools about the dividing line between actionable harassment that denies a victim equal access to education and mere inappropriate teasing is a profoundly unsettling one: On the facts of this case, petitioner has stated a claim because she alleged, in the majority's words, "that the harassment had a concrete, negative effect on her daughter's ability to receive an education." In petitioner's words, the effects that might have been visible to the school were that her daughter's grades "dropped" and her "ability to concentrate on her school work [was] affected." Almost all adolescents experience these problems at one time or another as they mature.

III

. . .

. . . The majority seems oblivious to the fact that almost every child, at some point, has trouble in school because he or she is being teased by his or her peers. The girl who wants to skip recess because she is teased by the boys is no different from the overweight child who skips gym class because the other children tease her about her size in the locker room; or the child who risks flunking out because he refuses to wear glasses to avoid the taunts of "four-eyes"; or the child who refuses to go to school because the school bully calls him a "scaredy-cat" at recess. Most children respond to teasing in ways that detract from their ability to learn. The majority's test for actionable harassment will, as a result, sweep in almost all of the more innocuous conduct it acknowledges as a ubiquitous part of school life.

The string of adjectives the majority attaches to the word "harassment"—"severe, pervasive, and objectively offensive"—likewise fails to narrow the class of conduct that can trigger liability, since the touchstone for determining whether there is Title IX liability is the effect on the child's ability to get an education. Indeed, the Court's reliance on the impact on the child's educational experience suggests that the "objective offensiveness" of a comment is to be judged by reference to a reasonable child at whom the comments were aimed. Not only is that standard likely to be quite expansive, it also gives schools—and juries—little guidance, requiring them to attempt to gauge the sensitivities of, for instance, the average seven year old.

. . . The problem is that the majority's test, in fact, invites courts and juries to second-guess school administrators in every case, to judge in each instance whether the school's response was "clearly unreasonable." . . .

. . .

There will be no shortage of plaintiffs to bring such complaints. Our schools are charged each day with educating millions of children. Of those millions of students, a large percentage will, at some point during their school careers, experience something they consider sexual harassment. A 1993 Study by the American Association of University Women Educational Foundation, for instance, found that "fully 4 out of 5 students (81%) report that they have been the target of some form of sexual harassment during their school lives." The number of potential lawsuits against our schools is staggering.

The cost of defending against peer sexual harassment suits alone could overwhelm many school districts, particularly since the majority's liability standards will allow almost any plaintiff to get to summary judgment, if not to a jury. In addition, there are no damages caps on the judicially implied private cause of action under Title IX. As a result, school liability in one peer sexual harassment suit could approach, or even exceed, the total federal funding of many school districts. Petitioner, for example, seeks damages of $500,000 in this case. Respondent school district received approximately $679,000 in federal aid in 1992–1993. . . .

. . .

The prospect of unlimited Title IX liability will, in all likelihood, breed a climate of fear that encourages school administrators to label even the most innocuous of childish conduct sexual harassment. It would appear to be no coincidence that, not long after the DOE issued its proposed policy guidance warning that schools could be liable for peer sexual harassment in the fall of 1996, a North Carolina school suspended a 6-year-old boy who kissed a female classmate on the cheek for sexual harassment, on the theory that "[u]nwelcome is unwelcome at any age." A week later, a New York school suspended a second-grader who kissed a classmate and ripped a button off her skirt. The second grader said that he got the idea from his favorite book "Corduroy," about a bear with a missing button. School administrators said only, "We were given guidelines as to why we suspend children. We follow the guidelines."

At the college level, the majority's holding is sure to add fuel to the debate over campus speech codes that, in the name of preventing a hostile educational environment, may infringe students' First Amendment rights. Indeed, under the majority's control principle, schools presumably will be responsible for remedying conduct that occurs even in student dormitory rooms. As a result, schools may well be forced to apply workplace norms in the most private of domains.

. . .

Disregarding . . . state-law remedies for student misbehavior and the incentives that our schools already have to provide the best possible education to all of their students, the majority seeks, in effect, to put an end to student misbehavior by transforming Title IX into a Federal Student Civility Code. I fail to see how federal courts will administer school discipline better than the principals and teachers to whom the public has entrusted that task or how the majority's holding will help the vast majority of students, whose educational opportunities will be diminished by the diversion of school funds to litigation. The private cause of action the Court creates will justify a corps of federal administrators in writing regulations on student harassment. It will also embroil schools and courts in endless litigation over what qualifies as peer sexual harassment and what constitutes a reasonable response.

In the final analysis, this case is about federalism. Yet the majority's decision today says not one word about the federal balance. Preserving our federal system is a legitimate end in itself. It is, too, the means to other ends. It ensures that essential choices can be made by a government more proximate to the people than the vast apparatus of federal power. Defining the appropriate role of schools in teaching and supervising children who are beginning to explore their own sexuality and learning how to express it to others is one of the most complex and sensitive issues our schools face. Such decisions are best made by parents and by the teachers and school administrators who can counsel with them. The delicacy and immense significance of teaching children about sexuality should cause the Court to act with great restraint before it displaces state and local governments. . . .

EXERCISE 8.2. The majority holds that students suing over student-on-student sexual harassment must show that the harassment "is so severe, pervasive, and objectively offensive that it effectively bars the victim's access to an educational opportunity or benefit." Is this standard too tough to take care of many of the real problems with sexual harassment that students face? Or is it too weak to prevent young people and their families from bringing federal court lawsuits over trivial issues like unwanted love poetry, overly sexual valentine cards, and the kind of sexual banter and horseplay that take place in school hallways all over America?

EXERCISE 8.3. Find out if there is a sexual harassment policy at your school. If there is, consider how well it implements the holdings of these cases and the rules of Title IX. If no policy is currently in place, gather some model school policies from the Internet and the Department of Education and draft one for your school; offer it to the principal as a public service. Create a list of the kinds of behaviors that you consider to be sexually harassing because they make people feel humiliated and depressed (unwanted pinching, leering, and teasing, for example). Now develop a list of the kinds of behaviors that you view acceptable because they make people feel good (nice compliments and mutual flirting, for example). Is it hard to draw a line? Compare your lists with those of your classmates. Do boys and girls have different perceptions about where the line should be drawn?

FOR THE CLASS

SEXUAL HARASSMENT? Consider the following examples of potentially objectionable behavior and try to determine whether each one constitutes Title IX sexual harassment—either quid pro quo or hostile environment—under the *Gebser* and *Monroe County* precedents. Could the students in each case sue?

A. Andy Algebra, the math teacher at North High, calls Sally Senior up on the phone every night to talk about their respective social lives and tries to engage her in phone sex. One night he asks her to meet him at the beach. Although Andy is, by far, her favorite teacher, Sally tells him that she thinks "the relationship is going in the wrong direction." He says, "Gee, I was planning to nominate you for the math award, but I guess you're not really my prize pupil after all." Sally is upset about the situation and receives a C+ on her next exam, the first time she has received below a B+ in the class. She tells her academic adviser, the assistant principal, about the situation, but he tells her to just "ignore his comments, he flatters all the pretty girls." A week later, Andy sends Sally an e-mail, saying: "I hope you meet me at the beach Friday night so we can discuss your poor grade on the last test. I know a way you can get your grades back up." Sexual harassment?

B. Albert Feinstein is slender and not athletically inclined. At gym, the other boys in the locker room tease him about his weight and clumsiness. Lately, they have taken to calling him "fag," "sissy," and "girl," and snapping their wet towels on his rear end. Several times when Albert has opened up his locker, he has found a bra or girl's panties with his name written on them. After another boy, forty pounds heavier than Albert, pounced on him on a wrestling mat and simulated sexual intercourse, Albert began to skip gym and complained about these events to his physical education teacher, who replied: "Come on, Albert, loosen up and take it like a man." Sexual harassment?

C. In a biology classroom discussion about the female reproductive system, Joe raised his hand and asked the teacher: "If girls are supposed to have mammary glands to feed their babies, why doesn't Mary have any?" The teacher immediately reprimanded Joe and demanded that he apologize to Mary, who was humiliated in front of her classmates. Sexual harassment?

D. Every day when girls at Reading High enter school, players on the football team sit on the curb with scorecards and hold up numbers, one through ten, "grading" them on their looks and appearance. Many girls felt embarrassed and humiliated by having to pass this gauntlet and began to come to school late to avoid being rated in this way. After receiving a number of "tardy" notices, several of the girls were given detention and other forms of discipline. When they objected to their discipline on the ground that they could not enter the school because of the rating game, the principal told them: "That's simply a fall homecoming tradition, and it's certainly no excuse for blatantly violating the rules of the school." The girls were disciplined. Meanwhile, the members of the team also took to pasting pictures of girls in the school onto the nude bodies of women pictured in pornographic magazines and placing them in the boys' locker room. After a few weeks, the coach took them down but no one was disciplined. Sexual harassment?

Discuss whether any of these cases are "actionable"—that is, whether any of the students could bring a lawsuit against their school under Title IX in federal court. What would be the strengths and weaknesses of each case? Pretend your class is a law firm and you must advise the students in each case on what to do. What advice do you give them?

The Right of Gay and Lesbian Students Against Harassment

Title IX's protections against sexual harassment apply to gay and lesbian students as well as to straight students. In 1996, an Ashland, Wisconsin, student named Jamie Nabozny received a $900,000 judgment against his school system for its failure to put an end to the violence Nabozny endured at the hands of classmates from grades 7 through 11. At one point, Nabozny was beaten so badly that he was hospitalized. Gay-bashing of this nature has, in some instances, led to murder.

Hostility toward gay, lesbian, and bisexual students—and anyone who others think may belong to one of these groups—can also take nonviolent forms. The ridicule, relentless teasing, and put-downs that can occur may also be actionable in court if they are sufficiently severe and pervasive. Many states and counties have passed specific laws and ordinances protecting students against harassment based on sexual orientation. California has such a law, as does Massachusetts, which also promotes the creation of gay and lesbian support groups in public high schools. The state now has 180 Gay/Straight Alliances on campus.

Many people think that passing laws to protect gays, lesbians, and bisexuals against harassment encourages or promotes homosexuality. Do you agree? Why or why not? (Do you think that a person's sexual orientation is learned behavior, and does this affect your position?) Should gay and lesbian students have the right to form Gay/Straight Alliances on campus alongside other student clubs? How does this question relate to the First Amendment?

What can be done to prevent harassment of gay and lesbian students? Discuss with your classmates. (An interesting video on this issue, *It's Elementary,* is available from *www.womedia.org.*)

Read On

American Association of University Women. *Hostile Hallways: The AAUW Survey on Sexual Harassment in America's Schools.* Washington, D.C.: The Foundation, 1993.

Department of Education, Office of Civil Rights. *Sexual Harassment Guidance: Harassment of Students by School Employees, Other Students, or Third Parties.* Washington, D.C.: Government Printing Office.

Langelan, Martha. *Back Off: How to Confront and Stop Sexual Harassment and Harrassers.* New York: Simon and Schuster, 1993.

Stein, Nan, and Lisa Sjostram. *Flirting or Hurting? A Teacher's Guide to Student-to-Student Sexual Harassment in Schools.* Washington, D.C.: NEA Professional Library Publication, 1994. [Available from the National Education Association at 1-800-229-4200.]

For Further Information

American Association of University Professors at *www.aaup.org.*

Lambda Legal Defense at *www.lambdalegal.org.*

Gay, Lesbian and Straight Education Network at *www.glsen.org.*

National Education Association at *www.nea.org.*

National Organization for Women's Legal Defense and Education Fund at *www.nowldef.org.*

National Women's Law Center at (202) 588-5180.

PRIVACY, SEXUALITY, AND THE FOURTEENTH AMENDMENT

9

Whether or not we condone it, however much we might prefer it not be true, the fact is millions of American teenagers have sex every year. Consider this startling statistic from the Alan Guttmacher Institute in New York: each year nearly one million U.S. teenaged girls become pregnant, and almost four out of five of these pregnancies are unintended. Some 55 percent of these pregnancies are carried to term, 31 percent end in abortions, and 14 percent end in miscarriage.

The pervasiveness of teen sexual activity, combined with the public's conflicted feelings about it, make it difficult to know what to do about the very high rates of teen sex, pregnancy, and abortion. One possibility is to promote abstinence. Another is to make condoms available to students who are having sex. As you can imagine, the latter approach is highly controversial; many people feel that making contraceptives available to students interferes with the right of parents to control their children's upbringing.

A related issue is whether or not young women seeking an abortion should first have to obtain the consent and authorization of one of their parents. A variation on this approach charges health care providers with notifying parents.

Currently, thirty states require some type of parental involvement. This is the tough issue to which we now turn.

POINTS TO PONDER

How do the privacy rights founded in the liberty interest protected in the Fourteenth Amendment affect issues of sexuality in the school setting?

- Should young women, minors under the age of eighteen, be required to have the consent of one of their parents or a judge before obtaining an abortion?
- Should high schools make condoms available to sexually active teens to try and curb the high rates of teen pregnancy, or does this practice violate the parents' right to control the raising of their children?

Abortion and the Privacy Rights of Teenagers

Few constitutional issues in our time have been as charged as the issue of abortion. In 1973, in *Roe v. Wade,* the Supreme Court upheld the fundamental right of a woman to choose an abortion in consultation with her doctor. In *Roe,* the Court derived the right to an abortion from the basic right to privacy. The right to privacy is founded in the liberty interest protected in the Fourteenth Amendment: "[N]or shall any state deprive any person of life, liberty, or property. . . ."

The controversy over abortion has never really subsided, and the Supreme Court has dealt with repeated attempts by states to restrict a woman's abortion options. In the following 1992 decision, *Planned Parenthood of Southeastern Pennsylvania v. Casey,* however, the Court reaffirmed the essential "core" right of a woman to make a decision about terminating a pregnancy. But it did this in a way that allows greater regulation of abortion—specifically, when teenagers, or minor females, seek to have one. In *Casey,* the Court upheld, among other restrictions, the Commonwealth of Pennsylvania's rule that females under the age of eighteen must obtain the consent of either one of their parents or a judge before having an abortion. As a matter of constitutional law, does this holding damage the rights of women or simply uphold the rights of parents?

PLANNED PARENTHOOD OF SOUTHEASTERN PENNSYLVANIA

v.

CASEY

Supreme Court of the United States
Argued April 22, 1992.
Decided June 29, 1992.

[The Court addressed the following sections of the Pennsylvania Abortion Control Act:]

Parental Consent for Abortion

. . . Except in the case of a medical emergency or except as provided in this section, if a pregnant woman is less than 18 years of age and not emancipated, or if she has been adjudged an incompetent . . . , a physician shall not perform an abortion upon her unless, in the case of a woman who is less than 18 years of age, *he first obtains the informed consent both of the pregnant woman and of one of her parents.* . . . In the case of a pregnancy that is the result of incest, where the father is a party to the incestuous act, the pregnant woman need only obtain the consent of her mother. (emphasis added)

. . . If both of the parents or guardians of the pregnant woman refuse to consent to the performance of an abortion or if she elects not to seek the consent of either of her parents or of her guardian, [the court] shall, upon petition or motion, after an appropriate hearing, authorize a physician to perform the abortion *if the court determines that the pregnant woman*

A young pregnant girl appears before a judge in a Philadelphia courtroom. In many states that today require girls seeking an abortion to obtain parental consent first, girls are exercising their right to a "judicial bypass" by appearing before a judge and asking the court's permission to terminate the pregnancy.

is mature and capable of giving informed consent to the proposed abortion, and has, in fact, given such consent. (emphasis added)

If the court determines that the pregnant woman is not mature and capable of giving informed consent or if the pregnant woman does not claim to be mature and capable of giving informed consent, the court shall determine whether the performance of an abortion upon her would be in her best interests. If the court determines that the performance of an abortion would be in the best interests of the woman, it shall authorize a physician to perform the abortion.

[Following is an excerpt from Justice O'CONNOR's majority opinion in *Casey* considering the above provision:]

. . .

V

. . .

D

We next consider the parental consent provision. Except in a medical emergency, an unemancipated young woman under 18 may not obtain an abortion unless she and one of her parents (or guardian) provides informed consent as defined above. If neither a parent nor a guardian provides consent, a court may authorize the performance of an abortion upon a determination that the young woman is mature and capable of giving informed consent and has in fact given her informed consent, or that an abortion would be in her best interests.

We have been over most of this ground before. Our cases establish, and we reaffirm today, that a State may require a minor seeking an abortion to obtain the consent of a parent or guardian, provided that there is an adequate judicial bypass procedure. Under these precedents, in our view, the one-parent consent requirement and judicial bypass procedure are constitutional.

The only argument made by [Casey] respecting this provision and to which our prior decisions do not speak is the contention that the parental consent requirement is invalid because it requires informed parental consent. For the most part, [Casey's] argument is a reprise of their argument with respect to the informed consent requirement in general, and we reject it for the reasons given above. Indeed, some of the provisions regarding informed consent have particular force with respect to minors: the waiting period, for example, may provide the parent or parents of a pregnant young woman the opportunity to consult with her in private, and to discuss the consequences of her decision in the context of the values and moral or religious principles of their family.

. . .

Justice BLACKMUN, concurring in part, concurring in judgment in part and dissenting in part.

. . . While the State has an interest in encouraging parental involvement in the minor's abortion decision, [the law] is not narrowly drawn to serve that interest.[1]

Chief Justice REHNQUIST, joined by Justice WHITE, Justice SCALIA, and Justice THOMAS, concurring in the judgment in part and dissenting in part.

. . . We believe that *Roe* was wrongly decided and that it can, and should be overruled. . . . [They argue that states should be free to regulate abortion without interference by the Supreme Court.]

. . .

We have treated parental consent provisions [very] harshly. Three years after *Roe,* we invalidated a Missouri regulation requiring that an unmarried woman under the age of 18 obtain the consent of one of her parents before proceeding with an abortion. We held that our abortion jurisprudence prohibited the State from imposing such a "blanket provision . . . requiring the consent of a parent." In [another case] the Court struck down a similar Massachusetts parental consent statute. A majority of the Court indicated, however, that a State could constitutionally require parental consent, if it alternatively allowed a pregnant minor to obtain an abortion without parental consent by showing either that she was mature enough to make her own decision, or that the abortion would be in her best interests. . . . We have never had occasion, as we have in the parental notice context, to further parse our parental consent jurisprudence into one-parent and two-parent components.

. . .

. . . [A] parental consent restriction certainly places very substantial obstacles in the path of a minor's abortion choice. . . . This may or may not be a correct judgment, but it is quintessentially a legislative one. . . . Under the guise of the Constitution, this Court will still impart its own preferences on the States in the form of a complex abortion code. . . .

Each year, more than one million young American women between the ages of twelve and nineteen become pregnant. These pregnancies are, in the vast majority of cases, unplanned. Studies show that most young women in this situation will approach one of their parents, usually their mother, to discuss their situation. But many young women do not consult their parents, citing fear, embarrassment, anxiety, and a desire not to upset them. Some young women are in abusive or dysfunctional families where they are afraid that their pregnancy will just further complicate family dynamics or even provoke violence against them or other family members.

As of July 1999, thirty states required some form of parental involvement in the teen's abortion decision—whether it was simple notice that the procedure was to take place or a requirement of actual consent (backed up by the "judicial bypass" option if consent was not forthcoming). The arguments for such laws

JUSTICE HARRY A. BLACKMUN (1908–1999) was born in Nashville, Illinois, and raised in St. Paul, Minnesota. Although he wanted to be a doctor rather than a lawyer, he went to Harvard Law School in 1929. He clerked on the Eighth Circuit Court of Appeals, practiced privately, and then actually took the place of his former employer and mentor, Judge Sanborn, on the Eighth Circuit. In 1970 President Richard Nixon appointed Blackmun to the Supreme Court after Nixon's two prior choices, both southern conservatives, were rejected by the Senate. Blackmun remained until his retirement in 1994.

HIGHLIGHTS

➤   Blackmun began a long-lasting friendship with fellow future Supreme Court justice Warren Burger in kindergarten and was even the best man at Burger's wedding. On the Court, the two were initially called "the Minnesota twins," but then their opinions began to diverge and their relationship cooled.

➤   In private practice, Blackmun was resident general counsel for the Mayo Clinic, a prestigious research hospital in Minnesota. He described those ten years as "the happiest years of [my] professional experience."

➤   Though he regretted not going to medical school, Justice Blackmun had more of an impact on the field of medicine than most doctors because of his famous opinion in *Roe v. Wade,* upholding the right of a woman to choose abortion in consultation with her doctor. This was the opinion of which Justice Blackmun was most proud.

focus on keeping parents closely connected to the lives of their children. Proponents of these laws say that children need help and support during times of crisis and that the parental involvement laws promote family decision-making and protect parental rights. Many parents say that, if they are asked to consent to any other form of surgery for their minor children, why not abortion? They consider it a matter of their fundamental right to raise their children and set family values. In cases where abuse is a real danger, the minor can find her way to a judge in family court to authorize the procedure.

Opponents of mandatory parental involvement argue that, while most young women facing an unwanted pregnancy will of their own accord talk to one or both parents, the laws traumatize and endanger precisely those young women who come from the most difficult family situations. They also argue that the laws turn many young women into criminals or outlaws who go to other states or jurisdictions to seek an abortion. The whole legal machinery here, they claim, delays the ability to get an abortion, increasing both the cost and the risk of the procedure. They also cite the embarrassment young women experience going before a judge (and a bailiff and a court reporter and anyone else who might be in the courtroom) to ask for the right to have an abortion. Some judges lecture and upbraid the young women and many have found the young women not mature enough to get an abortion.

What do you think of this difficult issue?

EXERCISE 9.1. What do you think of "parental consent" requirements that force young women to obtain the consent of their parents or a judge in order to have an abortion? Does this violate their right to privacy? Will it make it more difficult to exercise the right, or will it foster greater family support and harmony? Interestingly, while the *Casey* Court upheld the parental consent provision in the Pennsylvania law, it struck down the spousal notification provision that required women to attest that they had either notified their husbands of their plans to get an abortion or could not find them. Why do you think the Court treated the two provisions differently? One factor cited by Justice O'Connor was the high incidence of domestic violence and abuse by husbands of their wives, a problem often exacerbated by the decision of whether or not to proceed with a pregnancy. Does this argument sufficiently distinguish the two kinds of provisions? Do pregnant teenagers ever face domestic violence because of their predicament? On the other hand, if minors cannot obtain other kinds of surgery and medical procedures without parental consent, is there any reason to treat abortion differently from a constitutional perspective?

FOR THE CLASS

LEGISLATIVE DECISION-MAKING. Turn your class into a state legislature. In the wake of the Supreme Court's decision in *Casey*, which upheld parental consent laws, your state is considering whether or not to require all females, age eighteen and under, seeking an abortion to obtain the signature of both parents or, if her parents refuse, the consent of a state trial court judge before she is permitted to proceed. Would you vote for or against such a law? Using your classroom blackboard, make an inventory of all of the arguments available on both sides of the issue. Give speeches, have a debate, and then take a vote.

Birth Control

America experiences high rates of teen pregnancy. Some people place the blame for this on the saturation of media with sexual images; others attribute it to an appalling lack of proper sexual education and knowledge about contraception. Very likely, these two factors go hand-in-hand to create large numbers of unplanned pregnancies.

In response to this problem, many school systems have sought to promote sex education; some have gone so far as to distribute contraceptives—specifically condoms—to students when they ask for them. In the next case, the Supreme Judicial Court of Massachusetts held that a program of voluntary distribution of condoms to male or female students who request them, without parental notification, did not violate the family's or student's privacy interests. The court determined that, because the program was wholly voluntary and parents could instruct their children on whether or not to participate, there was no unlawful coercion or pressure for students to use the available contraceptive services.

CURTIS
v.
SCHOOL COMMITTEE OF FALMOUTH

Supreme Judicial Court of Massachusetts
Argued March 7, 1995.
Decided July 17, 1995.

Opinion: LIACOS, C.J.

The plaintiffs, students and parents of students in the Falmouth public school system, appealed from a grant of summary judgment in favor of the defendants, the school committee of Falmouth (school committee) and three individual defendants. We granted the school committee's application for direct appellate review. We affirm.

. . .

The plaintiffs alleged in their amended complaint, and now argue before this court, that the condom-availability program, as it stands, violates their right to familial privacy and their guaranteed liberties as parents in the control of the education and upbringing of their children, protected by the Fourteenth Amendment to the United States Constitution. . . . The plaintiffs ask us to reverse the judge's entry of summary judgment for the defendants and to enjoin the school committee from continuing to make condoms available to students without the inclusion of a provision which would permit parents to opt out of the program and without a system of parental notification of their child's requests for a condom.

The motion judge set forth the facts as follows: "On January 2, 1992, following an authorizing vote of the FSC [Falmouth school committee], the Superintendent of Schools issued a memorandum to the teaching staff of grades 7 through 12, detailing the condom availability program. At Lawrence Junior High School, students could request free condoms from the school nurse. Prior to receiving them, students would be counseled. The nurse was also instructed to give students pamphlets on AIDS/HIV and other sexually transmitted diseases. At Falmouth High School, students could request free condoms from the school nurse, or students could purchase them for $ .75 from the condom vending machines located in the lower level boys' and girls' restrooms. Counseling by trained faculty members would be provided to students who requested it, and informational pamphlets were available in the [school] nurse's office. The Superintendent's memorandum instructed the staff to reserve their own opinions regarding condom availability in order to respect students' privacy. The memorandum also indicates that the Superintendent's presentation of the condom availability to the student body would stress abstinence as the only certain method for avoiding sexually transmitted diseases. The condom availability program took effect on January 2, 1992.

"The FSC condom program does not provide for an 'opt out' for students' parents whereby the parents have the option of excluding their student child from the availability of condoms. Nor is there a parental notification provision in the FSC program by which parents would be notified of their children's requests for condoms.". . .

. . .

The judge concluded that the plaintiffs had failed to meet the threshold requirement for each of their claims because they were unable to demonstrate that the condom-availability program placed a coercive burden on their rights. . . . [T]hey argue, the State was required to prove the existence of a compelling State interest in maintaining the condom-availability program.

. . . [T]he condom-availability program in Falmouth is in all respects voluntary and in no way intrudes into the realm of constitutionally protected rights. Because no threshold demonstration of a coercive burden has been made, nor could have been made on these facts, the defendants properly were granted summary judgment.

. . .

We discern no coercive burden on the plaintiffs' parental liberties in this case. No classroom participation is required of students. Condoms are available to students who request them and, in the high school, may be obtained from vending machines. The students are not required to seek out and accept the condoms, read the literature accompanying them, or participate in counseling regarding their use. In other words, the students are free to decline to participate in the program. No penalty or disciplinary action ensues if a student does not participate in the program. For their part, the plaintiff parents are free to instruct their children not to participate. The program does not supplant the parents' role as advisor in the moral and religious development of their children. Although exposure to condom vending machines and to the program itself may offend the moral and religious sensibilities of the plaintiffs, mere exposure to programs offered at school does not amount to unconstitutional interference with parental liberties without the existence of some compulsory aspect to the program.

. . .

Because we conclude the program lacks any degree of coercion or compulsion in violation of the plaintiffs' parental liberties, or their familial privacy, we conclude also that neither an opt-out provision nor parental notification is required by the Federal Constitution. . . .

. . .

Judgment affirmed.

EXERCISE 9.2. Do you think that public high schools should participate in condom distribution programs? What if students are required to meet with counselors first and discuss safe sexual behavior and proper use of contraceptives? In an older case from New York state, an appeals court struck down a similar condom distribution program that also did not have a parental notification requirement or opt-out option. Two courts came to opposite conclusions on the same issue. Which case had the better outcome? Why?

FOR THE CLASS

Imagine that you and your classmates are members of the school board in a district that sees 15 percent of its female students drop out before graduation as a result of pregnancy. How should the school district tackle the problem of teenage pregnancy? Do you favor condom distribution? Abstinence education? GED programs? Discuss the issue and your options with your classmates and see if you can develop an approach that you believe will effectively deal with the problem.

Note

1. "A State may not place any restriction on a young woman's right to an abortion, however irrational, simply because it has provided a judicial bypass."

Read On

Rubin, Eva. *Abortion, Politics and the Courts:* Roe v. Wade *and Its Aftermath.* New York: Greenwood, 1987.

Tribe, Laurence. *Abortion: The Clash of Absolutes.* New York: Norton, 1992.

SUPREME COURT CONFIRMATION EXERCISE: YOU BE THE JUDGE!

10

"[The President] shall appoint . . . Judges of the supreme Court." ARTICLE II, SECTION 2

"The Judges, both of the supreme and inferior courts, shall hold their Offices during good behaviour . . . ." ARTICLE III, SECTION 1

Article II of the Constitution gives the president the power to appoint Supreme Court justices (and other federal judges) with "the Advice and Consent of the Senate." This means that the president's candidates for the Supreme Court have to receive a majority vote in the Senate in favor of confirmation before they are able to take office. Historically, the Senate has taken its duties seriously and closely scrutinized presidential nominees to the Court. Indeed, over the centuries, there have been many heated controversies over nominees, and many have been rejected by the Senate.

Because Supreme Court justices have life tenure and never have to face the public in an election to explain their views, Senate confirmation hearings are the single occasion upon which the Congress can carefully probe the ideas of Supreme Court nominees. It is also the only opportunity the public and press have to witness and indirectly participate in a public dialogue with nominees about the Supreme Court, the Constitution, and justice. This public educational function has become increasingly important since the 1939 confirmation hearing of Felix Frankfurter, the first nominee to appear personally before the Senate, and infinitely more important since the 1981 confirmation hearing of Sandra

The family of Supreme Court justice nominee Sandra Day O'Connor, the first woman ever to serve as a justice, attends her historic confirmation hearings before the Senate Judiciary Committee in 1981.

Day O'Connor, which was the first to be shown on television and broadcast on radio. Today, Supreme Court confirmation hearings draw intense public interest and media scrutiny.

In the following exercise, students will assume the roles of key actors in a mock U.S. Supreme Court confirmation hearing before the United States Senate's Committee on the Judiciary. Select three students to play the roles of the U.S. Supreme Court justice nominees, nine students to organize themselves into the Senate Committee on the Judiciary (with the teacher acting as the committee chair), three students to be television commentators, one student to act as the president of the United States, and three students to serve as counsel to the three Supreme Court nominees. In this exercise, we are assuming that there are suddenly three vacancies on the Supreme Court. In fact, this scenario is highly unlikely; vacancies, when they arise, almost always occur one at a time.

The confirmation process for U.S. Supreme Court judicial nominees typically involves the following four-part sequence: First, the White House and the Federal Bureau of Investigation undertake several background checks on individuals identified as potential nominees;[1] second, the president makes his or her selection based on the outcome of these checks and on ideological and political grounds; third, a confirmation hearing to judge the fitness of the president's nominee (or, in our case, nominees) is conducted by the Senate Judiciary Committee; and fourth, the full Senate takes a final vote on whether or not to confirm the president's choice.

Start by having the student who is playing the president spend some time with his or her nominees to elicit background information. The president should then write and present a speech in a mock press conference introducing his or her nominees and trumpeting their virtues as potential justices. What are the outstanding qualities and experiences that qualify these persons to sit on the most important court in the land? What are the considerations and characteristics that the president cites as having informed his or her decision? The members of the media should ask questions about the president's choices and raise any issues of controversy surrounding the nominees. How does the president respond? (Note that the nominees should not make comments on their views at this time, but should wait to do so at the Senate Judiciary Committee hearings.)

Next, move on to the Senate Judiciary Committee hearing process. The nominees should fill out the questionnaire on the facing page and distribute copies of their answers to every member of the Senate Judiciary Committee (and other students as well) for their consideration. Once the nominees' answers have been distributed, the confirmation hearing can begin.

QUESTIONNAIRE FOR JUDICIAL NOMINEES

1. Full Name (include any former names used)
2. Date and Place of Birth
3. Education
4. Marital Status
5. Health: The physical and mental requirements of this position require you to prove that you are currently capable, and do not foresee any likelihood of mental or emotional instability. Please disclose all information concerning this issue and provide the date of your last physical examination.
6. Memberships: List all organizations to which you belong and the positions you hold in each.
7. Public Service: Provide your record of public service over the past five years.
8. Net Worth: Provide a complete, current financial net worth statement.
9. Have you to your knowledge ever been under investigation for a possible violation of a civil or criminal statute? Have you ever been arrested or charged with a crime?
10. Please advise the Committee on any unfavorable information that may influence public or congressional response to your nomination.
11. What is your judicial philosophy? Do you believe in "judicial activism," the idea that federal courts should actively intervene to enforce people's rights, or do you think that the Court should generally defer to the political branches of government? What are your rules for the road?
12. What do you think are the best Supreme Court decisions involving the rights of students and young people? What do you think are the worst?

The committee should consider one nominee at a time. Each nominee should start off by making an opening statement thanking the president and the committee and generally describing his or her views and commitment to the

Supreme Court. The students on the Senate Judiciary Committee should take turns posing two or three questions each to the nominee. The chair of the committee should call on senators in order of seniority (perhaps by age?), always making sure that order and protocol prevail throughout the proceedings. The nominees' counsels should be seated next to them during the hearings and be prepared to aid the nominees as necessary.

Senators can ask any questions they want, but the nominees always have the option of choosing not to answer. In fact, many nominees refuse to answer questions about their views of specific cases that will come before the Court, saying that such pointed answers would be inappropriate. Notwithstanding these objections, most nominees do their best to address the concerns of the senators. Oftentimes, senators will try to nail nominees down on their specific commitments and beliefs. The following are sample questions that the senators might ask. Feel free to change them around or make up your own, depending on your concerns:

1. What are your main qualifications to serve on the U.S. Supreme Court?
2. What aspects of law do you find the most intriguing?
3. What do you think are the greatest Supreme Court cases of all time?
4. Do you think that minors and students have constitutional rights? Are those rights equal to the rights of adults, or are they of less weight?
5. Do you believe that the *Casey* Court was correct in holding that states may impose parental consent requirements on minors seeking to have abortions? Why or why not?
6. Do you consider yourself hard-working? How do we know that you have the commitment that this job demands?

When all of the senators have finished asking questions, the nominee should be given a moment to offer his or her closing thoughts. At this point, the chair of the Senate Judiciary Committee should thank the nominee and excuse him or her.

Now bring on the next nominee and repeat the above process.

When all of the nominees have had their hearings, the committee should take a break and the three television reporters and commentators should simulate a talk show and discuss how the various nominees fared in the hearing process. What were their strengths and weaknesses as candidates? How did they handle hot issues and controversial questions? How will the various senators react to their testimony?

The committee should then reconvene and discuss the various nominees and their legal philosophies and positions, and then vote on whether or not to confirm each of the nominees. At this point, the classroom exercise is at an end. Of course, the nomination process is not yet complete. Normally, the names of the nominees who have passed the committee process are sent to the full Senate for a final vote. If you have a large class, have those students who were not selected to play any of the previous roles act as the full Senate and put the issue to them for a final vote. Which nominee or nominees did the class select?

The Supreme Court nominees (now justices, perhaps!) should discuss their experience: what they found difficult about the process, what they enjoyed about the process, and what they learned from the process. What would they do differently next time? What about the other actors? What did they learn from the process? Do you think that you would ever like to be a judge or a justice on the Supreme Court? Why or why not?

EXERCISE 10.1. Write a one- or two-page essay indicating who in your class you think would make a good judge or justice. Why? What personal characteristics does this classmate display that you would seek in a judge? Read the essay aloud.

EXERCISE 10.2. Write a one-page essay on any or all of the following questions: What is the most important thing people should know about the Constitution? How do you think learning about constitutional rights and responsibilities has changed your thinking about citizenship? Do you think there is a difference between young people who are constitutionally literate and those who are not? How would you convince a fellow teenager that it is important to study constitutional law? Is it important? Read your essay aloud.

EXERCISE 10.3. Write a letter to a present Supreme Court justice telling him or her which decisions or opinions of his or hers you admire and why.

EXERCISE 10.4. Organize a class trip to your state supreme court. If you find the experience meaningful, why not organize a class trip to the United States Supreme Court? Washington, D.C., is a great place to visit. Write an article for your school and local newspapers about the experience.

Note

1. The first background check requires the nominee to complete numerous questionnaires that cover issues ranging from the nominee's address, education, and marital status to health conditions, legal activities, and ethical beliefs. The second background check is a computerized search for a nominee's criminal record or involvement in potentially embarrassing activities. The final background check is made by the FBI and includes a compilation of detailed interviews with current and previous employers and employees, family members, friends, colleagues, and neighbors. The FBI's background check is made available to the Senate Judiciary Committee chair and the ranking minority member only when the confirmation hearing exposes damaging information about the nominee.

UNITED STATES CONSTITUTION

We the People of the United States, in Order to form a more perfect Union, establish Justice, insure domestic Tranquility, provide for the common defence, promote the general Welfare, and secure the Blessings of Liberty to ourselves and our Posterity, do ordain and establish this Constitution for the United States of America.

Article I

SECTION 1. All legislative Powers herein granted shall be vested in a Congress of the United States, which shall consist of a Senate and House of Representatives.

SECTION 2. The House of Representatives shall be composed of Members chosen every second Year by the People of the several States, and the Electors in each State shall have the Qualifications requisite for Electors of the most numerous Branch of the State Legislature.

No Person shall be a Representative who shall not have attained to the age of twenty five Years, and been seven Years a Citizen of the United States, and who shall not, when elected, be an Inhabitant of that State in which he shall be chosen.

[Representatives and direct Taxes shall be apportioned among the several States which may be included within this Union, according to their respective Numbers, which shall be determined by adding to the whole Number of free Persons, including those bound to Service for a Term of Years, and excluding Indians not taxed, three fifths of all other Persons.][1] The actual Enumeration shall be made within three Years after the first Meeting of the Congress of the United States, and within every subsequent Term of ten Years, in such Manner as they shall by Law direct. The Number of Representatives shall not exceed one for every thirty Thousand, but each State shall have at Least one Representative; and until such enumeration shall be made, the State of New Hampshire shall be entitled to chuse three, Massachusetts eight, Rhode-Island and Providence Plantations one, Connecticut five, New-York six, New Jersey four, Pennsylvania eight, Delaware one, Maryland six, Virginia ten, North Carolina five, South Carolina five, and Georgia three.

When vacancies happen in the Representation from any State, the Executive Authority thereof shall issue Writs of Election to fill such Vacancies.

The House of Representatives shall chuse their Speaker and other Officers; and shall have the sole Power of Impeachment.

SECTION 3. The Senate of the United States shall be composed of two Senators from each State, [chosen by the Legislature thereof,][2] for six Years; and each Senator shall have one Vote.

Immediately after they shall be assembled in Consequence of the first Election, they shall be divided as equally as may be into three Classes. The Seats of the Senators of the first Class shall be vacated at the Expiration of the second Year, of the second Class at the Expiration of the fourth Year, and of the third Class at the Expiration of the sixth Year, so that one third may be chosen every second Year; [and if Vacancies happen by Resignation, or otherwise, during the Recess of the Legislature of any State, the Executive thereof may make temporary Appointments until the next Meeting of the Legislature, which shall then fill such Vacancies.][3]

No Person shall be a Senator who shall not have attained to the Age of thirty Years, and been nine Years a Citizen of the United States, and who shall not, when elected, be an Inhabitant of that State for which he shall be chosen.

The Vice President of the United States shall be President of the Senate, but shall have no Vote, unless they be equally divided.

The Senate shall chuse their other Officers, and also a President pro tempore, in the Absence of the Vice President, or when he shall exercise the Office of President of the United States.

The Senate shall have the sole Power to try all Impeachments. When sitting for that Purpose, they shall be on Oath or Affirmation. When the President of the United States is tried, the Chief Justice shall preside: And no Person shall be convicted without the Concurrence of two thirds of the Members present.

Judgment in Cases of Impeachment shall not extend further than to removal from Office, and disqualification to hold and enjoy any Office of honor, Trust or Profit under the United States: but the Party convicted shall nevertheless be liable and subject to Indictment, Trial, Judgment and Punishment, according to Law.

SECTION 4. The Times, Places and Manner of holding Elections for Senators and Representatives, shall be prescribed in each State by the Legislature thereof; but the Congress may at any time by Law make or alter such Regulations, except as to the Places of chusing Senators.

The Congress shall assemble at least once in every Year, and such Meeting shall [be on the first Monday in December],[4] unless they shall by Law appoint a different Day.

SECTION 5. Each House shall be the Judge of the Elections, Returns and Qualifications of its own Members, and a Majority of each shall constitute a Quorum to do Business; but a smaller Number may adjourn from day to day, and may be authorized to compel the Attendance of absent Members, in such Manner, and under such Penalties as each House may provide.

Each House may determine the Rules of its Proceedings, punish its Members for disorderly Behaviour, and, with the Concurrence of two thirds, expel a Member.

Each House shall keep a Journal of its Proceedings, and from time to time publish the same, excepting such Parts as may in their Judgment require Secrecy; and the Yeas and Nays of the Members of either House on any question shall, at the Desire of one fifth of those Present, be entered on the Journal.

Neither House, during the Session of Congress, shall, without the Consent of the other, adjourn for more than three days, nor to any other Place than that in which the two Houses shall be sitting.

SECTION 6. The Senators and Representatives shall receive a Compensation for their Services, to be ascertained by Law, and paid out of the Treasury of the United States. They shall in all Cases, except Treason, Felony and Breach of the Peace, be privileged from Arrest during their Attendance at the Session of their respective Houses, and in going to and returning from the same; and for any Speech or Debate in either House, they shall not be questioned in any other Place.

No Senator or Representative shall, during the Time for which he was elected, be appointed to any civil Office under the Authority of the United States, which shall have been created, or the Emoluments whereof shall have been encreased during such time; and no Person holding any Office under the United States, shall be a Member of either House during his Continuance in Office.

SECTION 7. All Bills for raising Revenue shall originate in the House of Representatives; but the Senate may propose or concur with Amendments as on other Bills.

Every Bill which shall have passed the House of Representatives and the Senate, shall, before it become a Law, be presented to the President of the United States; If he approve he shall sign it, but if not he shall return it, with his Objections to that House in which it shall have originated, who shall enter the Objections at large on their Journal, and proceed to reconsider it. If after such Reconsideration two thirds of that House shall agree to pass the Bill, it shall be sent, together with the Objections, to the other House, by which it shall likewise be reconsidered, and if approved by two thirds of that House, it shall become a Law. But in all such Cases the Votes of both Houses shall be determined by yeas and Nays, and the Names of the Persons voting for and against the Bill shall be entered on the Journal of each House respectively. If any Bill shall not be returned by the President within ten Days (Sundays excepted) after it shall have been presented to him, the Same shall be a Law, in like Manner as if he had signed it, unless the Congress by their Adjournment prevent its Return, in which Case it shall not be a Law.

Every Order, Resolution, or Vote to which the Concurrence of the Senate and House of Representatives may be necessary (except on a question of Adjournment) shall be presented to the President of the United States; and before the Same shall take Effect, shall be approved by him, or being disapproved by him, shall be repassed by two thirds of the Senate and House of Representatives, according to the Rules and Limitations prescribed in the Case of a Bill.

SECTION 8. The Congress shall have Power To lay and collect Taxes, Duties, Imposts and Excises, to pay the Debts and provide for the common Defence and general Welfare of the United States; but all Duties, Imposts and Excises shall be uniform throughout the United States;

To borrow Money on the credit of the United States;

To regulate Commerce with foreign Nations, and among the several States, and with the Indian Tribes;

To establish an uniform Rule of Naturalization, and uniform Laws on the subject of Bankruptcies throughout the United States;

To coin Money, regulate the Value thereof, and of foreign Coin, and fix the Standard of Weights and Measures;

To provide for the Punishment of counterfeiting the Securities and current Coin of the United States;

To establish Post Offices and post Roads;

To promote the Progress of Science and useful Arts, by securing for limited Times to Authors and Inventors the exclusive Right to their respective Writings and Discoveries;

To constitute Tribunals inferior to the supreme Court;

To define and punish Piracies and Felonies committed on the high Seas, and Offences against the Law of Nations;

To declare War, grant Letters of Marque and Reprisal, and make Rules concerning Captures on Land and Water;

To raise and support Armies, but no Appropriation of Money to that Use shall be for a longer Term than two Years;

To provide and maintain a Navy;

To make Rules for the Government and Regulation of the land and naval Forces;

To provide for calling forth the Militia to execute the Laws of the Union, suppress Insurrections and repel Invasions;

To provide for organizing, arming, and disciplining, the Militia, and for governing such Part of them as may be employed in the Service of the United States, reserving to the States respectively, the Appointment of the Officers, and the Authority of training the Militia according to the discipline prescribed by Congress;

To exercise exclusive Legislation in all Cases whatsoever, over such District (not exceeding ten Miles square) as may, by Cession of particular States, and the Acceptance of Congress, become the Seat of the Government of the United States, and to exercise like Authority over all Places purchased by the Consent of the Legislature of the State in which the Same shall be, for the Erection of Forts, Magazines, Arsenals, dock-Yards, and other needful Buildings; — And

To make all Laws which shall be necessary and proper for carrying into Execution the foregoing Powers, and all other Powers vested by this Constitution in the Government of the United States, or in any Department or Officer thereof.

SECTION 9. The Migration or Importation of such Persons as any of the States now existing shall think proper to admit, shall not be prohibited by the Congress prior to the Year one thousand eight hundred and eight, but a Tax or duty may be imposed on such Importation, not exceeding ten dollars for each Person.

The Privilege of the Writ of Habeas Corpus shall not be suspended, unless when in Cases of Rebellion or Invasion the public Safety may require it.

No Bill of Attainder or ex post facto Law shall be passed.

No Capitation, or other direct, Tax shall be laid, unless in Proportion to the Census or Enumeration herein before directed to be taken.[5]

No Tax or Duty shall be laid on Articles exported from any State.

No Preference shall be given by any Regulation of Commerce or Revenue to the Ports of one State over those of another; nor shall Vessels bound to, or from, one State, be obliged to enter, clear, or pay Duties in another.

No Money shall be drawn from the Treasury, but in Consequence of Appropriations made by Law; and a regular Statement and Account of the Receipts and Expenditures of all public Money shall be published from time to time.

No Title of Nobility shall be granted by the United States: And no Person holding any Office of Profit or Trust under them, shall, without the Consent of the Congress, accept of any present, Emolument, Office, or Title, of any kind whatever, from any King, Prince, or foreign State.

SECTION 10. No State shall enter into any Treaty, Alliance, or Confederation; grant Letters of Marque and Reprisal; coin Money; emit Bills of Credit; make any Thing but gold and silver Coin a Tender in Payment of Debts; pass any Bill of Attainder, ex post facto Law, or Law impairing the Obligation of Contracts, or grant any Title of Nobility.

No State shall, without the Consent of the Congress, lay any Imposts or Duties on Imports or Exports, except what may be absolutely necessary for executing it's inspection Laws: and the net Produce of all Duties and Imposts, laid by any State on Imports or Exports, shall be for the Use of the Treasury of the United States; and all such Laws shall be subject to the Revision and Controul of the Congress.

No State shall, without the Consent of Congress, lay any Duty of Tonnage, keep Troops, or Ships of War in time of Peace, enter into any Agreement or Compact with another State, or with a foreign Power, or engage in War, unless actually invaded, or in such imminent Danger as will not admit of delay.

Article II

SECTION 1. The executive Power shall be vested in a President of the United States of America. He shall hold his Office during the Term of four Years, and, together with the Vice President, chosen for the same Term, be elected, as follows

Each State shall appoint, in such Manner as the Legislature thereof may direct, a Number of Electors, equal to the whole Number of Senators and Representatives to which the State may be entitled in the Congress: but no Senator or Representative, or Person holding an Office of Trust or Profit under the United States, shall be appointed an Elector.

[The Electors shall meet in their respective States, and vote by Ballot for two Persons, of whom one at least shall not be an Inhabitant of the same State with themselves. And they shall make a List of all the Persons voted for, and of the Number of Votes for each; which List they shall sign and certify, and transmit sealed to the Seat of the Government of the United States, directed to the President of the Senate. The President of the Senate shall, in the Presence of the Senate and House of Representatives, open all the Certificates, and the Votes shall then be counted. The Person having the greatest Number of Votes shall be the President, if such Number be a Majority of the whole Number of Electors appointed; and if there be more than one who have such Majority, and have an equal Number of Votes, then the House of Representatives shall immediately chuse by Ballot one of them for President; and if no Person have a Majority, then from the five highest on the list the said House shall in like Manner chuse the President. But in chusing the President, the Votes shall be taken by States, the Representation from each State having one Vote; A quorum for this Purpose shall consist of a Member or Members from two thirds of the States, and a Majority of all the States shall be necessary to a Choice. In every Case, after the Choice of the President, the Person having the greatest Number of Votes of the Electors shall be the Vice President. But if there should remain two or more who have equal Votes, the Senate shall chuse from them by Ballot the Vice President.][6]

The Congress may determine the Time of chusing the Electors, and the Day on which they shall give their Votes; which Day shall be the same throughout the United States.

No Person except a natural born Citizen, or a Citizen of the United States, at the time of the Adoption of this Constitution, shall be eligible to the Office of President; neither shall any Person be eligible to that Office who shall not have attained to the Age of thirty five Years, and been fourteen Years a Resident within the United States.

In Case of the Removal of the President from Office, or of his Death, Resignation, or Inability to discharge the Powers and Duties of the said Office,[7] the Same shall devolve on the Vice President, and the Congress may by Law provide for the Case of Removal, Death, Resignation or Inability, both of the President and Vice President, declaring what Officer shall then act as President, and such Officer shall act accordingly, until the Disability be removed, or a President shall be elected.

The President shall, at stated Times, receive for his Services, a Compensation, which shall neither be encreased nor diminished during the Period for which he shall have been elected, and he shall not receive within that Period any other Emolument from the United States, or any of them.

Before he enter on the Execution of his Office, he shall take the following Oath or Affirmation:— "I do solemnly swear (or affirm) that I will faithfully execute the Office of President of the United States, and will to the best of my Ability, preserve, protect and defend the Constitution of the United States."

SECTION 2. The President shall be Commander in Chief of the Army and Navy of the United States, and of the Militia of the several States, when called into the actual Service of the United States; he may require the Opinion, in writing, of the principal Officer in each of the executive Departments, upon any Subject relating to the Duties of their respective Offices, and he shall have Power to grant Reprieves and Pardons for Offences against the United States, except in Cases of Impeachment.

He shall have Power, by and with the Advice and Consent of the Senate, to make Treaties, provided two thirds of the Senators present concur; and he shall nominate, and by and with the Advice and Consent of the Senate, shall appoint Ambassadors, other public Ministers and Consuls, Judges of the supreme Court, and all other Officers of the United States, whose Appointments are not herein otherwise provided for, and which shall be established by Law: but the Congress may by Law vest the Appointment of such inferior Officers, as they think proper, in the President alone, in the Courts of Law, or in the Heads of Departments.

The President shall have Power to fill up all Vacancies that may happen during the Recess of the Senate, by granting Commissions which shall expire at the End of their next Session.

SECTION 3. He shall from time to time give to the Congress Information of the State of the Union, and recommend to their Consideration such Measures as he shall judge necessary and expedient; he may, on extraordinary Occasions, convene both Houses, or either of them, and in Case of Disagreement between them, with Respect to the Time of Adjournment, he may adjourn them to such Time as he shall think proper; he shall receive Ambassadors and other public

Ministers; he shall take Care that the Laws be faithfully executed, and shall Commission all the Officers of the United States.

SECTION 4. The President, Vice President and all civil Officers of the United States, shall be removed from Office on Impeachment for, and Conviction of, Treason, Bribery, or other high Crimes and Misdemeanors.

Article III

SECTION 1. The judicial Power of the United States, shall be vested in one supreme Court, and in such inferior Courts as the Congress may from time to time ordain and establish. The Judges, both of the supreme and inferior Courts, shall hold their Offices during good Behaviour, and shall, at stated Times, receive for their Services, a Compensation, which shall not be diminished during their Continuance in Office.

SECTION 2. The judicial Power shall extend to all Cases, in Law and Equity, arising under this Constitution, the Laws of the United States, and Treaties made, or which shall be made, under their Authority;—to all Cases affecting Ambassadors, other public Ministers and Consuls;—to all Cases of admiralty and maritime Jurisdiction;—to Controversies to which the United States shall be a Party;—to Controversies between two or more States;—between a State and Citizens of another State;[8]—between Citizens of different States;—between Citizens of the same State claiming Lands under Grants of different States, and between a State, or the Citizens thereof, and foreign States, Citizens or Subjects.[8]

In all Cases affecting Ambassadors, other public Ministers and Consuls, and those in which a State shall be Party, the supreme Court shall have original Jurisdiction. In all the other Cases before mentioned, the supreme Court shall have appellate Jurisdiction, both as to Law and Fact, with such Exceptions, and under such Regulations as the Congress shall make.

The Trial of all Crimes, except in Cases of Impeachment, shall be by Jury; and such Trial shall be held in the State where the said Crimes shall have been committed; but when not committed within any State, the Trial shall be at such Place or Places as the Congress may by Law have directed.

SECTION 3. Treason against the United States, shall consist only in levying War against them, or in adhering to their Enemies, giving them Aid and Comfort. No Person shall be convicted of Treason unless on the Testimony of two Witnesses to the same overt Act, or on Confession in open Court.

The Congress shall have Power to declare the Punishment of Treason, but no Attainder of Treason shall work Corruption of Blood, or Forfeiture except during the Life of the Person attainted.

Article IV

SECTION 1. Full Faith and Credit shall be given in each State to the public Acts, Records, and judicial Proceedings of every other State. And the Congress may by general Laws prescribe the Manner in which such Acts, Records and Proceedings shall be proved, and the Effect thereof.

SECTION 2. The Citizens of each State shall be entitled to all Privileges and Immunities of Citizens in the several States.

A Person charged in any State with Treason, Felony, or other Crime, who shall flee from Justice, and be found in another State, shall on Demand of the executive Authority of the State from which he fled, be delivered up, to be removed to the State having Jurisdiction of the Crime.

[No Person held to Service or Labour in one State, under the Laws thereof, escaping into another, shall, in Consequence of any Law or Regulation therein, be discharged from such Service or Labour, but shall be delivered up on Claim of the Party to whom such Service or Labour may be due.][9]

SECTION 3. New States may be admitted by the Congress into this Union; but no new State shall be formed or erected within the Jurisdiction of any other State; nor any State be formed by the Junction of two or more States, or Parts of States, without the Consent of the Legislatures of the States concerned as well as of the Congress.

The Congress shall have Power to dispose of and make all needful Rules and Regulations respecting the Territory or other Property belonging to the United States; and nothing in this Constitution shall be so construed as to Prejudice any Claims of the United States, or of any particular State.

SECTION 4. The United States shall guarantee to every State in this Union a Republican Form of Government, and shall protect each of them against Invasion; and on Application of the Legislature, or of the Executive (when the Legislature cannot be convened) against domestic Violence.

Article V

The Congress, whenever two thirds of both Houses shall deem it necessary, shall propose Amendments to this Constitution, or, on the Application of the Legislatures of two thirds of the several States, shall call a Convention for proposing Amendments, which, in either Case, shall be valid to all Intents and Purposes, as Part of this Constitution, when ratified by the Legislatures of three fourths of the several States, or by Conventions in three fourths thereof, as the one or the other Mode of Ratification may be proposed by the Congress; Provided [that no

Amendment which may be made prior to the Year One thousand eight hundred and eight shall in any Manner affect the first and fourth Clauses in the Ninth Section of the first Article; and][10] that no State, without its Consent, shall be deprived of its equal Suffrage in the Senate.

Article VI

All Debts contracted and Engagements entered into, before the Adoption of this Constitution, shall be as valid against the United States under this Constitution, as under the Confederation.

This Constitution, and the Laws of the United States which shall be made in Pursuance thereof; and all Treaties made, or which shall be made, under the Authority of the United States, shall be the supreme Law of the Land; and the Judges in every State shall be bound thereby, any Thing in the Constitution or Laws of any State to the Contrary notwithstanding.

The Senators and Representatives before mentioned, and the Members of the several State Legislatures, and all executive and judicial Officers, both of the United States and of the several States, shall be bound by Oath or Affirmation, to support this Constitution; but no religious Test shall ever be required as a Qualification to any Office or public Trust under the United States.

Article VII

The Ratification of the Conventions of nine States, shall be sufficient for the Establishment of this Constitution between the States so ratifying the Same.

Done in Convention by the Unanimous Consent of the States present the Seventeenth Day of September in the Year of our Lord one thousand seven hundred and Eighty seven and of the Independence of the United States of America the Twelfth. IN WITNESS whereof We have hereunto subscribed our Names,

George Washington,
President and deputy from Virginia.

NEW HAMPSHIRE: John Langdon,
                   Nicholas Gilman.

MASSACHUSETTS: Nathaniel Gorham,
                   Rufus King.

CONNECTICUT: William Samuel Johnson,
                   Roger Sherman.

| NEW YORK: | Alexander Hamilton. |

NEW JERSEY:	William Livingston,
	David Brearley,
	William Paterson,
	Jonathan Dayton.

PENNSYLVANIA:	Benjamin Franklin,
	Thomas Mifflin,
	Robert Morris,
	George Clymer,
	Thomas FitzSimons,
	Jared Ingersoll,
	James Wilson,
	Gouverneur Morris.

DELAWARE:	George Read,
	Gunning Bedford Jr.,
	John Dickinson,
	Richard Bassett,
	Jacob Broom.

MARYLAND:	James McHenry,
	Daniel of St. Thomas Jenifer,
	Daniel Carroll.

| VIRGINIA: | John Blair, |
| | James Madison Jr. |

NORTH CAROLINA:	William Blount,
	Richard Dobbs Spaight,
	Hugh Williamson.

SOUTH CAROLINA:	John Rutledge,
	Charles Cotesworth Pinckney,
	Charles Pinckney,
	Pierce Butler.

| GEORGIA: | William Few, |
| | Abraham Baldwin. |

[The language of the original Constitution, not including the Amendments, was adopted by a convention of the states on September 17, 1787, and was subsequently ratified by the states on the following dates: Delaware, December 7, 1787; Pennsylvania, December 12, 1787; New Jersey, December 18, 1787; Georgia, January 2, 1788; Connecticut, January 9, 1788; Massachusetts, February 6,

1788; Maryland, April 28, 1788; South Carolina, May 23, 1788; New Hampshire, June 21, 1788.

Ratification was completed on June 21, 1788.

The Constitution subsequently was ratified by Virginia, June 25, 1788; New York, July 26, 1788; North Carolina, November 21, 1789; Rhode Island, May 29, 1790; and Vermont, January 10, 1791.]

Amendments

AMENDMENT I *(First ten amendments ratified December 15, 1791.)*

Congress shall make no law respecting an establishment of religion, or prohibiting the free exercise thereof; or abridging the freedom of speech, or of the press; or the right of the people peaceably to assemble, and to petition the Government for a redress of grievances.

AMENDMENT II

A well regulated Militia, being necessary to the security of a free State, the right of the people to keep and bear Arms, shall not be infringed.

AMENDMENT III

No Soldier shall, in time of peace be quartered in any house, without the consent of the Owner, nor in time of war, but in a manner to be prescribed by law.

AMENDMENT IV

The right of the people to be secure in their persons, houses, papers, and effects, against unreasonable searches and seizures, shall not be violated, and no Warrants shall issue, but upon probable cause, supported by Oath or affirmation, and particularly describing the place to be searched, and the persons or things to be seized.

AMENDMENT V

No person shall be held to answer for a capital, or otherwise infamous crime, unless on a presentment or indictment of a Grand Jury, except in cases arising in the land or naval forces, or in the Militia, when in actual service in time of War or public danger; nor shall any person be subject for the same offence to be twice put in jeopardy of life or limb; nor shall be compelled in any criminal case to be a witness against himself, nor be deprived of life, liberty, or property, without due process of law; nor shall private property be taken for public use, without just compensation.

AMENDMENT VI

In all criminal prosecutions, the accused shall enjoy the right to a speedy and public trial, by an impartial jury of the State and district wherein the crime shall have been committed, which district shall have been previously ascertained by law, and to be informed of the nature and cause of the accusation; to be confronted with the witnesses against him; to have compulsory process for obtaining witnesses in his favor, and to have the Assistance of Counsel for his defence.

AMENDMENT VII

In Suits at common law, where the value in controversy shall exceed twenty dollars, the right of trial by jury shall be preserved, and no fact tried by a jury, shall be otherwise re-examined in any Court of the United States, than according to the rules of the common law.

AMENDMENT VIII

Excessive bail shall not be required, nor excessive fines imposed, nor cruel and unusual punishments inflicted.

AMENDMENT IX

The enumeration in the Constitution, of certain rights, shall not be construed to deny or disparage others retained by the people.

AMENDMENT X

The powers not delegated to the United States by the Constitution, nor prohibited by it to the States, are reserved to the States respectively, or to the people.

AMENDMENT XI *(Ratified February 7, 1795)*

The Judicial power of the United States shall not be construed to extend to any suit in law or equity, commenced or prosecuted against one of the United States by Citizens of another State, or by Citizens or Subjects of any Foreign State.

AMENDMENT XII *(Ratified June 15, 1804)*

The Electors shall meet in their respective states and vote by ballot for President and Vice-President, one of whom, at least, shall not be an inhabitant of the same state with themselves; they shall name in their ballots the person voted for as President, and in distinct ballots the person voted for as Vice-President, and they shall make distinct lists of all persons voted for as President, and of all persons voted for as Vice-President, and of the number of votes for each, which lists they shall sign and certify, and transmit sealed to the seat of the government of the United States, directed to the President of the Senate;—The President of the Senate shall, in the presence of the Senate and House of Representatives, open all the certificates and the votes shall then be counted;—The person having the greatest number of votes for President, shall be the President, if such number be a majority of the whole number of Electors appointed; and if no person have such majority, then from the persons having the highest numbers not exceeding three on the list of those voted for as President, the House of Representatives shall choose immediately, by ballot, the President. But in choosing the President, the votes shall be taken by states, the representation from each state having one vote; a quorum for this purpose shall consist of a member or members from two-thirds of the states, and a majority of all the states shall be necessary to a choice. [And if the House of Representatives shall not choose a President whenever the right of choice shall devolve upon them, before the fourth day of March next following, then the Vice-President shall act as President, as in the case of the death or other constitutional disability of the President.—][11] The person having the greatest number of votes as Vice-President, shall be the Vice-President, if such number be a majority of the whole number of Electors appointed, and if no person have a majority, then from the two highest numbers on the list, the Senate shall choose the Vice-President; a quorum for the purpose shall consist of two-thirds of the whole number of Senators, and a majority of the whole number shall be necessary to a choice. But no person constitutionally ineligible to the office of President shall be eligible to that of Vice-President of the United States.

AMENDMENT XIII *(Ratified December 6, 1865)*

> *SECTION 1.* Neither slavery nor involuntary servitude, except as a punishment for crime whereof the party shall have been duly convicted, shall exist within the United States, or any place subject to their jurisdiction.

> *SECTION 2.* Congress shall have power to enforce this article by appropriate legislation.

AMENDMENT XIV *(Ratified July 9, 1868)*

> *SECTION 1.* All persons born or naturalized in the United States, and subject to the jurisdiction thereof, are citizens of the United States and of the State wherein they reside. No State shall make or enforce any law which shall abridge the privileges or immunities of citizens of the United States; nor shall any State deprive any person of life, liberty, or property, without due process of law; nor deny to any person within its jurisdiction the equal protection of the laws.

> *SECTION 2.* Representatives shall be apportioned among the several States according to their respective numbers, counting the whole number of persons in each State, excluding Indians not taxed. But when the right to vote at any election for the choice of electors for President and Vice President of the United States, Representatives in Congress, the Executive and Judicial officers of a State, or the members of the Legislature thereof, is denied to any of the male inhabitants of such State, being twenty-one years of age,[12] and citizens of the United States, or in any way abridged, except for participation in rebellion, or other crime, the basis of representation therein shall be reduced in the proportion which the number of such male citizens shall bear to the whole number of male citizens twenty-one years of age in such State.

> *SECTION 3.* No person shall be a Senator or Representative in Congress, or elector of President and Vice President, or hold any office, civil or military, under the United States, or under any State, who, having previously taken an oath, as a member of Congress, or as an officer of the United States, or as a member of any State legislature, or as an executive or judicial officer of any State, to support the Constitution of the United States, shall have engaged in insurrection or rebellion against the same, or given aid or comfort to the enemies thereof. But Congress may by a vote of two-thirds of each House, remove such disability.

> *SECTION 4.* The validity of the public debt of the United States, authorized by law, including debts incurred for payment of pensions and bounties for services in suppressing insurrection or rebellion, shall not be questioned. But neither the United States nor any State shall assume or pay any debt or obligation incurred in aid of insurrection or rebellion against the United States, or any claim for the loss or emancipation of any slave; but all such debts, obligations and claims shall be held illegal and void.

> *SECTION 5.* The Congress shall have power to enforce, by appropriate legislation, the provisions of this article.

AMENDMENT XV *(Ratified February 3, 1870)*

> *SECTION 1.* The right of citizens of the United States to vote shall not be denied or abridged by the United States or by any State on account of race, color, or previous condition of servitude.

> *SECTION 2.* The Congress shall have power to enforce this article by appropriate legislation.

AMENDMENT XVI *(Ratified February 3, 1913)*

The Congress shall have power to lay and collect taxes on incomes, from whatever source derived, without apportionment among the several States, and without regard to any census or enumeration.

AMENDMENT XVII *(Ratified April 8, 1913)*

The Senate of the United States shall be composed of two Senators from each State, elected by the people thereof, for six years; and each Senator shall have one vote. The electors in each State shall have the qualifications requisite for electors of the most numerous branch of the State legislatures.

When vacancies happen in the representation of any State in the Senate, the executive authority of such State shall issue writs of election to fill such vacancies: *Provided,* That the legislature of any State may empower the executive thereof to make temporary appointments until the people fill the vacancies by election as the legislature may direct.

This amendment shall not be so construed as to affect the election or term of any Senator chosen before it becomes valid as part of the Constitution.

AMENDMENT XVIII *(Ratified January 16, 1919)*[13]

> *SECTION 1.* After one year from the ratification of this article the manufacture, sale, or transportation of intoxicating liquors within, the importation thereof into, or the exportation thereof from the United States and all territory subject to the jurisdiction thereof for beverage purposes is hereby prohibited.

> *SECTION 2.* The Congress and the several States shall have concurrent power to enforce this article by appropriate legislation.

> *SECTION 3.* This article shall be inoperative unless it shall have been ratified as an amendment to the Constitution by the legislatures of the several States, as provided in the Constitution, within seven years from the date of the submission hereof to the States by the Congress.

AMENDMENT XIX *(Ratified August 18, 1920)*

The right of citizens of the United States to vote shall not be denied or abridged by the United States or by any State on account of sex.

Congress shall have power to enforce this article by appropriate legislation.

AMENDMENT XX *(Ratified January 23, 1933)*

➤ *SECTION 1.* The terms of the President and Vice President shall end at noon on the 20th day of January, and the terms of Senators and Representatives at noon on the 3d day of January, of the years in which such terms would have ended if this article had not been ratified; and the terms of their successors shall then begin.

➤ *SECTION 2.* The Congress shall assemble at least once in every year, and such meeting shall begin at noon on the 3d day of January, unless they shall by law appoint a different day.

➤ *SECTION 3.*[14] If, at the time fixed for the beginning of the term of the President, the President elect shall have died, the Vice President elect shall become President. If a President shall not have been chosen before the time fixed for the beginning of his term, or if the President elect shall have failed to qualify, then the Vice President elect shall act as President until a President shall have qualified; and the Congress may by law provide for the case wherein neither a President elect nor a Vice President elect shall have qualified, declaring who shall then act as President, or the manner in which one who is to act shall be selected, and such person shall act accordingly until a President or Vice President shall have qualified.

➤ *SECTION 4.* The Congress may by law provide for the case of the death of any of the persons from whom the House of Representatives may choose a President whenever the right of choice shall have devolved upon them, and for the case of the death of any of the persons from whom the Senate may choose a Vice President whenever the right of choice shall have devolved upon them.

➤ *SECTION 5.* Sections 1 and 2 shall take effect on the 15th day of October following the ratification of this article.

➤ *SECTION 6.* This article shall be inoperative unless it shall have been ratified as an amendment to the Constitution by the legislatures of three-fourths of the several States within seven years from the date of its submission.

AMENDMENT XXI *(Ratified December 5, 1933)*

➤ *SECTION 1.* The eighteenth article of amendment to the Constitution of the United States is hereby repealed.

➤ *SECTION 2.* The transportation or importation into any State, Territory, or possession of the United States for delivery or use therein of intoxicating liquors, in violation of the laws thereof, is hereby prohibited.

➤ *SECTION 3.* This article shall be inoperative unless it shall have been ratified as an amendment to the Constitution by conventions in the several States, as provided in the Constitution, within seven years from the date of the submission hereof to the States by the Congress.

AMENDMENT XXII *(Ratified February 27, 1951)*

➤   *SECTION 1.* No person shall be elected to the office of the President more than twice, and no person who has held the office of President, or acted as President, for more than two years of a term to which some other person was elected President shall be elected to the office of the President more than once. But this Article shall not apply to any person holding the office of President when this Article was proposed by the Congress, and shall not prevent any person who may be holding the office of President, or acting as President, during the term within which this Article become operative from holding the office of President or acting as President during the remainder of such term.

➤   *SECTION 2.* This article shall be inoperative unless it shall have been ratified as an amendment to the Constitution by the legislatures of three-fourths of the several States within seven years from the date of its submission to the States by the Congress.

AMENDMENT XXIII *(Ratified March 29, 1961)*

➤   *SECTION 1.* The District constituting the seat of Government of the United States shall appoint in such manner as the Congress may direct:

A number of electors of President and Vice President equal to the whole number of Senators and Representatives in Congress to which the District would be entitled if it were a State, but in no event more than the least populous State; they shall be in addition to those appointed by the States, but they shall be considered, for the purposes of the election of President and Vice President, to be electors appointed by a State; and they shall meet in the District and perform such duties as provided by the twelfth article of amendment.

➤   *SECTION 2.* The Congress shall have power to enforce this article by appropriate legislation.

AMENDMENT XXIV *(Ratified January 23, 1964)*

➤   *SECTION 1.* The right of citizens of the United States to vote in any primary or other election for President or Vice President, for electors for President or Vice President, or for Senator or Representative in Congress, shall not be denied or abridged by the United States or any State by reason of failure to pay any poll tax or other tax.

➤   *SECTION 2.* The Congress shall have power to enforce this article by appropriate legislation.

AMENDMENT XXV *(Ratified February 10, 1967)*

➤   *SECTION 1.* In case of the removal of the President from office or of his death or resignation, the Vice President shall become President.

➤   *SECTION 2.* Whenever there is a vacancy in the office of the Vice President, the President shall nominate a Vice President who shall take office upon confirmation by a majority vote of both Houses of Congress.

➤   *SECTION 3.* Whenever the President transmits to the President pro tempore of the Senate and the Speaker of the House of Representatives his written declaration that he is unable to discharge the powers and duties of his office, and until he transmits to them a written declaration to the contrary, such powers and duties shall be discharged by the Vice President as Acting President.

➤ *SECTION 4.* Whenever the Vice President and a majority of either the principal officers of the executive departments or of such other body as Congress may by law provide, transmit to the President pro tempore of the Senate and the Speaker of the House of Representatives their written declaration that the President is unable to discharge the powers and duties of his office, the Vice President shall immediately assume the powers and duties of the office as Acting President.

Thereafter, when the President transmits to the President pro tempore of the Senate and the Speaker of the House of Representatives his written declaration that no inability exists, he shall resume the powers and duties of his office unless the Vice President and a majority of either the principal officers of the executive department or of such other body as Congress may by law provide, transmit within four days to the President pro tempore of the Senate and the Speaker of the House of Representatives their written declaration that the President is unable to discharge the powers and duties of his office. Thereupon Congress shall decide the issue, assembling within forty-eight hours for that purpose if not in session. If the Congress, within twenty-one days after receipt of the latter written declaration, or, if Congress is not in session, within twenty-one days after Congress is required to assemble, determines by two-thirds vote of both Houses that the President is unable to discharge the powers and duties of his office, the Vice President shall continue to discharge the same as Acting President; otherwise, the President shall resume the powers and duties of his office.

AMENDMENT XXVI *(Ratified July 1, 1971)*

➤ *SECTION 1.* The right of citizens of the United States, who are eighteen years of age or older, to vote shall not be denied or abridged by the United States or by any State on account of age.

➤ *SECTION 2.* The Congress shall have power to enforce this article by appropriate legislation.

AMENDMENT XXVII *(Ratified May 7, 1992)*

No law varying the compensation for the services of the Senators and Representatives shall take effect, until an election of Representatives shall have intervened.

NOTES

1. The part in brackets was by section 2 of the Fourteenth Amendment.
2. The part in brackets was changed by the first paragraph of the Seventeenth Amendment.
3. The part in brackets was changed by the second paragraph of the Seventeenth Amendment.
4. The part in brackets was changed by section 2 of the Twentieth Amendment.
5. The Sixteenth Amendment gave Congress the power to tax incomes.
6. The material in brackets has been superseded by the Twelfth Amendment.
7. This provision has been affected by the Twenty-fifth Amendment.

8. These clauses were affected by the Eleventh Amendment.
9. This paragraph has been superseded by the Thirteenth Amendment.
10. Obsolete.
11. The part in brackets has been superseded by section 3 of the Twentieth Amendment.
12. See the Nineteenth and Twenty-sixth Amendments.
13. This Amendment was repealed by section 1 of the Twenty-first Amendment.
14. See the Twenty-fifth Amendment.

Source: U.S. Congress, House, Committee on the Judiciary, *The Constitution of the United States of America, as Amended,* 100th Cong., 1st sess., 1987, H Doc 100-94.

Glossary

ADVISORY OPINION. An opinion issued by a court in which it states how it would rule on a legal matter that is not actually ripe for decision; significantly, the Supreme Court and other federal courts do not issue advisory opinions.

APPELLANT. The party that appeals a lower court's decision. This party is usually seeking reversal of the lower court's decision. *See also* Petitioner.

APPELLEE. The party that responds to an appeal. This party is generally seeking affirmation of a lower court's decision. *See also* Respondent.

ATTORNEY GENERAL. Head of the Department of Justice, appointed by the president. Responsibilities include representation of the United States in legal matters, standing before the Supreme Court in cases where the United States is a party, and counseling the president and others within the executive branch as needed.

BILL OF RIGHTS. The first ten amendments of the Constitution guaranteeing citizens basic constitutional rights and liberties.

CERTIORARI. *See* Writ of certiorari.

CIVIL SUIT. A lawsuit undertaken to protect an individual's private legal rights. Also known as a civil action.

COMMON LAW. Body of law that develops over time from the judgments of courts. Contrasted with statutory law, which is written by legislatures.

CONCURRING OPINION. Opinion written by a justice or judge that agrees with the ruling of the majority opinion in a case but that offers a separate explanation or process of reasoning.

CONSTITUTIONAL INJURY. A harm caused by violation of an individual's constitutional rights that gives rise to standing to sue.

CRIMINAL PROSECUTION. Process by which the government charges a person with a criminal violation and brings him or her to trial.

DEFENDANT. Person or party that is sued in a civil case or prosecuted in a criminal case.

DISSENTING OPINION. Opinion written by a justice or judge that disagrees with the ruling of the majority opinion in a case.

DOUBLE JEOPARDY. The prosecution of an individual twice for the same criminal offense. This practice is outlawed by the Fifth Amendment to the Constitution.

DUE PROCESS CLAUSE. Clause in the Fifth and Fourteenth Amendments that declares that no person may be deprived of life, liberty, or property without due process of law. Interpreted to mean that every individual is entitled to a fair trial with significant protections, such as the right to be heard, to call witnesses, to cross-examine witnesses, and so forth.

EXPRESSIVE CONDUCT. Actions that do not literally involve speaking or writing but that nonetheless send a message. Picketing a store, wearing a political button, and painting a picture are all examples of expressive conduct.

FEDERALISM. The system of divided and allocated powers between the states and the federal government.

GENERAL COUNSEL. The most senior lawyer in a government or private legal department.

GRAND JURY. A body of citizens that sits to review relevant evidence and testimony in order to determine whether or not a person should be formally charged with a crime.

ILLEGAL. Actions or conduct that are in violation of municipal, state, or federal law.

INJUNCTION. An order from a court commanding or preventing an action.

INJURY. The violation of another party's legal rights or its legally protected interests. If the government puts you in prison without a trial, it has violated your Due Process rights and you have been injured by its actions.

IN LOCO PARENTIS. Literally, in the place of a parent; teachers and school authorities act in loco parentis in the school domain when there is no direct supervision by a parent or guardian.

JUDICIAL RESTRAINT. The theory and practice whereby judges defer to the political branches and strive not to invalidate democratically chosen public policies and laws.

JUDICIAL REVIEW. The constitutional power of a court to examine laws and policies made by other branches of government and to invalidate them if they are unconstitutional or unlawful.

LIABILITY. A legal obligation or responsibility. Liability is enforceable by a court in a civil or criminal trial.

MAJORITY OPINION. Opinion written by a justice or judge indicating the court's ruling in a case and offering an explanation for that ruling.

MANDAMUS. Latin for "we command." Usually, a writ of mandamus is issued from a court to force another court or government official to undertake a specific action.

MEDIATOR. A neutral party that helps to bring opposing sides to agreement by suggesting solutions and fostering productive negotiations.

MOOT. Descriptive of a case that is no longer fit for judicial resolution because an actual controversy no longer exists.

ORDINANCE. Local law enacted by a city, suburb, town, municipality, or other local entity.

PETITIONER. Party that presents a petition to a court in an effort to seek appeal of a judgment. *See also* Appellant.

PLAINTIFF. Party that brings original civil suit in a state or federal court.

POLITICAL QUESTION. Doctrine that compels federal courts to avoid deciding cases involving the discretionary powers of the executive or legislative branches.

PRECEDENT. Prior case law.

PRIOR RESTRAINT. The restriction of speech or press before it is actually published or expressed. Analogous to censorship.

RELIEF. The monetary benefit or other restitution that a court in a civil suit grants to a party that has suffered damages or injury.

RESPONDEAT SUPERIOR. Doctrine that allows an employer (or superior) to be liable for an employee's actions committed in the course of employment.

RESPONDENT. Party that answers to a petition for review in court. *See also* Appellee.

RIPENESS. Doctrine requiring that an actual live case or controversy be present—as opposed to a hypothetical or potential controversy—in order for a case to be heard. A case will not be heard unless it is ripe for adjudication.

SEPARATION OF POWERS. The constitutional doctrine establishing that each of the three branches of the government—legislative, executive, and judicial—is essentially independent and exercises unique powers.

SEXUAL HARASSMENT. Sexual conduct, sometimes accompanied by promises or threats, that (1) creates a hostile learning or workplace environment and/or (2) involves express or implied conditions in which rejection of, or submission to, said conduct will affect an individual's employment or academic status (quid pro quo harassment).

SOLICITOR GENERAL. Attorney in the Department of Justice who represents the government in cases that go before the Supreme Court.

STANDING. The doctrine requiring that an individual show that he or she suffered a direct and concrete injury that is traceable to the government and that can be redressed through court-ordered relief before a person's constitutional case against the government may be heard.

STATE ACTION. Action undertaken by a government agency or actor, whether federal, state, or local. State action is requisite to bringing a constitutional case against the government.

STATUTE. A law passed by a federal or state legislature.

STATUTORY. Relating to a statute.

TORT. A civil wrong. If you drive recklessly and knock down your neighbor's mailbox, he or she can sue you for committing a tort.

UNCONSTITUTIONAL. Descriptive of actions that are in violation of the commands or guarantees of the Constitution.

UNITED STATES CIRCUIT COURTS OF APPEAL. Body of courts consisting of thirteen federal circuits, including the Court of Appeals for the District of Columbia and the Court of Appeals for the Federal Circuit. These appellate courts try cases that have been appealed from the United States District Courts.

UNITED STATES DISTRICT COURTS. Body of trial courts in which cases involving federal lawsuits are first tried.

UNITED STATES SUPREME COURT. Highest court in the United States. The Supreme Court is made up of a chief justice and eight associate justices and is charged with ruling on appeals from the United States Circuit Courts of Appeal and from state supreme courts. The Court also functions as a trial court in specified disputes, including those that occur between states.

WRIT OF CERTIORARI. A writ issued by the Supreme Court to a lower court directing the lower court to deliver the case for review. *Certiorari* is Latin and means "to be more fully informed."

Index